TOTALLY
SUFFICIENT

Ed Hindson & Howard Eyrich
General Editors

HARVEST HOUSE PUBLISHERS
Eugene, Oregon 97402

TOTALLY SUFFICIENT

Copyright © 1997 by Harvest House Publishers
Eugene, Oregon 97402

Library of Congress Cataloging-in-Publication Data

Totally sufficient / Ed Hindson and Howard Eyrich, general editors.
    p. cm.
Includes bibliographical references.
ISBN 1-56507-630-3
1. Pastoral counseling. 2. Bible—Evidences, authority, etc. 3. Bible—Inspiration.
I. Hindson, Edward E.   II. Eyrich, Howard, 1939-   .
BV4012.T68   1997   96-51722
253'.5—dc21   CIP

*To the
pastor, elders, and members
of the
Kirk of the Hills Church
in St. Louis, Missouri,
who enabled us to
minister together
the Sufficient Word*

Contents

Foreword

This remarkable book on Christian counseling vis-à-vis psychological counseling carries an admirably accurate title: *Totally Sufficient*. Not only is its subject—the Bible—totally sufficient as a clinical tool in skillful hands for the treatment of behavioral disorders, but this compendium of twelve essays is also eminently adequate to the task which it confronts.

The first impression that reinforces reader confidence is the unquestionable credibility of the contributors themselves. A mere glance at the Table of Contents is convincing evidence that the debate is in the hands of professionals, all maximally credentialed and experienced. This is particularly comforting to those who know too well the shabby treatment customarily accorded by the mass media to almost any controversy centering on science and religion.

In comprehensive, yet penetrating, fashion and in language that is free of both psychotechnical and theological terms, here is a book that will prove to be of inestimable value to personal counselors, whether churched or unchurched, Christian or secular. Without denigrating the value of information provided by the textbooks of the social sciences, the consensus here is simply that man's truth is not always God's truth—and that the latter can only be discovered and put to productive use by practitioners who are grounded in the inerrant Word of God.

Generations who lived through the centuries preceding the recent dawning of psychology and psychiatry knew that the Scripture speaks to every area of human life. As Thomas Gray, the great poet of the eighteenth century, put it, it was Holy Writ "that taught the rustic moralist to die." It is just as efficacious, just as indispensable—and doubtless much more desperately needed—today, because it also teaches those who trust in it how to live, even under the most difficult of circumstances.

It has been my privilege to know many faithful physicians who have found the Bible to be an invaluable tool in physical and spiritual healing. As this splendid book about the total sufficiency of Scripture in the practices of medicine and counseling becomes widely read, I expect to meet many more.

— Dr. James Kennedy
Pastor, Coral Ridge Presbyterian Church
Fort Lauderdale, Florida

Preface

This is a book about Christian counseling—distinctively Christian counseling. It is, in fact, a book about *biblical counseling*. It is our intent to define, explain, and clarify the issues that are at the center of the debate within Christian counseling circles about the sufficiency of Scripture. Unfortunately, this debate has often produced more heat than light!

It is our prayer that this volume will allow those who are working within the field of biblical counseling to more clearly and effectively state the case for biblical counseling from the perspective of their own disciplines. Each contributor was selected because of his interest, expertise, and commitment to a ministry that is wholly consistent with biblical truth. These contributors worked separately, not collectively; therefore, the essays reflect the individuality of each contributor. They do not necessarily agree in totality with one another on every point, yet all are in agreement about the supremacy of Scripture in biblical counseling.

For too long now, biblical counseling has been misunderstood or misrepresented as a simplistic approach to the complex problems of human nature. Pejorative labels like "Bible Bangers," "Nothing Buttery," "obscurantist," and "irrelevant" have been used to criticize biblical counselors. They are generally represented as nonprofessionals interfering in various areas of the psychological domain, where they are said to have no business practicing their supposedly inadequate approach to counseling.

In contrast to this woeful stereotype, we have asked a team of ten professionals to discuss the issue of the sufficiency of Scripture in relation to counseling, psychology, psychiatry, medicine, biomedical research, the brain sciences, and pastoral ministry. Their observations may surprise you, as might their credentials and their expertise. This is no collection of undereducated, overzealous, misinformed pseudocounselors. These are real professionals, with great minds and great hearts, who are convinced the Bible still works today in speaking to the needs of real people.

It is our prayer that their essays will challenge and encourage you as you take a closer look at what biblical counseling is really all about. It is also our prayer that the essays will help sharpen the focus of the current debate over the Bible's sufficiency and produce more honest and conciliatory discussion in the future. We say that because all too often in the past, Christian biblical and psychological counselors have squared off, drawn lines, caricaturized one another, and in some cases misrepresented one another—all in the name of God and the truth! Our appeal is twofold: First, that Christians who prefer the psychological model would take the time to reexamine their own biblical roots. And second, that Christians who prefer the biblical model would ask themselves if they are truly biblical in their attitude and approach.

It has been our experience in more than 20 years of counseling that most Christian counselors, regardless of their theoretical viewpoint, sincerely want to help the people they counsel. The only real debate, then, is over the question of *how*. It is with this fact in mind that we offer these essays so that each reader, regardless of his or her theoretical viewpoint, may benefit from the issues discussed and debated in this volume.

Above all, may the *light* of God's truth outshine the *heat* of individual personality, preference, or distinction. May you find in this volume a better understanding of *what* biblical counselors believe, and *why* and *how* biblical counseling works. May God's sufficient grace be with us all!

Howard Eyrich, D.Min.
Ed Hindson, D.Phil.

TOTALLY SUFFICIENT

1

IS THE BIBLE REALLY ENOUGH?

Howard Eyrich, D.Min.
Ed Hindson, D.Phil.

There is a great debate raging in Christian counseling circles over the issue of the sufficiency of Scripture. While most Christian counselors profess belief in the inspiration of the Bible, many seem reluctant to trust the Scripture to speak authoritatively to their counseling profession.

Some prefer to view themselves as Christians who do counseling. Their approach and technique is essentially secular. They have little desire to make their counseling distinctively Christian. This may be because of the nature of their training or the setting in which they do their counseling. In addition, many Christians work for secular organizations that prefer to keep religion out of the counseling process.

Others feel very free to share their personal testimony and beliefs as part of their self-disclosure to their clients. But beyond this, they are reluctant to present their clients with a distinctively Christian view of their personal attitudes and behaviors.

Many Christian counselors today actively encourage the integration of psychology and theology as being

11

essential to a more adequate approach to counseling that is genuinely Christian in nature. Some, like Dr. Mark McMinn of Wheaton College, are also calling for a better understanding of the whole development of the spiritual life as a further aspect of effective integration. McMinn's book *Psychology, Theology and Spirituality*[1] has certainly broken new and important ground in this regard.

Then there are those of us who prefer to position ourselves as "biblical counselors." We strongly believe that theology (biblical truth) is the final determinant of the counseling process. We have often called for a more biblical and theological assessment of the validity or nonvalidity of psychological theories, practices, and techniques. No one has made this more clear than Jay Adams in his many works, including *Competent to Counsel* and *More Than Redemption*.[2]

Unfortunately, the posturing that took place in the early days of the Christian counseling movement tended to pit various proponents at such odds with one another that those on opposite sides of the debate often wrote one another off entirely. A person does not have to read many books on Christian counseling to discover that those who preferred a stronger biblical position were often viewed as less than credible in their approach to counseling.[3]

Complicating matters even further is the widespread and diverse nature of the current Christian counseling enterprise. A recent article in *Christianity Today* included a chart entitled "The Roots and Shoots of Christian Psychology," which touched off a storm of criticism in the Letters to the Editor column in the subsequent issue.[4] Almost half of the individuals whose names appeared in various categories on the chart wrote back to object to where and how they were included in the chart.

Ironically, the "Roots and Shoots" chart had secular psychology as the *roots* to the Christian psychology tree! The chart included some people who were grossly misplaced. But most telling of all were the *omissions*—such as Jay Adams, Tim LaHaye, Bill Gothard, biblical counselors in general, or Liberty University, which has the largest fully accredited counseling training program of any evangelical institution in the world!

WHY THE SUFFICIENCY DEBATE?

Psychology and theology have never been comfortable bedfellows. Their basic philosophical presuppositions are almost diametrically opposed to each other. Psychology rests upon a secular (humanistic or naturalistic) view of man's problems and the solution to those problems, and theology rests upon a biblical view of man and his problems. The basic anthropology (view of man) of psychology and theology is at opposite ends of the intellectual spectrum.

In many ways, John MacArthur and Wayne Mack are correct when they refer to "Christian psychology" as an "oxymoron" and secular psychology as a "pseudo-science."[5] At the heart of the sufficiency debate are the claims of Scripture versus the claims of psychology. Both presume to speak to the fundamental human condition and to suggest a cure for the inner conflicts in the souls of men. The way a person differentiates between psychological and biblical analysis determines the assessment that person makes of people, their problems, and the solutions to those problems.

The term *psychology* literally means "the study of the soul." Prior to Sigmund Freud's influence, psychology was largely viewed as a spiritual discipline. But Freud recast and redefined psychology in secular terms of human behavior.

Concepts like right, wrong, morality, immorality, obedience, and disobedience were soon replaced by terms like repression, regression, and ego formation. Psychologists began probing the unconscious mind instead of conscious behavior. Patients began to be analyzed and categorized, while biblical analyses and categories were discarded as irrelevant at best and incorrect at worst.

The "war" was on! Non-Christian secular psychologists virtually declared war on religion. Freud labeled it a form of neurosis, calling himself "a completely godless Jew" and a "hopeless pagan."[6] In many ways, Freud became the Father of the Great Psychological Excuse.

The psychologizing of modern culture is now a reality. As a result, the victim motif is so entrenched in our national thinking that the most blatant crimes are often excused by blaming the bad behavior on the failure of parents, friends, society, and even religion to meet the perpetrator's inner personal needs. Individual behavior is viewed as incidental. Society is asked to focus on the consequences rather than the causes of its ills. Welfare has replaced human responsibility. We are told that we need more abortion clinics, more condom distribution, and more aid to dependent children. But we dare not raise the "politically incorrect" cry for repentance, abstinence, or *morality*.

THE EVANGELICAL LOVE AFFAIR
WITH PSYCHOLOGY

Despite the glaring contradictions between secular psychology and biblical theology, the evangelical church has had a 30-year love affair with psychology. MacArthur observed that "evangelicalism is infatuated with psychotherapy. Emotional and psychological disorders supposedly requiring prolonged analysis have become almost fashionable."[7]

Why has this shift occurred? First, we must blame the modern church itself. Alien and anti-Christian ideologies have come and gone for centuries. But today's church is almost devoid of a clear-cut theology of any kind. Sermons are punctuated with a conglomeration of conflicting ideas regarding the very nature and task of the church itself. Christians in search of solutions for their problems have looked to the "insights" of secular psychology and brought them into a theologically illiterate church that has accepted those insights unwittingly and uncritically.

Second, we must recognize the failure of the twentieth-century church to make the Scripture relevant to the needs of individuals and families. It was not uncommon 20 to 30 years ago for people to attend church regularly but never hear a biblically relevant message on such issues as dating, marriage, family, divorce, singleness, or even personal spiritual growth. A number of popular Christian speakers and writers (such as Clyde Narramore, Henry Brandt, Tim LaHaye, Bill Gothard, and James Dobson) noticed this vacuum and began ministering to those in need. Soon terms like "Christian counselor" or "Christian psychologist" began to appear and found acceptability within Christian circles. *Christianity Today* recently observed that "popularizers such as authors James Dobson, Tim LaHaye and Larry Crabb convinced a whole generation of evangelicals that God cared about their psyches as well as their souls, opening the door for a marriage between theology and therapeutic thought."[8]

As a result, the church became involved in a debate over methodology in counseling. Jay Adams called for theologically trained counselors to fill the vacuum. Larry Crabb replied that it would take more than theology to fix damaged psyches and argued for better psychological training. Paul Meier and Frank Minirth began popularizing Christian psychiatry. Eventually, addiction recovery models became popular in evangelical circles. More and more Christians began seeking professional licensure in order to guarantee third-party insurance payments for their counseling services. The Christian counseling movement exploded, with clinics popping up everywhere: Rapha, Alpha Care, Minirth-Meier, and so on. Christian call-in programs came to fill the radio dial. Myriad books have been written. Counseling advice became available everywhere.

UNRESOLVED QUESTIONS

But with this explosion came some nagging questions that remained unresolved:

- Were theology and psychology really compatible?

- Did psychological labels really help people understand their struggles or merely excuse them?

- Was all this counseling really helping change people?

- How could psychologically trained counselors receive adequate biblical and theological training?

- Without biblical and theological training, how could Christian psychological counselors adequately deal with issues such as marriage, divorce, or child-rearing?

In response to those questions, Dr. Gary Collins, a leader in the Christian counseling movement, has admitted, "There are a number of people who have graduate school training in psychology, but Sunday school training in theology!"[9]

I (Howard) recently received a letter from one of my graduate students, who explained that he had to "set aside" his "previous training" at an evangelical institution to focus on the issues of conversion and character formation with a counselee who simply needed to "come to Christ." "That was one issue," he said, "no one ever dealt with in all my counseling training!"

From the time the Christian counseling movement began on up through today, the basic issues in the sufficiency debate have remained the same: If the Bible is really sufficient to meet man's needs, why do we need psychology? If psychology is sufficient, why do we need God or the Bible? Even so-called "integrationist" approaches—which profess to combine both the Bible and psychology—have not fully answered these basic questions.

Several key issues are still at stake in this debate:

1. How can secular training be viewed as adequate for counseling and theological training viewed as inadequate?

2. Can Sunday school "theology" adequately prepare Christian professionals to make intelligent theological judgments?

3. Why should Christian counselors abandon the Bible when many secularists actually applaud the Bible?

4. Are we not undermining our evangelical belief in biblical inerrancy by denying the sufficiency of Scripture in counseling?

5. How can we properly evaluate the challenges of multiculturalism and political correctness without a proper theological basis?

6. How does a person reconcile his own theology with competing theologies and remain consistent in his or her counseling?

7. Why should Christian counselors not offer to pray with their clients when many Christian doctors are now actively following this practice in the medical field?

THE DICHOTOMY BETWEEN BELIEF AND PRACTICE

What has happened to the modern Christian professional? Whether in the counseling professions, the practice of medicine, or in research, ministry, or education, many Christian professionals have adopted the modern mind-set of the world in which they live and have been trained. Theologian John Murray rightly observed that we need to "beware of the controlling framework of modern thinking lest its patterns and presuppositions become our own, and then, before we know it, we are carried away by a current of thought and attitudes that makes the sufficiency and finality of Scripture not only extraneous but akin to our way of thinking."[10]

An interesting dichotomy has arisen in the church today. During the 1970s a very successful organization developed under the leadership of James Montgomery Boice and several others: the International Council on Biblical Inerrancy. This organization produced a cohesive, scholarly, and distilled document that cogently states the doctrine of biblical inerrancy. Shortly after the final document was issued, it became evident that evangelicals could not relax in their defense of the Bible because the battle soon shifted its focus to the issue of the sufficiency of Scripture.

Today there is a dichotomy in the church on two levels. First, we have a church that professes to believe the Bible is inerrant, but it is not sufficient for matters of faith and life. It is not difficult to find evidence of this dichotomy. Survey, for example, the extracurricular offerings in many churches. On Sunday morning these churches uphold the Bible and its message of salvation through faith in Christ, but during the rest of the week there is a smorgasbord of self-help groups that meet to aid the Christian in his struggles with anything from worry to homosexuality. If you attend any of these self-help groups, you will discover that many offer advice that does not even come close to being biblical in nature. There is a dichotomy between the pulpit and the self-help groups, seminars, and classrooms within our own local churches.

Second, we have a church that professes to believe in an inerrant Bible that is sufficient for justification, but not for sanctification. Sid Galloway, who works closely with counselors in hospital settings, gave an example of this at a recent counseling convention. He reported about a conversation he had with one of his co-workers about the issue of biblical sufficiency. At one point Sid said, "I know you believe the Bible is sufficient for justification, but do you believe it is sufficient for sanctification?" After some discussion, the co-worker admitted that he did not believe that the Bible was sufficient for sanctification.

This dilemma is not true for all psychologists who are Christians. Psychologist Chris Thurman writes:

> Obviously . . . God helps us by providing truth in the form of His Word, the Bible. We don't have to wonder what the most important truths (true truth) in life are because God divinely inspired mortal man to write them down for our enlightenment and application. In a world where so much nonsense is passed off as wisdom, we don't have to be confused or in the dark about what truth is. If people need the truth to be set free, the Bible is God's way of giving us the truths we must believe for true freedom in life.[11]

The focus among evangelicals has shifted from inerrancy to sufficiency, and this shift has created a dichotomy with profound effects. The logical implication of this dichotomy is the concept that the Bible is sufficient to gain passage into heaven, but it is insufficient to deal with life on this earth.

THE PSYCHOLOGIZING OF EVANGELICALISM

How has the evangelical community arrived at this point? There are a number of factors that have contributed to the current dilemma. It is not the purpose of this book to trace the historical development of our present crisis; however, there is one issue that is essential to consider. It is the issue of *scientific methodology*, which has been extremely beneficial to the human community. There is no one alive today who would voluntarily wish to return to the prescientific era. The technology available to us in the medical sciences alone is cause for us to rejoice that the Lord has allowed us to live in this day and age. But many have endeavored to adapt scientific methodology to the social sciences, bringing about an unfortunate side effect. These individuals have given psychology the aura of the exactness of biology, chemistry, and the other hard sciences. This supposed credibility has too often translated debatable findings into truth. Phenomenological observations have become *laws.* "It *seems* to be true that . . ." has become "it *is* true that . . .". Unfortunately, many times it has been Christians who have been more prone to "deify" these findings, and not the secular community.

It is not uncommon today to hear Christians substantiating the concepts of psychology. Many Christians accept these concepts without any comprehension of whether they are biblically valid. For example, it is quite common to hear a Christian say, "I am a recovering alcoholic," or "I am codependent." They accept these conditions as having the same credibility as the substitutionary atonement of Christ. In doing so, these Christians embrace symptoms as conditions and end up locking themselves into living with these symptoms for the rest of their lives. Unfortunately, they never learn to deal with the root problem of their symptoms, which is sin.

Is Integration Desirable?

One popular writer has advocated "spoiling the Egyptians."[12] By this he means that Christians should take from the social sciences whatever "truth" has been discovered and bring it into their schema of Christian counseling. No doubt this writer intended to simply use this figure of speech in an allegorical sense. However, the allegory fails to do justice to the clear meaning of the biblical text from which the concept is taken. In the biblical text (Exodus 12:35-36), this spoiling of the Egyptians was clearly a matter of borrowing *material* things, not sociocultural concepts. In fact, when the Israelites did borrow such concepts they built a golden calf and an idol, and God punished them for it.

Several years ago, apologist and theologian Cornelius Van Til astutely anticipating the sufficiency debate, drew from the Scripture an illustration that is consistent with sound biblical exegesis and warned against turning to the world for any basis of knowledge. He wrote:

> To illustrate our attitude to modern science and its methodology we call to mind the story of Solomon and the Phoenicians. Solomon wished to build a temple to the covenant God. Did he ask those who were not of the covenant to make a blueprint for him? No, he got his blueprint from God. ... But was there nothing useful to do for those who were not of the covenant? Not at all. The Phoenicians were employed as laborers to cut the timber. These Phoenicians were even recognized as being far more skillful than the covenant people in fashioning and trimming the timbers. ... Solomon used the Phoenicians as his servants, not his architects. Something similar to this should be our attitude to science. We gladly recognize the detail work of many scientists (yes, even social scientists) as being highly valuable. ... But we cannot use modern scientists and their methods as the architects of our structures of Christian interpretation.[13]

When Van Til speaks of Christian interpretation, he is not talking about the interpretation of Scripture, though his premise also applies there, but rather about the Christian interpretation of life. All the sciences, especially the social sciences, are very much involved in the interpretation of life. When Carl Rogers worked with a client from the viewpoint that the client had within him the answer(s) to his problems, he was interpreting life. When Maslow set before us the goal of self-actualizing, he was interpreting life. When Aaron Beck and a host of other cognitive-behavioral therapists saw the change of cognitive structure and structured behavioral change as the key solution to life problems, they were interpreting life.

Van Til's position becomes poignant when we begin to realize that the adoption and adaption of the non-Christian conceptions of life, whether derived philosophically or through scientific methodology, is placing this interpretation of life on the same level as revelation.[14] Yet Scripture indicates that it alone is capable of making the person of God adequate (2 Timothy 3:16-17). Only the Bible can fully equip a Christian and enable him to perform every good work (that includes conducting one's life and profession within acceptable limits—the limits of Christ-like character).

As we were doing research for this chapter, we observed an interesting phenomenon. When the church was dealing with the issues of inerrancy and authority, a number of Christian writers who took an integrationist stance wrote convincingly that the Scriptures take precedence over all scientific data. There are dozens of volumes available on the inerrancy debate. But ever since the church's focus shifted from inerrancy to sufficiency, very little has been written in support of Scripture's preeminence. A literature review of the last ten years yielded several articles by John MacArthur, which were variations on his book *Our Sufficiency in Christ* (1991). Other resources included *How to Help People Change* by Jay Adams (1986); *The Sufficiency of Scripture* by Noel Weeks (1988); *Psychology, Theology and Spirituality* by Mark

McMinn (1996); and *Self-Help or Self Destruction?* by Chris Thurman (1996). There have been numerous articles on integration, but we expected to find many articles on sufficiency, and the discovery that so little had been written heightened our determination to produce this book.

THE ISSUE AT STAKE

It is important in this discussion to understand that the essence of this issue is not a particular school of counseling, nor a particular view of the Christian life, nor a particular theological perspective. The crux of the issue is this: When I put on my professional suit, has it been tailored by the pattern of Scripture? Does Scripture determine the parameters of my discipline? Regardless of what the evidence of my research may suggest, am I willing to subject my interpretation of that evidence to the parameters of Scripture?

In his book *The Sufficiency of Scripture*, Noel Weeks discusses two contemporary issues in the light of Scripture: homosexuality and divorce. He indicates that the reason the Bible is not seen to be sufficient with respect to these issues is that it is often assumed "that the writers of Scripture did not have the advantage of the knowledge of our day."[15] After some lengthy discussion of the implications of this premise, Weeks draws the following conclusion:

> If we believe that people are not responsible for their actions and that people cannot be changed, then we will not have any real incentive for trying to help such cases. If we believe that God does not act in this world, then we will believe that people cannot be changed. . . . If there is no hope for change, then there is no hope for marriages in difficulty or for homosexuals.[16]

The Christian interpretation of life is what is at stake. Is Scripture sufficient to interpret life? For example, is Scripture sufficient to understand the behaviors we call schizophrenia or homosexuality? Can the Bible help a Christian to change his behavior so that he becomes both an obedient Christian and a socially acceptable individual? Is Scripture sufficient to provide a framework out of which the biochemist or the geneticist can work? Is God's Word sufficient to provide a structure for the use of the knowledge that is learned within each given science?

In an endeavor to answer these questions, we approached a variety of Christian professionals and asked them to write on the sufficiency of Scripture for the parameters of their disciplines. You might readily expect the representatives of some of these disciplines to affirm such a proposition—for example, pastors Dr. Benton or Dr. Dobson. However, there are many men in evangelical ministry today who do not practice the sufficiency of Scripture for the parameters of their disciplines. Some of the contributors, such as biochemist Dr. Madtes and biologist Dr. Hyndman, may surprise you. Our intent in selecting these various authors was to drive home the reality that regardless of our vocation, Scripture must be the superior guide. In addition, we selected a larger number of contributors in the social sciences than in other areas because this is the field in which there is the greatest confusion and compromise among Christians. Writers like Jay Adams, Paul Vitz, William Kirkpatrick, and Ed Bulkley have addressed the problem with a broad stroke; we hope this more focused contribution will provide more substantive answers specifically related to the sufficiency debate.

Some people may suggest that our view of sufficiency invalidates any use of scientific methodology in the social setting. A careful reading of the essays, however, will show this is not true. We invite both groups of critics to enter this debate so that the role of the Scriptures in relation to human behavior and healing can be clearly and effectively articulated. With the exploding numbers of Christians who counsel—biblical counselors and Christian counselors—and the growing sophistication of these disciplines both in terms of professional associations and state licensure, it is imperative that counselors address the matter of Scripture's sufficiency. The same imperative exists for other professions. For example, the biochemical researcher faces various ethical issues in his or her work. How can those issues be adequately addressed without a sufficient word from God on such matters?

Ultimately, we believe in the sufficiency and the subjecting of all humanly derived knowledge to the scrutiny of the Scriptures. We unhesitatingly call upon Christians involved in the counseling fields to reclaim their biblical heritage and to construct their theory and practice of counseling in the light of biblical truth. Fads and theories come and go, but the Word of God abides forever. God does not call us to be trendy, but truthful. Not fashionable, but faithful. His Word promises to provide us "everything pertaining to life" (2 Peter 1:3). Either it does, or it doesn't. Either it is totally sufficient or utterly insufficient.

Although there is a wide diversity in the professions represented by the contributors to this book, there is an exceptional common thread that binds these authors and their professions together. Each writer has professed a commitment to the inerrancy, authority, and sufficiency of the Scriptures. At the same time, you will notice that not all the contributors have equally worked out the implications of their commitment. You may even find yourself questioning a specific contributor's commitment to sufficiency. However, we do not find such a criticism to be a threat to the premise of this book. Rather, we welcome the challenges that will help each of us to better refine the implications of our commitment to the sufficiency of the Scriptures. And we trust that you will welcome the useful insights of those Christian writers who may still be struggling with a commitment to the sufficiency of Scripture. We ourselves warmly acknowledge the scholarship, the Christian commitment, the genuine care, and the effectiveness of those Christian professionals who have not come to a full appreciation of the sufficiency of God's Word. We recognize that many sincere believers are struggling with this issue, and our hope is that this work will help people on both sides of the debate to see more clearly exactly what role Scripture plays in our lives.

TOTALLY SUFFICIENT

2

WHAT IS BIBLICAL COUNSELING?

Wayne A. Mack, D.Min.

The Chicago Statement on Biblical Inerrancy states that "the authority of Scripture is a key issue for the Christian church in this and every age. Those who profess faith in Jesus Christ as Lord and Savior are called to show the reality of their discipleship by humbly and faithfully obeying God's written Word. To stray from Scripture in faith and conduct is disloyalty to our Master. Recognition of the total truth and trustworthiness of Holy Scripture is essential to a full grasp and adequate confession of its authority."

As a Christian, I wholeheartedly agree with every aspect of this general statement on biblical inerrancy and authority. I believe in both the inerrancy and authority of Holy Scripture. For me, the inerrancy and authority of Scripture are like Siamese twins—they are inseparably joined to each other. Holy Scripture, being God's law and testimony, is true and should therefore serve as our standard for all matters of faith and practice (Isaiah 8:19-20; 2 Peter 1:3). God's Word being both truthful (John 17:17) and authoritative calls us to humble and faithful obedience in every area on which it speaks. There is no authority that is higher than the one found in Scripture. Wherever and on whatever subject the Scriptures speak, they must be regarded as both inerrant and authoritative.

As a Christian, it is because I affirm the preceding convictions that I believe in the sufficiency of Scripture in the area of counseling. Scripture is not silent about the matter of its sufficiency for both understanding man and his non-physical problems, and resolving those problems. To me, it is crystal-clear about those issues. And because this is what I understand Scripture to be teaching about itself, my profession of faith in Jesus Christ as Lord and Savior compels me to submit to this sufficiency teaching. As I see it, doing anything less would amount to me being disloyal to my Master.

There have always been people who have affirmed the inerrancy and authority of Scripture in matters of faith and practice, but who would not affirm the sufficiency of Scripture for understanding and resolving the spiritual (non-physical) problems of man. They believe that we need the insights of psychology to understand and help people. In essence, they believe that when it comes to these matters, the Bible is fundamentally deficient. They believe that God did not design the Bible for this purpose, and consequently we must rely on extrabiblical psychological theories and insights. For many Christians, the Bible has titular (given a title and respected in name) rather than functional (actual, practical, real, respected in practice) authority in the area of counseling. It is acknowledged to be the Word of God and therefore worthy of our respect, but when it comes to understanding and resolving many of the real issues of life, it is considered to have limited value.

A DEFINITION OF CHRISTIAN COUNSELING

Christian Counseling Is Christ-Centered

The attitude that many Christians have toward Scripture was vividly illustrated by a person who visited to interview me about the kind of counseling I did. This person was traveling around the United States questioning various Christian counselors and asking them about their views on what constitutes Christian counseling. In the interview, I said I believed that any counseling that was worthy of the name "Christian" should be *conscientiously and comprehensively Christ-centered.* It will make much of who and what Christ is, and what He has done for us in His life, death, and resurrection. It will emphasize what He is doing for us right now in His intercession for us at the Father's right hand and what He will do for us in the future. It will also emphasize the Holy Spirit's present ministry in the believer's life.

In Christian counseling, the Christ of the Bible is not to be an appendage. He is not a "tack on" for surviving life in the "fast lane." He needs to be at the core, as well as the circumference, of our counseling. If we want to understand the nature and causes of a person's human difficulties, we need to understand the ways in which that person is unlike Christ in his or her values, aspirations, desires, thoughts, feelings, choices, attitudes, actions, and responses. Resolving a person's sin-related difficulties requires him to be redeemed and justified through Christ, receive God's forgiveness through Christ, and acquire from Christ enabling power to replace unChristlike (sinful) patterns of life with Christlike (godly) ways of life.

In his book on *Our Sufficiency in Christ,* John MacArthur tells a story about a man who was shut out of a house on a cold night. He suffered some unpleasant consequences during the ordeal, all of which he could have avoided had he known he had, in his pocket, a key to the house. Dr. MacArthur writes:

> That true story illustrates the predicament of Christians who try to gain access to God's blessings

through human means, all the while possessing Christ, who is the key to every spiritual blessing. He alone fulfills the deepest longing of our hearts and supplies every spiritual resource we need.

Believers have in Christ everything they will ever need to meet any trial, any craving, any difficulty they might ever encounter in this life. Even the newest convert possesses sufficient resources for every spiritual need. From the moment of salvation each believer is in Christ (2 Corinthians 5:17) and Christ is in the believer (Colossians 1:27). The Holy Spirit abides within as well (Romans 8:9)— the Christian is His temple (1 Corinthians 6:19). "Of His fullness we have all received, and grace upon grace" (John 1:16). So every Christian is a self-contained treasury of divinely bestowed spiritual affluence. There is nothing more—no great transcendental secret, no ecstatic experience, no hidden spiritual wisdom—that can take Christians to some higher plane of spiritual life. "His divine power has granted us *everything* pertaining to life and godliness, through the knowledge of Him who called us" (2 Peter 1:3, emphasis added). "The true knowledge of *Him*" refers to saving knowledge. To seek something more is like frantically knocking on a door, seeking what is inside, not realizing you hold the key in your pocket. . . .

No higher knowledge, no hidden truth, nothing besides the all-sufficient resources that we find in Christ exists that can change the human heart.

Any counselor who desires to honor God and be effective must see the goal of his efforts as leading a person to the sufficiency of Christ. The view that man is capable of solving his own problems, or that people can help one another by "therapy" or other human means, denies the doctrine of human depravity and man's need for God. It replaces the Spirit's transforming power with impotent human wisdom.[1]

For Christian counseling to take place, the people doing the counseling must be individuals who are *conscientiously and comprehensively Christian* in their outlook on life. Truly Christian counseling is done by people who have experienced the regenerating work of the Holy Spirit, come to Christ in repentance and faith, acknowledged Him as Lord and Savior of their lives, and want to live in obedience to Him. Their main concern in life is to exalt Him and bring glory to His name. They believe that because God did not spare His own Son (from the cross) but delivered Him up (to the cross and death) for us (on our behalf as our substitute), He will freely give us—through Christ—all that we need for effective and productive living (for transforming us into the likeness of His Son). Truly Christian counseling is done by those whose theological convictions influence, permeate, and control their personal lives and their counseling theory and practice.

Christian Counseling Is Church-Centered

Another major distinctive of truly Christian counseling that I mentioned to my interviewer was that it is *conscientiously and comprehensively church-centered.* The Scriptures clearly teach that the local church is the primary means by which God intends to accomplish His work in the world. The local church is His ordained instrument for calling the lost to Himself. It is also the context in which He sanctifies and changes His people into the likeness of Christ. According to Scripture, the church is His household, the pillar and ground of the truth (1 Timothy 3:15), and the instrument He uses to help His people put off the old manner of life (pre-Christian ways of thinking, feeling, choosing, and acting) and put on the new self (a new manner of life with Christlike thoughts, feelings, choices, actions, values, and responses—Ephesians 4:1-32).

Even a cursory reading of the New Testament will lead a person to the conclusion that the church is at the center of God's program for His people. Jesus Christ, who proclaimed that He would build His church

(Matthew 16:18), invested in it authority to act with the *imprimatur* of heaven (Matthew 18:17-20) and ultimately revealed that His plan was to fill the world with local bodies of believers (Matthew 28:18-20).

When trying to capture and project his conception of the role of the church in God's program and with God's people, John Calvin made this impassioned assertion:

> Because it is now our intention to discuss the visible church, let us learn from the simple title "mother" how useful, indeed necessary, it is that we should know her. For there is no other way to enter life unless this mother conceive us in her womb, give us birth, nourish us at her breast, and lastly, unless she keep us under her care and guidance until, putting off mortal flesh, we become like the angels (Matthew 22:30). Our weakness does not allow us to be dismissed from her school until we have been pupils all our lives. . . . God's fatherly favor and the especial witness of spiritual life are limited to his flock, so that it is always disastrous to leave the church (John Calvin, *Institutes of Christian Religion*, 2:1012).

This statement about the church by John Calvin was not specifically directed toward the issue of counseling, but it does indicate Calvin's perspective on the importance of the church in the lives of believers. His view concurs with the ideas that the church is responsible for providing counseling and Christians are responsible for seeking care and guidance for their personal lives. Calvin's study of the Scriptures convinced him that the nurture, edification, and sanctification of believers was to be church-centered. I wholeheartedly agree with this emphasis because I believe that is the unmistakable teaching of Holy Scripture.[2]

Christian Counseling Is Bible-Based

As I continued to explain my views on Christian counseling, I told my visitor that truly Christian counseling is *conscientiously and comprehensively Bible-based*, deriving from the Bible an understanding of who man is, the nature of his main problems, why he has these problems, and how to resolve them. For counseling to be worthy of the name of Christ, the counselor must be conscientiously and comprehensively committed to the *sufficiency of Scripture* for understanding and resolving all of the non-physical personal and interpersonal sin-related difficulties of man.

QUESTIONING THE SUFFICIENCY OF SCRIPTURE

At this point, the individual who had come to ask about my views on Christian counseling responded by saying, "Well, what you're saying about all of these things is nice, but what do you think should be done when people have really serious problems?"

Now, consider what this person—who claimed to be a Christian—was implying by asking that question. She was implying that the factors I had mentioned might prove to be helpful for people who have minor problems, but certainly they are not enough for resolving the really serious problems of life. She was intimating that the approach I had described was rather simplistic. She was suggesting that the resources that God prescribes in His Word for ministering to needy people are not adequate. She was insinuating that the substantial insights necessary for ministering to people with major difficulties must be gleaned from sources other than the ones I had mentioned.

Unfortunately, at least from my perspective, her views represent the opinions of many professing Christians. In a book entitled *Introduction to Biblical Counseling*, Douglas Bookman describes the way such Christians think about the sufficiency of Scripture in relation to counseling:

Any Christian who sets out to counsel another individual is aware that the counsel offered must be true. Counseling is by definition and impulse a helping ministry. It assumes that someone is confronted with some measure of confusion, disappointment, or despair and that a second person endeavors to help by analyzing the counselee's situation, sorting out the issues involved, and then offering helpful and healing advice and direction. But the efficacy of all that the counselor undertakes to do is dependent at least on this one thing: that his analysis and counsel is *true*. Thus, any thoughtful consideration of the ministry of counseling must begin with the most basic of all philosophical questions, that question articulated by a Roman procurator two thousand years ago, "What is truth?"

Ever since its genesis as a distinguishable discipline almost four decades ago, the school of thought and ministry broadly known as Christian psychology has been convulsed by the issue of its own epistemological construct. (That is, where ought/may Christians go to find the *truth* necessary to help people who are hurting?) Because that discipline grew up largely within the broad limits of evangelical Christianity, there has been a universal acknowledgment of the veracity of Jesus' answer to the question of truth when, as He addressed His heavenly Father in prayer, He stated simply, "Thy Word is truth."

But for most that answer alone has not sufficed. The persuasion continues—articulated, justified, and applied in various ways—that there is *truth* that is at least *profitable* and perhaps even *necessary* to the counseling effort. This truth is to be discovered *beyond the pages of Scripture*. Christians who are thus persuaded are anxious to affirm Jesus' simple but profound declaration, yet they feel compelled to qualify that affirmation with the proposition that scriptural truths may (or even must) be supplemented by truths that have been discovered by human investigation and observation. This persuasion lies at the heart of the integrationist impulse of Christian psychology.

By all accounts, this integrationist tendency is rather recent in origin. Throughout much of the twentieth century a spirit of mutual mistrust and even contempt existed between the worlds of secular psychology and Christian theology. But that hostility began to thaw in certain circles sometime in the middle of this century, and by this last decade of the twentieth century there exists an obvious attitude of reconciliation between Christianity and psychology in many quarters. Indeed, many devotees of Christian psychology evidence a greater measure of fraternity with the secular psychological community than with those Christians who are compelled by their theology to reject the discipline of secular psychotherapy.[3]

The Two-Book Approach

Bookman then proceeds to delineate several ways in which Christians who don't believe in the Scripture's sufficiency for counseling actually do regard and use God's Word in counseling. One approach they use is called the *two-book* or the *general versus special revelation approach.* The argument that is often used to support this theory is that God reveals truth to us in two primary ways: through "nonpropositional truth deposited by God in the created order of things" which "must be investigated and discovered by mankind" and through "the propositional truth recorded in Scripture." The emphasis is that since all truth is God's truth, it really doesn't matter where that truth is found. Those who hold to this view believe that "the truth accurately derived from the consideration of the natural order of things (general revelation) is just as true as that derived from Scripture." When applied to the area of counseling, the proponents of this approach affirm that "any defensible truth that is derived by means of psychological research into the order of mankind is truth derived from general revelation, thus truth derived from God, and thus truth as dependable and authoritative as truth exegeted from Scripture."[4]

A representative quote from Harold Ellens, a defender of this two-book view, clearly illustrates the thinking behind this position. Ellens asserts:

Theology and psychology are both sciences in their own right, stand legitimately on their own foundations, read carefully are the two books of God's Revelation. . . .

Wherever *truth* is disclosed it is always *God's truth*. Whether it is found in General Revelation or Special Revelation, it is *truth* which has equal warrant with all other *truth*. Some *truth* may have greater weight than other *truth* in a specific situation, but there is no difference in its warrant as *truth*.[5]

In another publication, Ellens gives additional information about the nature of and rationale for this two-book perspective. In keeping with this idea that *general* and *special revelation* are complementary, serving different purposes and being *equally* authoritative, he makes the following comments:

I believe the Bible to be an internally coherent testimony of the believing community throughout a 2000- to 3000-year period regarding the mighty acts of God's redemption in the community's experience. I believe that testimony is normative and authoritative for us in matters of faith and life because it is a warrantable testimony and is God's universalized truth. This does not, however, force me to agree that the Bible is authoritative truth in matters which are not the focus and burden of that spirit-inspired, redemptive testimony of the historic believers. Moreover, because the Bible is a testimony incarnated in the human fabric of historical and cultural material, just as God's testimony in the Son of God himself was incarnated in that same human stuff, it is imperative that its human limitations and historical anomalies be differentiated from its redemptively revelational material. Jesus, for example . . . spoke quite erroneously in terms of a three-storied universe, an imminent second coming, and the like. Humanness radically conditioned Him with cultural-historical limitations as regards issues that were not central to the single truth of God's testimony in Him, that is, that God is for

us, not against us. Why are those who insist on inerrancy as the only foundation for authority in Scripture afraid to have a Bible that is at least as
culturally bound as was the incarnate Son of God
himself . . . ?

Sound psychological theory and practice genuinely enhance the patient's personhood. God designed what
that is. Christians perceive it to varying degrees. Full-
orbed personhood may be achieved by patients to
varying levels of functionality. Sound psychology,
which brings the patient, for example, out of depression
to emotional resilience and stability, is just as Christian
at that level as at the level affording the final stages of
maturity. . . . Even if that deliverance from depression is
done by a secularist, it is a Kingdom act and a Christian
enterprise. . . .

What matters in the helping of professing Christians is
less the imparting of biblical information or religious
practices to the patient, and more the enhancement of
healthy functionality of the human as person: in the direction of completeness in body, mind and spirit. That
practice of the helping professions that is preoccupied
with the final step of wholeness, spiritual maturity, will
short-circuit the therapeutic process and put the religious dynamic of the patient or therapist straight into
the religious person's pathology.[6]

The No-Book Approach

Another approach taught by integrationists might be
called the no-book approach, which suggests that we
can't really be sure our understanding of the Bible is accurate because our interpretive efforts are always colored
by our own perspectives. Bookman explains this approach in this way:

All human knowledge is flawed by definition.
These is no reason to be any more suspicious of science than of theology (i.e., of the theories and facts
derived by human investigation than of supposed

truths derived from Scripture) simply because Scripture is no less liable to the limitations of human participation than is any other truth source.

> Regardless of the authority and/or veracity of the truth source, human knowing of truth can only approach greater and greater levels of probability; certainty is propositionally unthinkable.[7]

While this viewpoint may seem incredulous to most Christians, it is likely to become the dominant view of so-called "Christian counseling" in the years ahead. This viewpoint already dominates post-critical hermeneutics and will most likely continue to filter down into the arena of pastoral and religious counseling.

The Filtering-Device Approach

Some Christians who aren't comfortable with either of the previously mentioned perspectives assert that the Bible should be used as a rule book or filtering device for identifying counseling truth. According to the advocates of this view,

> All truth claims that are the result of human cogitations, investigations, and theorizing must be subjected to the Word of God that alone will be allowed to pass judgment on the veracity and applicability of those truth claims. The Bible and the Bible alone will be granted the role of falsification; that is, if a truth-claim is discerned to contradict or compromise a truth established in Scripture, that competing truth-claim is to be adjudged false.[8]

> Truth derived from the study of any segment of general revelation, whether psychology or any other field, is not as trustworthy as the truth found in Scriptures. This is the reason that the integrationist will filter psychological truth through biblical truth and will accept only that which is not contradictory to God's special revelation.[9]

This view is sometimes called *"spoiling the Egyptians"*—a phrase that comes from Exodus 12:36 and is used in reference to what the Israelites did when they were delivered from Egyptian captivity. This incident is used to illustrate and give some biblical warrant to the practice of accepting and benefiting from extrabiblical insights in the realm of counseling theory and practice. Those who promote this view say that because the Israelites didn't reject the silver and gold that came from the ungodly Egyptians (in fact, they were commanded by God to take all of the silver and gold they could get—Exodus 3:21-22), we shouldn't reject counseling theories and practices that are discovered and used by unbelievers.

While the proponents of these three major approaches to Christian counseling differ on some issues, they are all agreed on one major point: The traditional biblical resources for dealing with man's problems are not enough; they simply are not adequate. We must make use of insights and ideas and techniques that are not taught by nor found in God's Word. Bookman and others have written excellent resources that expose the errors of such thinking, and I recommend their writings to you for further illumination and refutation.[10]

THE SHORTCOMINGS OF EXTRABIBLICAL INSIGHTS

Limitations of Human Knowledge

There are three reasons why I reject the idea that Christian counselors need extrabiblical insights to do truly effective counseling. The first reason is related to the *finiteness of man's knowledge*. The fact that man is finite necessarily limits the extent and validity of his knowledge. Even Adam, the first man, was a finite human being who needed God's revelation to rightly understand God, himself, what was right and wrong, what was true and what was false, what should be believed and what should not be believed (Genesis 1:26-28; 2:15-17, 24).

An old fable about six blind men who all bumped into and felt different parts of the same elephant illustrates the futility of man's attempts to find absolute truth by the usual means of intuition, reason or logic, or empirical research. As the story goes, one man approached the elephant from the front and grasped his trunk and said, "An elephant is like a fire hose." The second blind man happened to touch one of the animal's tusks and said, "An elephant is like a thick spear." The third blind man felt the elephant's side and said, "An elephant is like a wall." The fourth blind man, who approached the elephant from the rear and gripped its tail, said, "An elephant is like a rope." The fifth man grabbed hold of one of the elephant's legs and said, "An elephant is like the trunk of a tree." The sixth man, who was tall, grabbed one of the elephant's ears and said, "An elephant is like a fan."

Which of these depictions of an elephant was correct? None of them! And why? Because each blind man encountered or experienced only a limited portion of the whole elephant. Their knowledge of what an elephant was like was restricted and even erroneous because of the limitations of their experience and perception. And so it is and always must be with finite mortal man when it comes to the matter of discerning absolute truth apart from revelation from the living God, who knows all things and sees the whole picture clearly and perfectly.

A recent newspaper article reminded me of the futility of thinking that finite man can discover absolute truth apart from divine revelation. In this tongue-in-cheek article entitled "Education's Duplicity, Uselessness," Russell Baker writes:

> Pluto may not be a planet. Can you believe it? Is everything we learn in school a lie?

> This Pluto business is the last straw in the duplicity and uselessness of education. Now I have to deal with Plutonic revisionism, and I haven't even recovered from the discovery that you should not eat a good breakfast.

"Always eat a good breakfast." That's what they taught us in school. They said it was good for us.

Well, you know it, I know it, we all know it: they were wrong. We now know a good breakfast is bad for you. Those eggs sunny side up, that crisp bacon, the butter-soaked toast covered with jelly—bad for you.

So now we always eat a bad breakfast because they say a bad breakfast is good for you.

And remember the milk? Remember paying the milk money and having milk served right there in the classroom? What kind of milk was it?

Was it skim milk? Was it low-fat milk? Ha! You know it wasn't. It was milk with all the evil left in.

And they said it was good for you. Good for you! It was clogging your arteries and hastening your trip to the grave.

And they called that an education!

The older you get the clearer it becomes that education for the young may not only be useless, but downright dangerous.[11]

At this point in the article, Baker goes on to make a few more tongue-in-cheek remarks about the way what we once considered to be truth has been revised. After having done this, he concludes with these words:

Many people become as irked as I do about the incessant need to keep up with today's wisdom by abandoning or revising yesterday's. And of course today's wisdom will just as inevitably have to be abandoned or revised as the future bears down upon us.

You can bet the world has not faced the last revision of knowledge about Pluto, or about what constitutes a good breakfast. The revising of what we think of as knowledge goes on forever, and always has.

The truth about knowledge seems to be that its truth is only a sometimes thing, that what we accept as truth this year will have to be abandoned as the world turns.

This endless abandonment and revision is usually said to result from progress. But suppose progress is also an idea doomed to be abandoned. What if there is no such thing as progress, but only change?[12]

In his article, Baker astutely identifies the tentative nature of our humanly discovered knowledge or "truth" as he asserts that "what we accept as truth this year will have to be abandoned or revised." And why is humanly discovered "truth . . . only a sometimes thing"? One reason is because man's finiteness necessarily limits the extent and validity of his knowledge.

Depravity of Human Nature

A second factor that causes me to reject the idea that Christian counselors should welcome and depend on extrabiblical insights and therapies is connected to the biblical teaching about the *depravity of man's nature* since the fall of Adam in Genesis 3. Any biblical discussion of how man comes to know truth must include a consideration of what theologians often refer to as the "noetic"[13] effects of sin. Scripture clearly teaches that every aspect of man's being has been affected by sin. Man's character, speech, and behavior have all been perverted by sin[14]— as well as his emotions and desires, his conscience and will, his intellect, his thought processes, his goals and motives, and the way he views and interprets life. None of man's faculties have escaped the corrupting, corrosive, perverting, and debilitating impact of sin.

In reference to the cognitive, motivational, and emotional aspects of man's being, Scripture asserts that:

The heart is more deceitful than all else and is desperately sick; who can understand it? (Jeremiah 17:9).

God has looked down from heaven upon the sons of men, to see if there is anyone who understands (Psalm 53:2).

The wrath of God is revealed from heaven against all ungodliness and unrighteousness of men, who suppress the truth in unrighteousness. . . . Professing to be wise, they became fools. . . . For they exchanged the truth of God for a lie, and worshiped and served the creature rather than the Creator, who is blessed forever. . . . And just as they did not see fit to acknowledge God any longer, God gave them over to a depraved mind (Romans 1:18,22,25,28).

The mind set on the flesh is hostile toward God (Romans 8:7).

You were formerly alienated and hostile in mind (Colossians 1:21).

To the pure, all things are pure; but to those who are defiled and unbelieving, nothing is pure, but both their mind and their conscience are defiled (Titus 1:15).

Out of the heart come evil thoughts (Matthew 15:19).

In commenting on the noetic effects of sin, Edward Reynolds wrote:

Look into the mind; you shall find it full of vanity, wasting and wearying itself in childishness, impertinent, unprofitable notions, "full of ignorance and darkness," no man knoweth, nay no man hath so much acknowledged, as to enquire or seek after God in the way whereby he will be found. *Nay more, when God breaks in upon the mind, by some notable testimony from his creatures, judgments, or providence— yet they like it not, they hold it down, they reduce themselves back again to foolish hearts, to reprobate and undiscerning minds, as naturally as hot water returns to*

its former coldness. Full of curiosity, rash, unprofitable enquiries, foolish and unlearned questions,
profane babblings . . . perverse disputes, all the
fruits of corrupt and rotten minds. Full of pride and
contradiction against the truth, "oppositions of science," that is, setting up of philosophy and vain
deceits, imaginations, thoughts, fleshly reasonings
against the spirit and truth which is in Jesus. Full
of . . . fleshly wisdom, human inventions . . . of rules
and methods of its own to . . . come to happiness.
Full of inconstancy and roving swarms of empty
and foolish thoughts, slipperiness, and unstableness
. . . (emphasis added).[15]

What a clear description of sin's effects on the mind
of man! "But," you may ask, "what does this teaching
about the noetic effect of sin have to do with whether or
not Christian counselors should accept and use extrabiblical insights in their counseling efforts?"

The answer to that question is simple: Scripture teaches
that the minds of unredeemed men have been adversely affected by sin and, as a result, even if they observe something accurately, they are likely to interpret it wrongly.
Because they have the kind of mind (including all the cognitive, motivational, and emotional aspects previously
mentioned) described in the preceding Bible verses, unregenerate—and even to some extent, regenerate—men will
tend to distort truth. The only way we can think rightly is
to allow the Holy Spirit to renew our minds so that we will
learn to look at, interpret, and understand life through the
lens of Scripture (Psalm 36:9; 119:104; Isaiah 8:19-20; Romans 1:18-32; 12:2; Ephesians 4:23).

When he commented on the role that secular disciplines should play in biblical counseling, David
Powlison vividly described the noetic impact of sin on
man's thinking processes:

Secular disciplines may serve us well as they describe people; they may challenge us by how they
seek to explain, guide, and change people; but they

seriously mislead us when we take them at face value because they are secular. They explain people, define what people ought to be like, and try to solve people's problems without considering God and man's relationship to God. Secular disciplines have made a systematic commitment to being wrong.

This is not to deny that secular people are often brilliant observers of other human beings. They are often ingenious critics and theoreticians. But they also distort what they see and mislead by what they teach and do, because from God's point of view the wisdom of the world has fundamental folly written through it. They will not acknowledge that God has created human beings as God-related and God-accountable creatures. The mind-set of secularity is like a power saw with a set that deviates from the right angle. It may be a powerful saw, and it may cut a lot of wood, but every board comes out crooked.[16]

Because of our finiteness and sinfulness, our understanding of man and his problems can be trusted only when our thoughts and insights reflect the teaching of Holy Scripture. We simply are not able to ascertain truth apart from divine revelation. In another work, I wrote:

> We have no standard by which we can evaluate whether something is true or false except the Word of God. Thus while we can be confident that whatever we share with our counselees from the Word of God is true, we should have a healthy skepticism about any theory or insight that does not proceed from Scripture. If it is not taught by the Word of God alone, it may be error.[17]

In his book *Every Thought Captive*, Richard Pratt explains man's epistemological predicament apart from divine relation this way:

> All that can properly be called truth, not just "religious truth," resides first in God and men know

truly only as they come to God's revelation of Himself as the source of truth . . . (Psalm 94:10). . . . This dependence on God in the area of knowledge does not mean that men are without the true ability to think and reason. . . . Men do actually think, yet true knowledge is dependent on and derived from God's knowledge as it has been revealed to man.[18]

"But," someone may ask, "what about those statements that finite and sinful men make that seem to be a reiteration of concepts and ideas taught by Scripture? Must we regard these observations as false because people did not get them from the Bible?" These questions may be answered in these ways:

1. People may have been influenced by biblical teaching through various means and not even be aware of it, nor give the Bible credit for their insights. But even if this occurs, they will always distort scriptural teaching and put their own spin on it. They may, for example, talk about the importance of God, prayer, forgiveness, dealing with guilt, taking responsibility, love, confession, or the spiritual dimension in life. On the surface, a person's teaching on these concepts may seem biblical, but upon further investigation the theologically, biblically trained person will discover that not everything that sounds the same is the same. People may be using the same words or presenting the same concepts that God mentions in His Word, but they may also be filling those words and concepts with completely different meanings. In fact, the Bible tells us that men will suppress, deny, and distort the truth even if it is staring them in the face (Romans 1:18; 1 Corinthians 2:14).

2. Extrabiblical statements that seem to reflect biblical truth must be regarded as false because, as Richard Pratt states, "they are not the result of voluntary obedience to God's revelation."[19]

3. "Beyond this," Pratt continues, "the statements are falsified by the non-Christian framework of meaning and therefore lead away from the worship of God. If nothing else, the mere commitment to human independence falsifies the non-Christian's statements."[20]

The Sufficiency of Scripture

My third reason for rejecting the idea that Christian counselors need extrabiblical insights is that the Bible says God has given us—in our union with Christ and in His Word—everything that is necessary for living and for godliness (2 Peter 1:3). Scripture clearly says that it contains all the principles and practical insights that are necessary for understanding people and their problems (as we'll see in a moment). So apart from the question of whether it is possible to integrate the ideas of man with the truths of God's Word is the issue of whether or not it is necessary. On this matter, I am convinced the Scripture's own testimony about its sufficiency, adequacy, and superiority is abundantly plain.

To demonstrate this I could cite numerous passages of Scripture, but for the sake of time and space I will refer to only three representative passages: one from the Old Testament and two from the New. Psalm 19:7-11 makes numerous statements about the Bible that no one would ever consider making about the ideas of any man. In this text, assertions are made that set the Bible in a class all by itself—statements that unmistakably demonstrate the Bible's sufficiency and superiority over any of man's theories. Consider carefully what this passage says about what Scripture is and what it can do, and then think of the counseling implications of these assertions. According to Psalm 19:7-11, Scripture:

1. Is *perfect* (whole, complete, sufficient, lacking nothing) and therefore able to restore (transform, renew, restore) the soul (the inner man, the real self)—verse 7.

2. Is a *sure* (trustworthy, reliable, dependable) witness and therefore able to make wise the simple (people who lack a proper understanding of life, God, themselves, others)—verse 7.

3. Contains precepts (principles, guidelines, rules for character and conduct) that are *right* (correct, in accord with what is just and good, appropriate and fitting) and therefore able to cause the heart (the totality of man's inner non-physical self) to rejoice (to experience a sense of well-being, serenity, tranquility, and peace)—verse 8.

4. Is *authoritative* (it gives mandates and directives that are always correct) and pure (clear, untainted with evil or error) and therefore able to bring light into man's chaos and confusion, to replace man's ignorance and lack of understanding with clear direction, perspective, and insight—verse 8.

5. Is *clean* (uncontaminated, free from impurity, defilement) and enduring (permanent, unchanging, relevant, up to date, never outdated, never in need of alteration) and therefore able to produce the fear of the Lord (a wholesome and incredibly practical and positive reverence for God)—verse 9.

6. *Provides insights* about God, man, life, and everything needed for living and godliness that are altogether true (they correspond to and accurately reflect reality, they tell it like it really is) and righteous (they reflect that which is right, good, and holy, that which is truly just and fair) and therefore lead men to understand and practice what is truly real and right—verse 9.

7. Being "more desirable than gold, yes, than much fine gold," is able to produce in us a kind of *prosperity* that is more valuable than all the material riches of the world—verse 10.

8. Being "sweeter also than honey and the drippings of the honeycomb," is able to remove the sourness,

acidity, and bitterness caused by sin and to produce in us a *sweetness* of life that surpasses anything the world can provide—verse 10.

9. Possessing all of the previously noted qualities, is able to infallibly *warn and protect* us from the many dangers and disasters that can result from an ignorance of what is truly right—verse 11.

10. Possessing all of the previously noted characteristics, is able to *preserve* us from temptation, sin, error, false teaching, and every other threat to the health and well-being of our inner man—our thoughts, emotions, affections, and attitudes—verse 11.

Believing as I do in the inspiration, inerrancy, and authority of the Scriptures, Psalm 19:7-11 settles the sufficiency issue for me. If words mean anything, how could I come to any other conclusion? But there's more—much more. And some of that "more" is found in 2 Timothy 3:1-17. In the 13 verses of this chapter, Paul delineates a host of problems representative of what counselors often encounter in their attempts to help people. Many people who require counseling do so because they are struggling with difficulties that stem from one or more of the sinful attitudes, desires, and actions that Paul mentions in this rich passage.

Some people seek counseling because of problems that are associated with being "lovers of self, lovers of money, boastful, arrogant, revilers, disobedient to parents, ungrateful, unholy, unloving, irreconcilable, malicious gossips, without self-control, brutal, haters of good, treacherous, reckless, conceited, lovers of pleasure rather than lovers of God" (verses 2-4). Some individuals need counseling because they are "holding to a form of godliness, although they have denied its power" (verse 5). Some are struggling because they are "weighed down with sins, led on by various impulses" (verse 6). Many experience severe difficulties in their lives that are related to pride, opposition to and rebellion against God's truth, ungodly thoughts, deceitful patterns of living, and relating to people. Unpleasant, distressing difficulties that motivate people to seek counseling occur because they are "always learning and never able to come to the truth" or because they live in the midst of a society of people who are vile and hypocritical—people who are going "from bad to worse" (2 Timothy 3:6-13). People need counseling either because they are personally experiencing and manifesting sinful attitudes, desires, and behaviors; or they are personally suffering from the influence of people who manifest the sinful patterns depicted in this passage.

Where do we turn for resources to minister to these kinds of people? What do we need for understanding and resolving their problems? Paul answers that question in verses 14-17. At this point in his epistle, he turns from a description of the kinds of problems that people experience in this sin-cursed world to a description of the resources Christians have for ministering to the people he has just described in the first 13 verses. In clear and unmistakable words, Paul tells us that the resources we need for ministering to people who live in a 2 Timothy 3:1-13 society are found in Scripture. In concise, direct terms, Paul extols the Bible's total adequacy for ministering to people whose lives are characterized or affected by the things mentioned in verses 1-13.

WHY IS SCRIPTURE ADEQUATE?

According to Paul, the Scripture is totally adequate because:

1. *It is holy or sacred* (verse 15). It is set apart from any other writing or literary production; it is unique; it is in a class all by itself. No other writing can compare with what is written in the Scriptures.

2. *It is able* (verse 15). It has power to do things to and in people. "It is," as Jay Adams has written, "the Holy Spirit's tool for working in the minds

and hearts of men and women to make them like Christ. Being peculiarly associated with the Spirit both in its composition and in its use, the Bible is powerful, able to transform our lives."[21]

3. *It is inspired by God* (verse 16). Literally, the Greek word translated "inspired" means "God breathed." So Paul is telling us that the Bible is unique and able because its truths had their origin in God; they are not merely some man's opinions or discoveries or insights. As Peter said, "no prophecy of Scripture is a matter of one's own interpretation, for no prophecy was ever made by an act of human will, but men moved by the Holy Spirit spoke from God" (2 Peter 1:20-21). That is why, when quoting a portion of Psalm 2 (a psalm written by David), the early Christians said that the truth found in this psalm came to us from God by the Holy Spirit through the mouth of David (Acts 4:24-26). To the early Christians, the words of Scripture were authoritative and sufficient because, even though they came through the agency of holy men, they ultimately had their origin in God.

4. *It is profitable or useful* (verse 16). God's Word has utilitarian value; it enhances life; it is profitable in every way—for time and eternity, for our relationships with God and our fellow man, for our spiritual and emotional and mental well-being, for our marriages and families, for our goals and motivations, for guidance and direction, for comfort and challenge, for preventing and resolving our inner and interpersonal problems, for all of life. It is useful for teaching; it is the instrument the Holy Spirit uses to provide for us a standard of what is right and wrong, good and bad, true and false about all the truly important matters of life. Scripture is useful for reproof; the Holy Spirit uses it to convict us of sin and show us when we are wrong in our thinking, motives, desires, attitudes,

feelings, values, actions, and reactions. It is the instrument the Holy Spirit uses to bring us under conviction and motivate us to want to repent and change.

God's Word is also useful for correction; the Holy Spirit uses it to point us in the right direction and correct our sinful thoughts, motives, feelings, actions, and speech. It not only shows us what we need to change, but also tells us how to change and what to change to. And Scripture is profitable for training; it is the instrument the Holy Spirit uses to help us to develop new patterns of life. Scripture makes that which is unnatural—living righteously—natural; and makes that which is difficult—living God's way—easier. It helps us to develop strength in the areas in which we are weak.

5. *It can thoroughly equip the man of God for every good work* (verse 17). Through Scripture, the Holy Spirit thoroughly equips His servants—people of God— to do everything He wants them to do in the kind of society described in 2 Timothy 3:1-13. Do God's people need anything more than Scripture to effectively minister to the people living in the world described in verses 1-13? Is anything else really necessary? Absolutely not! Through Scripture, every believer can be thoroughly equipped. In Scripture, Christians have everything they need to understand people and their problems and to help them resolve those problems.[22]

John Murray draws the following conclusion about 2 Timothy 3:15-17: "There is no situation in which we (as men of God) are placed, no demand that arises for which Scripture as the deposit of the manifold wisdom of God is not adequate and sufficient" (Murray, *Collected Writings*, 3:261).[23]

OUR SUFFICIENCY IN CHRIST

Perhaps there is no better summary of the Bible's teaching about our complete sufficiency in Christ than the one given by the apostle Peter when he wrote that by His divine power, God "has granted to us everything pertaining to life and godliness" (2 Peter 1:3). "Life" has to do with everything related to living effectively and biblically in our daily activities and relationships with our environment and other people. "Godliness" has to do with our relationship with God—with living a God-centered, God-conscious life marked by godly character and conduct.

In 2 Peter 1:4-8, Peter defines "everything pertaining to life and godliness" as *"becom[ing] partakers of the divine nature"* (emphasis added). It involves being born again or from above; becoming a new creation in Christ Jesus; receiving from God a new nature with new dispositions, desires, interests, potential, and power; putting on the new self; and being renewed in the image of God (Romans 6:1-11; 2 Corinthians 5:17; Colossians 3:10; 1 Peter 1:23; 2 Peter 1:4; 1 John 3:1-18). It involves the capacity to "escape the corruption in the world caused by evil desires" (2 Peter 1:4 NIV). It involves developing the qualities of faith, moral excellence, true knowledge, self-control, perseverance, godliness, brotherly kindness, and Christian love (2 Peter 1:4-7) so that you might live a useful life for Christ (verses 8-10).

Life and godliness also involves being able to deal successfully with the issues that are present in the lives of people who seek counseling. People who are in need of counseling lack the qualities Peter mentions in 2 Peter 1:4-7 and need help in developing them. It's interesting to observe that people whose lives do reflect these qualities don't need much formal counseling. This passage, then, is pregnant with counseling implications.

Notice that Peter said that God has, by His divine power, "granted to us *everything* pertaining to life and godliness" (2 Peter 1:3, emphasis added). *Everything* that is needed to develop this kind of life and acquire the qualities in verses 4-7 has been granted to us by God. And how do we tap into these powerful, all-sufficient resources? Peter declared that these divine resources become ours through the true knowledge of God and of Jesus our Lord, and through the medium of His precious and magnificent promises (2 Peter 1:2-4). In other words, the repository of the *everything* we need for life and godliness is found in our glorious and excellent God and His precious and magnificent Word.

Our sufficiency as Christians is found in a deeper, fuller, life-changing knowledge of the glory and excellence of God and the magnificence and preciousness of His promises. Derek Kidner observed that God has called us to share "something of His moral excellence in this life, and of His glory hereafter. . . . The triple agency of the promises, the power and the Person of the Lord regenerate a man and make him a sharer in God's own nature, so that the family likeness begins to be seen in him."[23]

WORTHY OF FULL CONFIDENCE

In light of what we've learned from Psalm 19:7-11, 2 Timothy 3:15-17, and 2 Peter 1:3-7 I ask this question: Could God have stated more clearly the sufficiency of our resources in Christ and in His Word? What more could He have said to get the message through to us that we do not need any extrabiblical resources to understand people and their problems and help them to develop the qualities, attitudes, desires, values, feelings, and behavior that are proper for relating to and living before God in a way that pleases and honors Him?

A consideration of the truths presented in those three passages and many other sections of Scripture forces me to draw three conclusions:

1. The inerrant Bible to which Christians are committed as an authority in life teaches that God has provided for us in His Word whatever is true and necessary for successful living. It declares that God has given us, in the Bible, everything we need for living in right relationship with God, ourselves, and other people.

2. Because that is true, professing Christians have two options: either they must yield to the Bible's teaching on this matter or they must abandon the idea that the Bible is inerrant and authoritative. It is either inerrant and authoritative and also sufficient, or it is none of those things. If the Bible claims to be sufficient and it isn't, then you cannot say it is inerrant and authoritative. Given what the Bible teaches about itself, you simply cannot have it both ways.

3. This final conclusion is a natural concomitant of accepting the truthfulness of the first conclusion: Because the Bible asserts its own sufficiency for counseling-related issues, secular psychology has nothing to offer for understanding or providing solutions to the non-physical problems of people. When it comes to counseling people, we have no reason to depend on the insights of finite and fallen men. Rather, we have every reason to place our confidence in the sure, dependable, and entirely trustworthy revelation of God given to us in Holy Scripture because it contains a God-ordained, sufficient, comprehensive system of theoretical commitments, principles, insights, goals, and appropriate methods for understanding and resolving the non-physical problems of people. It provides for us a model that needs no supplement. God, the expert on helping people, has given us in Scripture counseling perspectives and methodology that are wholly adequate for resolving our sin-related problems.

THE NEED FOR CAUTION

David Powlison has stated well the danger of including extrabiblical ideas in the counsel offered to or by Christians:

> Let us clarify first what we mean by counseling methodology. A counseling methodology is a *system*

of theoretical commitments, principles, goals, and appropriate methods. It is a set of interconnected things; it is not a collection or random and eclectic bits of observation or technique. A counseling methodology is an organized, committed way of understanding and tackling people's problems.

Do secular disciplines have anything to offer to the methodology of biblical counseling? The answer is a flat no. Scriptures provide the system for Biblical counseling. Other disciplines—history, anthropology, literature, sociology, psychology, biology, business, political science—may be useful in a variety of secondary ways to the pastor and the biblical counselor, but such disciplines can never provide a system for understanding and counseling people.

God is the expert when it comes to people, and He has spoken and acted to change us and equip us to help others change.[24]

Secular psychology may play an *illustrative* (providing examples and details that, when carefully and radically reinterpreted, illustrate the biblical model) or *provocative* (challenging us to study the Scriptures more thoroughly to develop our model in areas we have not thought about or have neglected or misconstrued) function, but, because of man's finiteness and fallenness, the insights, methodologies, and practices of secular psychology are in many instances dangerously unbiblical, dishonoring to God, and harmful to people. Other aspects of secular psychology are at best neutral and therefore unnecessary.

None of the illustrations, observations, or details that secularists present are necessary for the task of understanding and helping people. We already have all we need—the authoritative, indispensable, perspicuous, sufficient, and superior revelation of God in His Word (Isaiah 8:19-20). Why, then, would any Christian think that we must turn to the extrabiblical theories or the practices of men for understanding and promoting change in people?

BIBLE-BASED RESOURCES FOR MAN'S PROBLEMS

Because the purpose of this chapter was to demonstrate that the Bible asserts its sufficiency for understanding and resolving the kinds of issues that counselors (Christian or non-Christian) deal with in their attempts to help people, I have not taken time to provide specific examples of how the Scriptures actually do help us or to provide details about a biblical methodology for counseling. Should you desire to pursue "the how to" more fully, I have listed some recommended resources.[25]

In these resources, you will find information about a biblical counseling methodology for understanding and resolving the problems of people. You will find case studies and teaching that illustrates the sufficiency of Scripture for people who claim to be suffering from multiple personality disorder (MPD); various kinds of eating disorders; sexual sins such as incest, homosexuality, transvestism, transsexualism, slavery to pornography and lust; depression; anxiety; anger; bizarre, schizophrenic behavior; drug abuse, including alcoholism; and what secularists would call obsessive, compulsive disorders. You will find biblically based information about problems of the past, self-esteem problems, chronic fatigue, demon possession, chemical imbalance, victimization, suffering, human defensiveness, women in menopause, women and PMS, confidentiality in counseling, crisis counseling, guilt, panic attacks, inordinate fears, psychological testing, ADHD, rebuilding a marriage after adultery, counseling various kinds of marriage and family problems, and other counseling issues.

TOTALLY SUFFICIENT

3

DOES BIBLICAL COUNSELING REALLY WORK?

David Powlison, Ph.D.

W hen I was asked to write about the sufficiency of Scripture for my discipline, I felt both excitement and uncertainty. The excitement came because I believe in the sufficiency, authority, and relevancy of Scripture for what I do. The uncertainty came because I don't know how to define my "discipline"! For the most part, I am a biblical counselor. I talk to people about their problems: interpersonal conflicts, hopelessness, confusion, frustration, fear, suffering, shyness, guilt, self-centeredness, false beliefs, decision making . . . the gamut. I also teach people to think biblically and presuppositionally about secular psychology. All those tasks come roughly under the heading of pastoral counselor and pastoral theologian.

But I also wear another disciplinary hat. I am a historian of science, medicine, and technology. I read scholarly articles and books that describe, interpret, and assess the "scientific" endeavor to comprehend and fix the world. Within this large field, I've concentrated on the history of efforts some people make to help other people with their problems in living: the activities that are known as counseling, psychology, psychiatry, and psychotherapy. Perhaps I could use the old theological phrase "the cure of souls" to describe what both secular and religious people attempt to do. If history shows one thing, it shows that each of the varied forms of the "cure" is wedded to a different interpretation of the "disease." The cure of souls displays an ever-shifting mosaic of conflicting ideas and practices.

The history of psychotherapy and psychiatry shows something else. The different fads and fashions in theory and therapy have been unified by two things: 1) human beings *are not* fundamentally sinful, and 2) the answer to people's problems lies *within* the individual or *within* human relationships. Secular theories view God's law and gospel as irrelevant for understanding and helping people. After the Civil War, people who did not believe that the Bible was sufficient, necessary, relevant, or true took over the care and treatment of problems in living. And today, many people believe that the Bible is flatly wrong and harmful. For example, it is hard to square the goals of a "positive mental attitude," "a robust mental health," and a "buoyant self-esteem" with a Bible that takes great pains to state that every person is a sinner and God has come as a Savior.

So what is my discipline? In a nutshell, I counsel biblically and study the history and ideas of people who disagree with me! These two professional strands—practitioner and scholar—actually unite toward a common mission. My desire is for Christians to become confident that Scripture is *about* what counseling is about. I also desire that Christians would become skilled in applying Scripture to life—first, to understand human problems accurately, and second, to address human problems wisely. The theme of this essay, then, is the theme of my life work.

This essay will defend the notion that Scripture is about what counseling is about. The Bible's relevance and sufficiency for the cure of souls is immediate and practical. This is more than abstract theory or the affirmation that counseling must proceed within the general boundaries of a Christian worldview. In the counseling discipline, Scripture gives much more than the contours of a worldview. The instructions Paul wrote in his epistles were designed to *change* lives in particular ways. Jesus taught His disciples with the intention of *changing* their motives, actions, words, attitudes, beliefs, and priorities. The same is true about the writings of the prophets, Moses, David, and Solomon. History and prophecy, law and gospel, epistle and meditation, psalm and proverb all are given to provide counsel, teaching, reproof, encouragement, enlightenment, and challenge. God didn't talk and act to fill up pages. He spoke in order to transform the way we live: "The secret things belong to the LORD our God, but the things revealed belong to us and to our sons forever, that we may observe all the words of this law" (Deuteronomy 29:29).

The relevance and sufficiency of Scripture is also not just a matter of rhetoric: "The Bible, the Bible, the Bible." Such rhetoric is also easy to pay lip service to without translating into practical help. Rhetoric gets stale, mean, or defensive. And rhetoric is uninformative. But Scripture goes into action and changes people. *How* does the Bible apply to people? *How* does change take place? *How* should counselors proceed to obey God and genuinely assist people?

In this essay, I want to demonstrate that Scripture is about what counseling is about. First, I will present a case study to demonstrate biblical thinking in action. The Bible says of itself that the Word of God discerns the thoughts and intentions of the heart (Hebrews 4:12). In the details of a life, Scripture enables us to understand what makes a person tick. The law of God exposes both a person's "false gods" and "the evil works of his hands." The gospel of God brings comprehensive change, instating the true God and Savior, and empowering new obedience. Biblical counseling is the instrument God says He uses to accomplish such a cure of souls. Robust, biblical Christianity speaks a better and truer word to the problems of living.

Second, I will look at how secular psychologies and psychotherapies shape the way Christians view people and counseling. The popular catchword is *integration*, as in "the integration of psychology and Christianity." What generally happens in such "integration" is that the Christianity is not robust enough to address the field of counseling as an independent and free-thinking voice. Rather, the psychology is robust, so it ends up dictating the vision of people and counseling. The net effect is "the accommodation of Christianity to psychology" or "the syncretism of Christianity with psychology" or "the subversion of Christianity by psychology."

Third, if Scripture teaches us God's own positive approach to counseling, how should biblical Christians interact with secular psychology, or with any other set of distorted observations, interpretations, and practices? Truth generates a penetrating criticism of counterfeits and lies. But commitment to the sufficiency of Scripture does not hermetically seal the mind to all further input or interaction. Far from it. Such commitment is a standpoint on the world, not a blindfold to the world. God's point of view places a paradigm shift, a radical reinterpretation, on what worldly people think they see. C.S. Lewis put it charmingly: "We believe that the sun is in the sky at midday, not because we can clearly see the sun (in fact it's too bright to see!), but because by it we can see everything else."[1]

Fourth, I will discuss how to convert "integrationists" to biblical wisdom. Most Christians who embrace psychology do so unwittingly, not knowing the power, sufficiency, relevance, and persuasiveness of the biblical alternative. Our goal must not simply be to stake out turf against encroachers; we must also aim to win psychologized people to God's glory. The counseling field is ripe for powerful evangelism. Such evangelism addresses not only the individual's moral life and religious commitments, it also addresses the intellectual and professional outworking of those morals and commitments. Because Scripture is about what counseling is about, it makes sense that the cure of souls will continue to be a major cultural and religious battlefield as we enter the twenty-first century—a battlefield where God will greatly glorify Himself by changing lives.[2]

CASE STUDY: "LOIS"[3]

Lois is a 39-year-old woman. She married at 19 because she was pregnant, and became divorced at 22. She subsequently got her bachelor's degree in elementary education, and has been teaching for 12 years in a local public school. She has found a lot of meaning and stability in her job, and has received consistently good evaluations from supervisors. Lois had a number of short-term sexual relationships with men over the years, but never remarried. Her daughter, Reneé, left home after high school, became employed at a beauty shop, and moved in with her boyfriend. Lois' relationship with Reneé was basically positive, and she looked to that as a source of stability and "being forced to be responsible" over the years.

At various times she drank heavily and used marijuana recreationally. She never considered herself an alcoholic, for she could stop at will when she became alarmed at what seemed to be excessive use. She was slightly pudgy, and was concerned about a recent ten-pound weight gain that she attributed to "snacking to calm my nerves." She dressed modestly and "middle of the road"—neither flashy nor dowdy—and used makeup only occasionally and sparingly. "I try to keep myself looking reasonably well, but I've never been too obsessed with what I look like." She used to watch TV for a couple of hours every night, but that tapered off to only two or three nights a week.

At one time she had gotten herself rather deep into debt. But for the last five years, she was basically free of debt, despite occasional "binge" purchases that set her back temporarily. She earned enough to live "hand-to-mouth," and said she didn't have enough money to put any aside into savings. She worried that she was unable to save up for an IRA or a down payment on a house. She viewed her teacher's pension as an important source of security.

At various times she struggled with depression, even seeking psychiatric help on one occasion. She frequently oscillated between fearful "mousiness" and angry rages with her husband and boyfriends. Feelings of anxiety, failure, and self-hatred were "endemic and sometimes became epidemic." The intensity and frequency of these reactions and feelings lessened somewhat as she "grew up" in her thirties.

Her family upbringing was, in her words, "bizarre." Her father was "brilliant, and he'd always tell us that he failed to get his Ph.D. only because he insulted his advisor, who was a total jerk and deserved to be told so. My father was a believer in telling people exactly what he thought of them, which wasn't too pleasant for me because he didn't think too much of me." Her father was an alcoholic who was constantly losing jobs and alienating people by his aggressive and "paranoid" ways. "I think I inherited some of his intelligence, for I always did well in school. I think I would have felt more hurt by him if I hadn't seen him as a 'crazy man' even from when I was in elementary school. I usually tried to keep my distance." Lois saw herself as a lot like her mother in personality—"only not so extreme"—in being prone to passivity, fear, anxiety, and only occasional anger. "I'm a pleaser and a follower, not an initiator, leader or aggressor. I'm like her, but I was never close to her." The family lived in eight different towns during Lois' school years. "I basically got pregnant and married in order to have an excuse to get out of the house. I never really had any friends, and I fell for the first person who was nice to me." She had no formal religious upbringing.

At the present time, Lois' father is living 3000 miles away. "Since I became a Christian I've been able to forgive him, and start up a reasonably cordial relationship—I write or phone every few months, and have visited for a couple days on two occasions. He's still a bit of a trial, and it would take a miracle for us to ever really be close. He's the same old self, though each of his negative ways is less intense." Lois' mother had divorced him after the children left home, and she died ten years ago. "I grieved. I coped. I think I feel sadder and feel regrets more now that I'm a Christian, because we were never really close. She was too wrapped up in her own problems."

Lois has a brother seven years older than her with whom she has never been close. "We each tried to make the best of it, and were too far apart to ever be more than next-door neighbors who feel a kind of arm's-length curiosity about each other. He's had a couple divorces, but seems to be doing pretty well running his small business."

Lois had converted to Christ four years ago through the testimony of a neighboring woman who had become a friend. Her involvement with the sexual immorality and substance abuse stopped immediately. The slow curve of improvement in negative feelings and actions—anger, depression, anxiety, low self-esteem, fearfulness, emotional volatility—took a rather marked positive jump, though she is still plagued by these from time to time. Lois came to know other Christian women who could serve as role models and help her to grow both personally and in having some confidence to think about getting involved with a man again. She now wants to serve the Lord with her gifts, and has gotten active in teaching Sunday school and attending a few courses in her church's weekly Bible school. She knows three Christian women whom she counts as close friends, all of whom are married. One of the couples hosts a weekly Bible study and fellowship group, which Lois attends regularly. She describes the study as a place where "people are honest and pray for one another."

Lois' present problem is twofold: "I'm depressed, afraid, and panicky in my own heart. I know that Jesus died for my sins, but sometimes I just don't feel it and I tell myself that God must hate me. And sometimes things get angry, tense, and depressing between me and Willy. I just react and either see red or see blue!" She has been dating Willy for about eight months. He is a Christian man her age, and has never married. He has been a Christian since his teens, and is both knowledgeable in the Bible and committed to ministering as a deacon. He is a high school graduate and works as a foreman in a factory.

Lois and Willy met at the Bible study. They had both found it easy to talk with one another—until recently. They have the same basic goals for lifestyle and ministry, and have felt a real "click" with one another. They would like to marry, and their mutual friends think they're a natural pair. But their relationship is having problems. "He's the one, I know it, but why am I getting so uptight?" She has become very picky about his shortcomings, and both of them are distressed about that. They have had arguments that they have not been able to solve, so their trust for each other has been diminishing. There are "taboo topics" that they can't approach without becoming tense: setting a date for the marriage, talking about having children, and so on. Lois is afraid that she will later be abandoned and rejected, "and that she will fail for the umpteenth time, and this time as a Christian." There is no sexual impropriety in their relationship.

They have prayed, read the Bible and Christian books, attended several seminars and retreats, and sought the advice and prayers of friends. "Maybe this sounds contradictory, but my devotional life has actually become more regular and more meaningful since we've been having problems. I always had trouble being consistent, and I think I feel closer to the Lord now than I did a year ago," she claims. Willy does not want to seek counseling at this time. Lois says, "That's OK, because I really think that a lot of the problem is me, not us, and if I can change, it will make a big difference. I've tried to do the right things, and I think I've improved, but I still become easily angered and negative. Then I feel so guilty. I always ask for Willy's forgiveness afterward, because the Lord convicts me instantly. But even after Willy forgives me, I still tend to wallow around being depressed. I can tell he's got his guard up and is confused about whether I love him or not and whether he can trust me."

That's the case study. What do you make of Lois? Beware! "Lois" is a minefield for the unwary and psychologized. Or, better, she is an inkblot test who will reveal *your* philosophy of counseling and working view of people. "Lois" can accommodate many different theories. The data of her case study is plastic. For example, is Lois compensating for a deep sense of inferiority and inadequacy? Does she suffer from low self-esteem? Is she an Adult Child of an Alcoholic and of a Dysfunctional Family? Is she codependent? Is she an anxiety neurotic? Does she have certain borderline personality characteristics? Or is Lois a DSM-IV 301.82, suffering an Avoidant Personality Disorder? Is she an Aries? Is she a Melancholic? Does she have hormonal imbalances? Does she have a demon of fear? Have contingencies of reinforcement conditioned her to react to men with fearful, hostile and avoidance behaviors? Is she suffering from repressed infantile trauma that created conflicting internalized object relations? Does her life lack mythical and archetypal meaning? Is she a purveyor of bourgeois propaganda to her students because she herself has been victimized by male-dominant and upper-class-dominant ideology? Do cognitive distortions fill her self-talk? Any and all of the above can be argued plausibly. Who is "Lois"?

Your diagnosis of choice will determine your therapy. Mainstream, eclectic psychotherapy? Psychoanalysis? Primal scream? Cognitive-behavioral therapy? Exorcism? Relaxation and guided imagery? Xanax t.i.d. and p.r.n.? Subscribe to an astrology magazine? Reclaim her inner child? Repeat affirmations that boost self-esteem? Codependents Anonymous 12-step group? Treatment options are as plastic as diagnostic options. How do the Scriptures make sense of Lois and then help her?

First, Lois' problems are specifically sin problems.
The two great commandments and their elaborations
throughout Scripture probe both the depths of Lois'
motivation and the nooks and crannies of her behavior,
thoughts, and emotions. God has revealed His law for
the express purpose of putting an accurate mirror up to
ourselves.

Sinful patterns of motivation can be discerned by examining what Lois loves, hopes in, fears, trusts, believes,
desires, takes refuge in, pursues, is preoccupied with,
obeys, listens to, and so forth. The Bible typically summarizes the worldly choices under the headings "idolatry" (Old Testament) or "desires of the flesh" (New
Testament). In the details of her life, who or what is her
god?[4] One writer puts it like this:

> There is something to which every knee bows. This
> is the person's god. As a matter of theory, one may
> deny that any concern deserves ultimacy. But as
> a matter of practice, no one escapes ceding ultimacy
> to something, whether it deserves ultimacy or
> not. . . . One need not be conscious of his god, or
> even conscious that he has a god. One might think
> he has no god, or that he is "looking for" or
> "waiting for" a god. One may even be converted
> from one god to another. But one will have a god.[5]

People cede such ultimacy to some god or other not only
in the "tidal drift" of their lives, but also in the "tiny ripples." Look closely at Lois' life as a whole, or at an incident in her life, or the arousal and expression of an
emotion, or a train of thought, or a choice made, and you
will find either a god or God. Scripture attunes us to notice this. And God then gives us eyes to understand in
His eyes what we've noticed. Scripture equips us to evaluate what we find: sin, idolatry, lusts of the flesh, or false
beliefs.

Patterns of the heart issue in a discernible lifestyle.
Sinful patterns of behavior, emotion, and thinking can be
discerned by noticing where Lois specifically lives out a

lifestyle that the Bible criticizes, summarized, for example, as "disorder and every evil practice" in James 3:16. In the details of her life, what does she do, feel, and think?[6] Looking at Lois through biblical eyes, we find many things. Here is a sampling—meant to provide illustrative hints, not exhaustive coverage:

- desire for approval, fear of rejection, "I *need* your approval" (e.g., Proverbs 29:25) leads to social anxieties, people-pleasing, and conformist behavior, avoidance of difficult topics and commitment to relationships;

- trust in money (e.g., Matthew 6:19-34) issues in brooding over finances, fantasies of security, subjective sense of either anxiety or security from looking at bank account;

- desire for pleasure or escape, wanting to feel good and comfortable, seeking "false refuge" (2 Timothy 3:4; inverse of psalms of refuge in God) leads to compulsive snacking, binge purchases;

- demands that others do her will, "I *demand* your approval or agreement" (e.g., James 4:1f, 11f), which issues in manipulation and anger outbursts;

- pride, playing the judge (e.g., Matthew 18:21-35; Romans 12:19) leads to unforgiving bitterness, hostile gossiping.

Wise counseling will explore and tackle these sorts of issues, for *these* are Lois' problems. The Bible diagnoses us through God's law. Clearly, her problem is sin: blinding gods, deceitful desires, habitually self-centered behaviors and attitudes. What are the resources to tackle such problems?

Second, God meets Lois in the gospel of His beloved Son. The Holy Spirit takes the self-humbling evaluation of the law and empowers Lois by the promises of His gospel to change her. There is indeed "mercy and . . . grace to help [us] in our time of need" (Hebrews 4:16). This grace issues progressively in concrete new obedience in the details and trials of each particular life situation, or into the "ripples." There is a bright side to God's work. Lois is able to find evidence that God's promises have become real to her. She knows His grace and forgiveness are real.

For example, Lois can see that God has already transformed her life. Her worldview, addictions, and morals have changed drastically for the better. She once was convinced that she was a victim; she now knows she is responsible for her choices and their consequences. Her emotions, which once were volatile and dominated by fear, anger, depression, anxiety, and self-hatred have changed. She used to live entirely on the roller coaster of her feelings about the immediate situation. But now she's learning to get off the roller coaster. At one time, when relationships failed, she simply blamed everything on boyfriends; now she has the humility to examine herself when problems arise.

What do the promises of God say about the stresses and pressures that impinge on Lois? Does Scripture make sense of them? Of course! From the abuses of her past to Willy's current sins, from PMS to hardship in the workplace, from financial pressure to Reneé's godlessness, life deals hard blows. But the truths of Romans chapters 5 and 8 and James 1 have been transforming Lois' understanding of what God is up to in these hardships. They are no longer random unpleasantries or brutalities. Lois has started to become a "wise" person, heeding and acting on the pattern Psalm 107:43 places on life's hardships.

What should a counselor say to Lois? There are many areas where she stands in need of renewing her mind. In these areas, she can turn to God for mercy and grace. And she can continue to refashion her responses to life as Christ works His image in her. For example, in her current relationship with Willy, she plays out at least three themes: "I need you (but you're unreliable)," "I demand of you (but you don't obey me)," and "I escape you (when the pressure cooker heats up)." Among other things, Lois expresses anxiety, avoidance, nitpicking anger, and a mild obsession with food. By facing these things for what they are and embracing Christ, she can learn patterns of loving, biblical communication (e.g., Ephesians 4:15f, 25-32). She can learn how to face Willy's sins and limitations as realistically and mercifully as her own. She can gain a foundation of godliness from which to make a wise decision about marriage. The Holy Spirit will enable her to do these things.

Ultimately the questions we should ask about biblical counseling are these: Is God real? Has He spoken? If not, biblical counseling is a way of attempting to delude people into a joyful, humble, hopeful, and loving lifestyle! *Biblical* counseling, by definition, hinges on the reality and truth of the God of the Bible. In my disciplines, counseling and the history of counseling, I am convinced that the God of the Bible *is* real. The other options available to people are deluded, shallow, deceitful. Biblical truth explains Lois and her life situation in depth—right to the details. The Bible tells her things about herself and her life circumstances that none of the secular theories touch. Biblical counseling is different, better, and truer because it rests on a true understanding of human nature—from God's perspective.

CRITIQUING INTEGRATIONISTS [7]

Biblical counseling was founded in the confidence that God has spoken comprehensively about and to human beings. His Word reveals sufficient and relevant truth. The Holy Spirit enables effective, loving ministry. Our positive call has been to pursue and then to promote biblical truth and methods in counseling. As a secondary application of this positive call, biblical counselors have consistently opposed the "integrationist" movement.

Integrationists attempt to wed secular psychology to conservative Christianity because they believe that

Scripture is not comprehensively sufficient. They say that Scripture, the Word of the Holy Spirit, is in some essential way *deficient* for understanding and changing people. The church therefore needs systematic and constitutive input from the social sciences in order to know what is true and to enable effective, loving counseling ministry. Integrationists claim that they are able to import the theoretical contents and psychotherapeutic practices of psychology into the church in a way that is consistent with biblical faith.

Biblical counselors have claimed, on the contrary, that the imports consistently hijack biblical faith and ministry. This is not to say that biblical counselors should ignore or dismiss the various secular psychologies.[8] Secular people—whether psychologists or anything else—can be perceptive observers and brilliant thinkers. But when we look at psychology we take seriously the pervasiveness of secular presuppositions and the spiritual malignancy of secular intentions: secularists, by definition, have a warped brilliance. To use an old expression of their own, they have "neurotic insights," observations that are dazzling but utterly distorted and self-serving. They systematically excise God when they look at people. But because all of human life can be understood only with-respect-to-God, *coram Deo*, they thus commit themselves to systematic error. Any utility secular psychology may have must be carefully qualified. Integrationists, however, are not careful enough, and they import fundamental and systematic falsehoods. I must also say that any potential utility of psychology must be subordinate to three far more fundamental tasks:

- articulating positive biblical truth in the counseling field;

- discerning the antithesis between secularism and biblical truth;

- converting psychologized people in a psychologized culture.

Integrationists have exacerbated the psychologization of human life, not remedied it. We can see how that has happened by critiquing the current state of integrationist thinking and practice. First, however, let me give a bit of historical background. The integrationist movement has developed through three phases.[9]

First, there was the preliminary phase, which went from the 1950s to the end of the 1960s. The integration movement among professedly Bible-believing Christians dates to the 1950s, with the prominence of Clyde Narramore and the founding of the Christian Association for Psychological Studies (CAPS). The founding of Fuller Graduate School of Psychology in the mid-1960s was the culmination of this early phase. The integrationist agenda had found its first institutional niche.

The second phase has been the professionalization phase. Over the past 25 years—partly as it has reacted to Jay Adams's criticisms—the integration movement has consolidated intellectually and institutionally. The current leaders have emerged into positions of influence through their writings and their institutional affiliations.

The following are noteworthy institutions that have developed to disseminate integrationist thinking and practices: Fuller Graduate School of Psychology; Rosemead School of Professional Psychology and *The Journal of Psychology and Theology*; Christian Association for Psychological Studies and *The Journal of Christianity and Psychology*; American Association of Christian Counselors and *The Christian Counselor*; integrationist departments at seminaries and Christian colleges such as Wheaton College, Dallas Seminary, Trinity Evangelical Divinity School, and Liberty University; and counseling ministries such as Minirth-Meier Clinics, Rapha, and Focus on the Family. The following individuals are among the leaders in the self-consciously integrationist movement: Clyde Narramore, H. Newton Maloney, Paul Tournier, Bruce Narramore, John Carter, Harold Ellens, Gary Collins, Frank Minirth, Paul Meier, James

Dobson, Vernon Grounds, David Seamands, Robert Schuller, David Benner, and Robert McGee.

Most recently the integrationist movement has entered a third phase: popularization. In the mid-1980s integrationist thinking broke out of the confines of educational institutions and professional psychotherapy. Pop psychology swept into evangelical churches through the recovery movement, which popularized terms such as codependents, adult children, dysfunctional families, 12-steps, support groups, and healing of memories. With increasing frequency the pulpit, the pew, and Christian publishing houses are speaking the same psychological language when they attempt to explain human experience and solve life's problems.

The stated intent of frank integrationists is to borrow theories and practices from secular psychology and weave them into the tenets of the Christian faith. Covert or unwitting integrationists do not state this intention, but simply borrow. The net effect in every integrationist's system is that secular error eats up biblical truth, so that false views of human nature and of the change/counseling process control the system.

What is the current state of integrationism? The integrationist movement is neither static nor monolithic. Though there are recurrent themes, there are often divergent and conflicting emphases and styles. I see three major styles. Within each I will flag two crucial issues where the recurrent themes appear. First, what is at the bottom of the heart of man? and, What is the view of human nature (anthropology)? Second, how do we know what is true? and, What is the view of knowledge (epistemology), particularly in regard to secular psychology? These are signal issues in regard to the issue of Scripture's sufficiency. Do the Scriptures have enough detail and penetration to get at the issues that matter? Or must we get crucial *knowledge* about the human *heart* from other sources?

The Basic Styles

1. "The Flea Market": Chaotic Integrationism

This is the integrationism that sells on the street, that jumps off the bookstore shelves into the hands and hearts of Christians looking to solve their life problems. Here are several examples among scores that could be cited; I chose these not because they are particularly bad or good, but because they are typical and popular:

- Frank Minirth, Paul Meier, and Robert Hemfelt, *Love Is a Choice: Recovery for Codependent Relationships*

- David Seamands, *Healing for Damaged Emotions*

- Robert Schuller, *Self-Esteem: The New Reformation*

- William Backus and Marie Chapian, *Telling Yourself the Truth* [10]

What is at the bottom of the heart of man? Here is a sampling of the answers offered in the Flea Market:

- Minirth, Meier, Hemfelt: legitimate need to be loved, love hunger, an empty love tank because of the failures of others to love us (e.g., pp. 33-40)

- Seamands: the need to feel good about yourself, the heart as a storehouse of repressed hurts and deprivations (e.g., pp. 48-54, 60, 138)

- Schuller: an unfulfilled need for self-esteem underlies every human act; the need for self-love, dignity, self-worth, self-respect, self-esteem is the deepest of all human needs; the core of sin is a lack of self-esteem; at the deepest level sin is self-rejection and psychological self-abuse, which leads to the more outward sins (e.g., pp. 15, 33f, 98ff.)

- Backus and Chapian: the need to feel good about yourself, be happy, and feel loved and important (e.g., pp. 9ff., 40, 51, 109, 111).

In each case, some variety of "the heart as needy and/or wounded" undergirds the theory. Needs for love and for self-esteem predominate in the Flea Market literature. Sin and misery are secondary consequences of deep, unmet needs.

How do we know what is true? Each of the books above is an eclectic hodge-podge of personal experiences, gleanings from various psychologies, and Bible verses (almost invariably misused). The criterion for truth is a slipshod version of "every man did what was right in his own eyes." There is no attempt to think systematically about human beings in a way that is exegetically careful, emerging out of Scripture (*exegesis*) rather than reading into Scripture (*eisegesis*).

2. "The Big Umbrella": Sophisticated Integrationism

The latest, high-culture integrationism articulates the intellectual cutting edge of integrationist philosophy. This is the integrationism of the Christian graduate schools of psychology. It seeks to appropriate and evaluate secular psychological theory in an eclectic manner under the guidance of Christian "control beliefs." The Big Umbrella seeks to carefully integrate everything— from Freud to Skinner, from exorcism to healing of memories, from Carl Rogers to Jay Adams.

Those who are proponents of this form of integrationism tend to be critical of the Flea Market pop psychologies. For example, Stan Jones and Richard Butman wrote, "Too much of what passes off as integration today is anemic theologically or biblically, and tends to be little more than a spiritualized rehashing of mainstream mental health thought" and "Christians doing integration have deserved much of the criticism they have received from the psychology-bashers."[11] A related development in modern, sophisticated integrationism is that it attempts to enfold Jay Adams under the Big Umbrella. Scholarly integrationists often do not have the knee-jerk hostility to Adams that characterized the integrationism of the 1970s.

They believe they have domesticated the "radically biblical" message, assimilating Adams as one further contributor, a fundamentally eclectic model. For example, Siang-Yang Tan's laycounseling system is a syncretism of Jay Adams, Larry Crabb and Gary Collins. Two examples of recent Big Umbrella writing include:

- Siang-Yang Tan, *Lay Counseling: Equipping Christians for a Helping Ministry*[12]

- Stanton Jones & Richard Butman, *Modern Psychotherapies: A Comprehensive Christian Appraisal*

What is at the bottom of the heart of man? Here is the way in which these authors speak of the essential issues of human nature:

- Tan: psychological and spiritual longings or needs for significance, love, and hope (pp. 34-37, 50f).

- Jones & Butman: "the Bible gives no direct message about the nature of human motivation," but we can glean from Genesis 2 that people have fundamental needs for purposeful activity and loving relatedness to others (pp. 47-49). But, "biblically the term *heart* is . . . what psychologists and philosophers often call our self" (p. 46). "Human beings are first and foremost agents" (p. 47). Rebellion against God, the desire to be gods ourselves, now becomes an operative motive in all that we do (p. 55).

Some variety of need theory may undergird the view of human motivation, as with Tan, though it is not stated with the blatant self-centeredness of the Flea Market. In other cases, such as Jones and Butman, the stated view may be more orthodox, though the orthodoxy is underutilized in the chapters that follow.

There are differences between Tan, and Jones and Butman. Tan's view has overt affinities with what was said previously about the Flea Market type of integrationism and what will be said below about Larry Crabb's view of the heart. The problem with Jones and Butman's view is more subtle; I'd like to call attention to two revealing aspects of their view of motivation.

First, the comment, "The Bible gives no direct message about the nature of human motivation" stopped me in my tracks. How could they say that, recognizing as they do that human beings compulsively play God? The Bible that I read is fundamentally and pervasively *about* human motivation! So why do Jones and Butman perceive Scripture as relatively empty? What they look for —and do not find in the Bible—is the sort of definition of motivation that secular psychologists pursue. Secularists want to define some list of drives, needs, or core desires that motivate people *irrespective of their relationship to God.* They seek to define human nature in and of itself, not with-respect-to-God; to analyze the heart *per se,* not *coram Deo.* Examples of discussions of motivation that might fit Jones and Butman's criteria for a "direct message" would include: Maslow's hierarchy of needs, the behaviorists' distinction between primary and secondary drives, and Freud's eros and thanatos and conflict between id and superego compulsions. The Bible does not say much about human motivation in the sense Jones and Butman pursue because God defines the issues of the heart as pervasively with-respect-to-God or, in other words, as "covenantal."

Jones and Butman go on to define "the action" of human motivation as a creational need for purposeful activity and loving relatedness to others. I believe these are better understood as self-evident spheres of human activity. Certainly human beings operate in the channels of interpersonal relationships and productive accomplishment. That is a truism, but it's not a significant system-aligning truth. Jones and Butman believe it but do not trace out how *the* issue of motivation, and relationship to God, gets played out in these spheres and every other sphere of human functioning. If spheres of activity are so important, why limit the list to man as a social being (attuned to being loved) and a productive being (attuned to accomplishing something)? We could easily add many other spheres of significant and instinctive human activity. Man is obviously a somatic being, continually oriented towards sensual comfort or discomfort, pleasure or pain. Man is a meaning-maker, always ordering and interpreting life. Man is an economic being, oriented towards money and possessions. Man is a political being, instinctively attuned to issues of power, authority, and submission. Man is a moral being, always evaluating according to criteria of fair or unfair, good or evil. Man is a glory being, alert to issues of relative status and success. Man is an aesthetic being, creative and sensitive to beauty, metaphor, rhythm, and order. Man is . . . The pie can be sliced many ways.

Each of these spheres of human activity is abundantly illustrated within the Bible. However, listing or prioritizing them turns out to be relatively inconsequential for understanding human motivation. Scripture subordinates all under its master category of motivation: man is a *religious creature* who worships, serves, loves, hopes in, seeks, trusts, fears . . . something—either God or God-substitutes. So there is a great divide in man's social nature, between whether people are attuned to being loved or to loving. There is a great divide in man's economic nature, between whether people are attuned to financial advantage and disadvantage or to gratitude, contentment, and generosity. There is a great divide, a *religious* divide, in every sphere. Jones and Butman, like the secular psychologists on whom they model their idea of what a motivation theory should accomplish, detail secondary matters and largely ignore primary matters. They view Scripture as deficient with regard to human motivation because God is not concerned with providing a systematic catalogue of secondary things.

Second, how should we understand Jones and Butman's comment about the equivalence of the biblical *heart* with the secular idea of *self*? This comment nicely illustrates the fundamental weakness in integrationist anthropology and epistemology. Integrationists see synonyms, whereas a closer look reveals antonyms. In biblical anthropology, *heart* has to do with man's relationship either to God or to the false gods of the world, the flesh, and the devil. The issue of the heart is the question, "Who or what rules me?" Or, "For which voice(s) do I have ears?" Contrary to Jones and Butman's assertion, not a single one of the psychologists or philosophers they refer to mean man-with-respect-to-God when they speak of self as the core of human identity. They mean man-in-and-of-himself, an idea absolutely foreign to the Bible except as a description of the way sinners would *like* to think of themselves. Secular thinkers would prefer to interpret man as self rather than as heart-before-God, because they are secular. The idea of self in secular philosophy and psychology is not an equivalent term for the biblical idea of heart; it is a *functional* equivalent— that is, a counterfeit and substitute. To say, "Biblically, *heart* is what psychologists and philosophers often call our *self*" is like saying, "Chemically, *sugar* is what dieters call *saccharine.*" The two are different things, and the latter is a substitute for and a counterfeit of the former. Hence it is completely logical that no secular thinker sees repentance unto Jesus Christ, the new heart, and the power of the Holy Spirit as central to significant change. Their faulty anthropology forbids such answers and prescribes other answers. Jones and Butman underestimate the noetic effects of sin on systems of thought that seek to describe, explain and change human beings.

How do we know what is true? Jones and Butman (chapter 15) teach—and Tan (chapters 3 and 4) exemplifies—a frank but avowedly "responsible" eclecticism. It "makes infinite sense" to select and combine in orderly fashion "compatible features from diverse sources, sometimes from otherwise incompatible theories and systems; the effort to find valid elements in all doctrines and theories and to combine them into a harmonious whole" (p. 382). The integrity of the individual integrator is the ultimate guarantor of truth; the mind and practice of the individual integrator is the ultimate location where truth is forged. In so doing, the Big Umbrella denies that Scripture gives the "harmonious whole" up front, as God's point of view (truth) about human beings.

Specific exegesis plays no role in the trenches of counseling theory and practice for Jones and Butman. Their Christian control beliefs are theological generalities, open to speculative and idiosyncratic application. After stating the obvious fact that the Bible is not exhaustively encyclopedic (it does not contain every fact), they go on to conclude that therefore the Bible is useful only in a very general way:

> While the Bible provides us with life's most important and ultimate answers as well as the starting points for knowledge of the human condition, it is not an all-sufficient guide for the discipline of counseling. The Bible is inspired and precious, but it is also a revelation of limited scope, the main concern of which is religious in its presentation of God's redemptive plan for His people and the great doctrines of the faith (p. 27).

Sentiments aside, the Bible is deficient. Jones and Butman, however, misunderstand the nature of the Word of God. While their theology is full of true but sweeping generalizations, the theology of the Bible rivets us to the details of the real life struggles of human beings. Jones and Butman ignore the very things the Bible is useful *for* when they discuss the supposed teaching of 2 Timothy 3:16-17 that the Bible is only a "useful" resource among many resources (p. 26).

Of course, biblical counselors should agree that the Bible is not exhaustively encyclopedic. We use and pursue extrabiblical information continuously. For example, we gather data from a bickering couple, eagerly pursuing those extrabiblical details that are grist for the mill of biblical truth. We may freely comment without apology, "Bill, when you said those things to Sue in an angry tone . . .," and string together four extrabiblical things in a row (Bill, the things said, Sue, the angry tone). But when we as biblical counselors say that Scripture is not an exhaustive catalogue of every fact about every person in every time and every place, we come to the opposite conclusion that Jones and Butman hold to.

We believe—and they do not believe—that the Bible is comprehensively sufficient as a guide for the discipline of counseling. Scripture guides the questions asked in gathering data; it explains and exposes the motives for Bill's anger; it maps out in detail the way of peacemaking. For example, James 3–4, Ephesians 4, Matthew 7–18, and Galatians 5–6 are *about* what is going on between Bill and Sue and between the two of them and God. In fact, it is the breadth of Scripture's scope and the relevance of Scripture's details that impresses us. Human life is essentially religious down to the details of behavior, thought, emotion, and motivation. Those great doctrines of the faith —and the hosts of tiny instructions as well—include all the categories for understanding human beings and all the pastoral practices that God the Holy Spirit uses to change people. Jones and Butman's "responsible eclecticism" in the last analysis is simply a sophisticated version of "every man did what was right in his own eyes."

Sophisticated integrationists seek to distance themselves from the grotesque wares hawked in the Flea Market. But they do not take the theology they believe and apply it to the details of human existence and the counseling process.

3. "Good Intentions Notwithstanding": Covert Integrationism

This is a seemingly unwitting integrationism—it claims to oppose psychology and to work in biblical categories. But psychological categories slip into the very foundation stones. The chief example is Larry Crabb's book, *Understanding People: Deep Longings for Relationship.*[13]

To his credit, Crabb is very critical of both the careless integration of the Flea Market and the careful integration of the Big Umbrella. But the systematic parallels between Crabb and other integrationists are hard to miss.

What is at the bottom of the heart of man? Crabb's explanation of human motives posits needs or yearnings for relational love and significant accomplishment. Idol-atrous demands and sinful life strategies are secondary reactions and compensations, wrong ways of going about getting these needs met.

Crabb's need theory is not stated with the blatant, sin-less self-centeredness of the Flea Market. But his system still pivots around the human experience of inner unful-fillment or pain, taking those experiences at face value; the needy, wounded, longing heart of Crabb's "personal circle" underlies sin.[14] The Bible's view of the heart is the opposite; life pivots around our relationship with God or false gods, not around the felt needs of sinners.

How do we know what is true? For Crabb, exegesis of Scripture is the avowed starting point (pp. 65f). "Bib-lical categories are sufficient for answering the questions a counselor will ask. . . . (Our task) is to think about life within the categories that the Scriptures provide. . . . The authority for our thinking depends on the degree to which it *necessarily emerges from clearly taught biblical cate-gories*" (p. 70, emphasis his). These are statements to which every nouthetic counselor subscribes.

But where does Crabb in fact get his system-shaping categories? Scripture nowhere yields Crabb's view of "deep yearnings/needs for relationship and impact"; his Jesus who encounters us primarily as the meeter of our needs; his distinction between casual, critical, and crucial longings; his definition of ontological maleness and fe-maleness. These ideas are the drive train and steering mechanism of Crabb's distinctives. These ideas are ex-plicit betrayals of Crabb's stated epistemological goal because they are exegetically and theologically insup-portable. "Every man did what was right in his own eyes." Good intentions are not necessarily a hedge against the noetic effects of sin on systems of thought.

The Basic Problems

What unifies these outwardly diverse forms of integrationism? The proponents of both the Big Um-brella and Good Intentions Notwithstanding abhor the excesses of the Flea Market, and seek to distance themselves from such conspicuously bad theology and careless uses of psychology. But in the last analysis, all integrationism evidences a defective view of human nature and a defective functional epistemology. For them sin is never the *specific* issue that underlies problems in living. And the categories that emerge from specific exegesis of Scripture are never the significant categories these proponents use for understanding and helping people.

Often a "naive" outsider sees more clearly what clothing the emperor wears. Sociologist James Hunter's *American Evangelicalism* analyzed the accommodation of contemporary evangelicalism to modern culture.[15] In one section he compares the differences between the crude and the sophisticated psychologizers of evangelical faith:

> (Their) analyses differ in degree of sophistication. At one level there is the crude psychologizing of biblical language and imagery. . . . At the highest level, there is the synthesis of biblicism and humanistic or Freudian psychology. . . . Yet the substantive difference is superficial, for what they all share is a *psychological Christocentrism*—a view of authentic mental and emotional health as rooted in the "establishment of a harmonious relationship with God through Jesus Christ. . . ."[16]

Hunter describes this psychologized faith as subjective, preoccupied with the self and "mental health," hedonistic, narcissistic, and oriented to address the "sensitivities and 'needs' of modern man."[17] It teaches a type of self-examination that departs from ways traditional Protestants searched their lives because of their paramount concern for "the rule of sin in the life and the process of mortification and sanctification."[18] For all the differences between various types of integrationists, they have major tendencies in common: 1) a man-centered view of what is deep in the core of man, and 2) a systematic embrace of secular psychology's "riches" because of

Scripture's deficiency and inadequacy for the task of significant self-understanding and change. Logically, they also tend to share a third major tendency: a revised gospel that alters or ignores Christ. He is either made the servant of the emotional and psychological "needs" of human beings or is made relatively irrelevant. Wherever sin is not seen as the specific problem, the Redeemer of sinners and sufferers will not be seen as the specific solution.

"What is at the bottom of the heart of man?" The question of anthropology. Biblically, the heart of man is the crucible where the first great commandment plays out: Do you love, fear, trust, serve, and listen to God? Or do you love, fear, trust, serve, and listen to idols, self, other people, your own performance, mammon, Satan, and cravings (for love, importance, self-esteem, control, among a horde of other things)? In other words, the law of God cuts to the very deepest issues of human life not just in high-flown theory, but in the trenches of daily life.

Most false teachings originate from unsound views about the corruption of human nature. Wrong views of a disease inevitably bring with them wrong views of the remedy. Wrong views of the corrupt nature of human beings always carry with them wrong views of the great cure for that corruption: Jesus Christ. It is striking how all three forms of integrationism—chaotic, sophisticated, and covert—converge in their view of the core of man. For all their differences, they are all fundamentally man-centered, either overtly (need theories) or subtly (by failure to develop the biblical view). Most integrationists systematically make human needs and desires fundamental. They baptize certain lusts of the flesh as "needs," and build their counseling endeavors around need theories rather than sin theories. These need theories typically focus attention on people's supposed basic needs for love or to feel good about themselves or to accomplish something worthwhile. In the logic of each theory, the human heart is fundamentally good, but because of the rough sledding of life in a fallen world, hearts become empty, needy, yearning, wounded.

All integrationists subscribe by profession of Christian faith to the fact of sin. All profess to believe in human responsibility. Many make incidental comments along the way that are wise and perceptive. (Naturally, such "happy contradictions" are more frequent in some cases than in others.) All profess to believe Mark 7:21-23: "From within, out of the heart of men, come . . ." But the logic of a psychologized system defines that heart in such a way that "out of the wounded, needy, legitimately yearning heart come . . ." The ultimate *why* for our problems is attributed to those other people who wounded us, who did not meet our needs, who left our longings unfulfilled.

The "happy contradictions" in these integrationist writers are matters for which God can be praised. But it is hard to cheer authors who so relentlessly attempt to build on faulty foundations. At the same time, I acknowledge that we biblical counselors have our failings as well. But I believe that, by the grace of God, we are fundamentally right because of our starting point (Scripture); yet on occasion we may be wrong, foolish, and ignorant in our understanding and application. That's why it's important for us to hold fast to what we have been given, repent of our sins, and grow in wisdom. Integrationists, by contrast, are fundamentally wrong because of their starting point, but by the grace of God, they may be occasionally right, wise, and perceptive. That difference is a world of difference—a matter we cannot take lightly because we are accountable for how our counsel affects people's lives.

"How do we know what is true?" The question of epistemology. Scripture is comprehensively sufficient for understanding those aspects of human nature and those processes of change that are essential for wise and effective counseling. That is because Scripture is about what counseling is about; Scripture was given for this express purpose.

All three forms of integrationism—chaotic, sophisticated, and covert—ultimately converge in the way they construct their basic ideas. Beyond their surface differences, each is fundamentally eclectic and self-willed rather than exegetically and systematically submissive to the Word of God. Each is receptive to secular misinterpretations of human life. Each fails to build a consistently biblical system that stands up exegetically and theologically. The great doctrines of the faith are variously ignored, compromised, amalgamated with man's own thinking, or unbalanced by picking and choosing. The eclectic tendency of the integrationist mindset does not yield nourishing food for the body of Christ. Integrationists do not exegete Scripture; they eisegete and proof-text, sometimes recklessly. Reading books by integrationists is a frustrating experience for anyone who loves the Bible and whose life-experience (both personal and in counseling ministry) has vindicated the truth, power, and wonders of God's eternal Word.

As you can see, then, my concern about psychology's subversion of Christian counseling is not mere rhetoric and contrariness. I am convinced that positive biblical truth about people makes more sense, true sense, and useful sense. It gives sense that lets us interact with psychology carefully for the ultimate purpose of converting psychologized people to biblical wisdom.

How Should Biblical Christians View and Use Psychology?

A positive understanding of biblical truth does many things for us. First, it enables us to understand and help Lois as well as ourselves. Biblical truth makes sense of people. Second, it enables us to critique the epistemological and theological problems both with secular psychology and with integrationism. Error wraps itself in darkness; truth makes error visible. And third, biblical truth lets us interact with and even learn from error.

How should biblical Christians view and use psychology? That is a crucial question because my critique of integrationism emerges from a positive understanding of how the Bible calls us to interact with error. That is also a large question, and what I say here will only sketch the broad contours of an answer.

The so-called "truths" of psychology are analogous to the "truth" an angry pagan wife might say as she curses out her sinning, Christian husband, "You're married to your job, not to me, you idiot! Every word out of your mouth is sniping and mean. I wish you would show even a little bit of kindness and consideration for me and the kids." Has she spoken "truth"? We who are biblical counselors would answer both yes and no, and carefully unpack what we mean. This may be devastatingly accurate about her husband in certain respects. She sees the speck in his eye (analogous to the descriptive accuracy of many psychological observations and case studies). But she ignores many other relevant facts about him (just as psychologists do). And her conclusions are shot through with deadly error and demand drastic reinterpretation from a wise counselor. She has no idea that what she so perceptively describes is his sin against God first. Neither does she know that her explanation ("You are chiefly offending *me*"), and the implications she draws ("I have a right to bring wrath against you") reflect her sin against God. She has no idea of the gospel's way of changing both her and him. She has no idea of how to win or confront her husband in a godly way. Her interpretive schema is godless—or, rather, places the human interpreter in the place of God. The "counseling" implications she draws serve the interests of her own autonomy from God.

How would biblical counselors approach this angry wife? They would turn her observations and concerns inside out and upside down.

From her words, we can learn a number of useful and provocative things about both her and her husband. But we don't buy her schema for a minute, because Scripture gives us a different set of eyeglasses.

Psychologists, however, are like this angry counselee as they observe, theorize, and practice. They notice many things, but bend everything to evade the God-relatedness of what they see. The cornerstone of the biblical interaction with psychology is to recognize the pervasive antithesis between biblical truth and secular psychology. Contrary to how biblical counselors are caricatured, we did not initiate this hostility! Psychologists initiated the antithesis to God's truth as they systematically express the noetic effect of their sin.[19] The *a priori* assumption that they can explain people truly without reference to God commits psychologists to a systematic error. Integrationists wash away or pay lip service to this antithesis; biblical counselors restore the antithesis.

Psychology's Role in Counseling

What role, if any, should psychology then have in our model of counseling? It should play *no* role in our *model* of counseling. But, radically reinterpreted, secular observations could play an *illustrational* role, providing examples and details that illustrate the biblical model and fill out our knowledge. They could also play a *provocative* role, challenging us to develop our model in areas we may never have thought about or may have neglected. Jay Adams states this succinctly in his book *Competent to Counsel.* Psychology can be a "useful adjunct" in two ways: 1) "for the purposes of illustrating, filling generalizations with specifics"; and 2) "to challeng[e] wrong human interpretations of Scripture, thereby forcing the student to restudy the Scriptures."[20] Indeed, there are biblical counselors who have written about the fundamental antithesis between biblical and secular presuppositions and utilized secular psychology (and other secular sources) in illustrational and provocative roles.[21]

Using psychology's observations in illustrational and provocative roles is no different from the way wise biblical counselors utilize other sources of extrabiblical knowledge. Here are a few examples of distorted, extrabiblical knowledge that the eyeglasses of Scripture equip us to utilize by reinterpreting constructively:

- the observations of an angry counselee or any coun-selee who is not thinking biblically. Biblical counselors continually reinterpret the data they hear, filling out their categories with fresh details. This reinterpretive labor is at the heart of counseling: renewing minds to understand the world God's way. It is also at the heart of the counselor's growth in becoming case-wise and mature. Counselees say, feel, believe, and do an un-searchable variety of things that wise counselors learn to interpret biblically.

- Shakespeare plays, mystery novels, and other litera-ture in which greed, pride, fear, lust, and other fleshly motives are portrayed in action. Fiction of any kind is not to be read as epistemologically authoritative. But if biblical categories control our focus, such literature can extend the range of our application of Scripture and force us to think about things or notice things we might not have considered previously.

- the daily newspaper, which wallows in mammon wor-ship, power politics, and gossip about sin. Biblical counselors, like preachers, may quote newspapers not because the papers are authoritative, but because they illustrate biblical truth and may make us stop and think about things we've never considered.

- medical research into "psychosomatic" relationships and their prevalence. We don't buy their categories, but can appreciate—and reinterpret—their observa-tions as illustrations of "spiritual-physiological" rela-tionships.

- sociology, history, archaeology, comparative anthro-pology, and so on. As with psychology, the consistent Christian refuses to accept these as norm-setting disciplines. Such studies of human life—when explicitly based on biblical presuppositions or when consistently reinterpreted through the lens of biblical presuppositions—may be of use in describing a given people at some point in time.[22]

- self-knowledge of my own sins and temptations. My personal application of 1 Corinthians 10:12-13 does not create truth, but illustrates, amplifies, and personalizes truth.

None of these sources *adds* anything to a biblical model of human nature and counseling. Each of those sources illustrates, unwittingly or wittingly, a biblical model of people in lush detail: "Now there's an aspect of anger I've never seen before." Each may provoke me to think biblically about something I haven't really considered: "How would I take *that* problem or help *that* person?" When we debunk psychologists of their pretensions to expert knowledge, to "science," we find they have the same twisted and blinkered perceptiveness of any other group of sinners. They may perhaps do empirical legwork that we do not have to repeat. But we must radically reinterpret what they see according to biblical truth. This reinterpretive labor—whether in the counseling office, in our closet, or in our reading—is a logical extension of grasping the pervasive antithesis between biblical truth and human error. What are psychologists—and counselees, novelists, medical doctors, and others—*really* looking at?[23]

Let me give one final example. The constructive reinterpretation of psychological observation is no different than the possible "usefulness" of reading a novel such as Thomas Wolfe's *Bonfire of the Vanities*. Wolfe portrays in action many generic human idolatries and sins (things I know from the Bible), giving them their particular "New York City, 1980s" color and detail (things I did not know previously, not having lived in New York). Could *Bonfire of the Vanities* "help" me counsel a jet-set New Yorker? It has already, not because I buy Thomas Wolfe's interpretive grid or relish the sleaze he depicts, but because the biblical model readily explains his observations of people.

The Biblical Counselor's Challenge

Biblical counselors face a twofold challenge: to hold faithfully to the categories of biblical truth *and* to grow casewise about diverse human beings. Jay Adams put it this way:

> Sin, then, in all of its dimensions, clearly is the problem with which the Christian counselor must grapple. It is the secondary dimensions—the variations on the common themes—that make counseling so difficult. While all men are born sinners and engage in the same sinful practices and dodges, each develops his own style of sinning. The styles (combinations of sins and dodges) are peculiar to each individual; but beneath them are the common themes. It is the counselor's work to discover these commonalities beneath the individualities.[24]

Scripture alone makes us systematically wise into the commonalities of human life. That wisdom then matures and becomes casewise through practice in applying Scripture to our own lives, to counselees, and to the things we read. Every wise biblical counselor engages in lifelong empirical research, informally if not formally. In this process, psychologists, sociologists, historians, counselees, the non-Christians who live next door, *USA Today*, Agatha Christie, and our own ongoing repentance may all contribute to our grasp of the styles and how they develop. Often in counseling or reading—and even as part of our own repentance!—we will have to take the *re*interpretive step that turns everything upside down and inside out.[25]

Biblical counselors who fail to think through carefully the nature of biblical epistemology run the danger of acting as if Scripture were exhaustive, rather than comprehensive; as if Scripture were an encyclopedic catalogue of all significant facts, rather than God's revelation of the crucial facts, richly illustrated, that yield a worldview sufficient to interpret whatever other facts we encounter; as if Scripture were the whole bag of marbles rather than the eyeglasses through which we interpret all marbles; as if our current grasp of Scripture and people were triumphant and final.

Defining the Bible's Sufficiency

Integrationists view Scripture as a small bag of marbles and psychology as a large bag of marbles. The *functional* logic of most integrationist epistemology is this: Put the two bags together, weed out the obvious bad marbles in psychology, and you end up with more marbles. Lip service is paid to Christian beliefs or "theology." It is easy for would-be biblical counselors to fall into the mistake of viewing Scripture as simply a huge bag of marbles. This epistemological position differs from the epistemology of integrationists only in quantity, not quality. It leads either to absurd forms of proof-texting ("There must be a verse somewhere in here on anorexia.") or to substituting pat answers for carefully thought-out wisdom ("First Timothy 4:3-5 says to eat with thankfulness; repent of not eating and follow this eating plan.") or to capitulating to integrationism in the wake of counseling failures ("Maybe the Bible doesn't contain all the marbles after all; it is only one useful resource for acquiring marbles, among many other sources.")

While the Bible does provide both the eyeglasses (interpretive categories that are true) and a vast number of concrete examples, it never pretends to provide all the examples. God demands that we put on our eyeglasses and think hard, well, and biblically about people. For example, ponder the implications of Galatians 5:19-21. Paul lists 15 representative examples of the works that are produced by the flesh's desires. He brackets that list with two comments that remind us to put on our biblical glasses, to look around us, and to notice numerous additional examples: "The works of the flesh are *obvious . . . and the like*" (emphasis added). Consider 1 Timothy 6:10: What are the *countless specific forms* of sin that a craving for money produces? And James 3:16: What countless *variations and permutations* of chaos and sin arise when people are self-absorbed in pride and demandingness? The sufficiency of Scripture challenges us to hard thinking and close observation of both individuals and cultures.

The fact that Scripture is sufficient should not be taken to mean that we can relax into the encyclopedia or concordance mentality. I have met biblical counselors who operated as if a problem not listed in the concordance is not a problem. They fail to appreciate the scope of biblical sufficiency. They fail to grasp that such problems *are* listed—within phrases such as "and the like" (Galatians 5:21 NIV) and "every evil practice" (James 3:16 NIV). They fail to do the hard thinking to demonstrate *how* the common themes of biblical truth underlie the idiosyncrasies and complexities of human sin, misery, and confusion.

I have also met a number of people who once were "biblical counselors" but became disillusioned, turning toward integrationism and the "riches" of secular psychology. These are people, however, whose epistemology had grave defects. Their bag-of-marbles epistemology made the Bible promise both more (an exhaustive encyclopedia) and less (a limiting concordance) than the real Bible promises. They had the rhetoric of the sufficiency of Scripture without the casewise reality of seeing *how* the Bible explains and changes people. When their grasp of the Bible proved disappointing in the face of human sin and suffering, psychology stepped persuasively into the gap. Psychology's abundance of hitherto unrecognized marbles made psychology's theories and techniques—its distorting glasses and fun-house mirrors—seem wonderfully convincing. We must remember that most integrationists were once conservative "Bible Christians." Their bag-of-marbles epistemology came in for rude shocks during their higher education or when they struggled with personal problems or the problems of counselees. Their suddenly insufficient Bible yielded to seemingly greater secular "wisdom." This same dynamic will continue to occur among biblical counselors unless we accurately define the meaning of Scripture's sufficiency.

Is the Bible a bag of marbles or the all-sufficient eyeglasses of truth—and lots of illustrative marbles—by which God corrects our sin-tainted vision? Our ability, as biblical counselors, to deal wisely with our own sins, to counsel wisely, and to defend our position effectively hinges on the answer. The fields are white for a harvest of psychologized people to be converted to biblical wisdom.

MINISTERING TO THE PSYCHOLOGIZED

I believe that Scripture is about what counseling is about, and that it makes utter good sense out of confused and confusing lives. But how do you convince people who don't believe that? How do you convince them that there is a better way of viewing and helping people? Typically you will run into two sorts of integrationists in your church or school: Christians with problems and Christians who want to help those who have problems. Usually these people will be naive integrationists— chaotic or unwitting—rather than philosophically committed integrationists. Typically they are Christians who have not thought systematically about what they believe, and so have accumulated an eclectic mix of contradictory ideas about life, problems, and solutions. Many of them, however, prove very responsive to biblical truth. From time to time you may encounter someone who is a committed integrationist. Even some of these people prove responsive when they see the cogency, penetration, pastoral skill, and love that biblical counseling entails.

How do we minister from the Word to people who hold to integrationist views? Let me sketch a worst-case scenario. Imagine "Lois" comes to you and says, "I'm a codependent with low self-esteem and I really need to learn to love myself because of the deep wounds to my inner child. I've just read John Bradshaw's *Homecoming* and Helmfelt, Minirth, and Meier's *Love Is a Choice.* I said,

'That's me! That's how I feel. That's what happened to me.'" Or, as a variant, perhaps a would-be counselor in your church says of Lois, "She's a codependent with low self-esteem . . . and I gave her *Love Is a Choice*. . . ." What a mouthful of jargon and confusion!

What method should you use to convert and bring about a biblical reinterpretation of Lois? As a biblical counselor, you want to make better—biblical—sense of the things Lois sees, does, experiences, feels, and believes. You want to challenge the distortions by offering explanations and help that cut deeper and wider. Such an approach is simply a matter of effective persuasion. You can't change a person's commitment to error; but you can hold out the carrot of sweet truth and apply the stick that exposes error's defects.

In this particular situation, how will you proceed? There are several historical facts and biblical convictions that serve as important foundational elements on which you can construct a pastoral strategy adapted to your hearer:[26]

1. The Bible never teaches that low self-esteem is the crucial issue. Gaining biblically accurate self-knowledge and knowledge of God is crucial. True self-knowledge entails, among other things, knowledge of sinfulness. The innocent inner child is a self-satisfying fiction.

2. The Bible never teaches that we have a need to love ourselves. It assumes we love ourselves inordinately and are self-absorbed (even when we "hate" ourselves). We need to learn to love God and our neighbor. To be obsessed with acquiring human "love" is not a disease or emotional dysfunction of "codependency"; it is idolatry against God and manipulative hatred towards people.

3. The categories that this psychologized person uses are an eclectic potpourri imbibed from godless sources: Alcoholics Anonymous, the recovery movement, psychodynamic psychology, and humanistic psychology.

How do you use these truths? Few psychologized people are convinced by hearing these three foundational truths served up as raw meat. How will you cook, garnish, serve, and so *apply* truth in effective ministry?

First, gather the facts that truth calls you to know. Remember, you are not debating with a book or in a lecture hall where ideas are kicked about as intellectual abstractions. You are talking to a person—Lois or Lois' counselor—who is committed, at least temporarily, to falsehoods. You must climb into Lois' life. For example, "Tell me everything you mean by those words you just described yourself with. What specific actions, emotions, thoughts, and experiences do you have in mind? When are you depressed? When do you hate yourself? What do you say to yourself? What do you do or not do because you feel so insecure? In what ways are you a relationship junkie? When, where, and with whom do such reactions show up?" As you, the counselor, dig behind the distorted labels you will find concrete realities that can be reinterpreted biblically. You will find the story of Lois that the case study told.

You will frequently find, for example (an implication of foundational truth #1), that Lois *does not know* that she lives sinfully, pursuing human approval and her own standards of accomplishment as a form of self-righteousness, and attempting to control her life's circumstances in order to maximize personal advantage and comfort. But when the dawn of accurate self-knowledge arrives, reigning ignorance—in the biblical sense—can yield to true self-knowledge as Lois sees the god she substituted for God.

You will frequently find (an implication of foundational truth #2) that Lois *loves* those many things just described: human approval, success on the job, being in control, the feelings associated with eating. She loves them inordinately, "heart, soul, mind, and might," more than God, and she "loves (her)self" more than her neighbors. Such attitudes and desires give birth to many specific sins (James 1:14f): anger, grumbling, fear, anxiety, self-pity, blameshifting, escapism, manipulating, fawning, playing the chameleon, immorality, materialism, gluttony, abiding frustration, hopelessness, and more.

Only when a person has a "fear of the LORD" does wisdom begin to dawn. Only then does intelligent repentance and humbling before God become possible; only then will light pierce the darkness. Get the diagnosis of the problem straight, and the Scripture brims full and overflows with relevant promises! You will find (implication of foundational truth #3) that Lois has imbibed, from the culture around her, false explanations that have left her deceived and stuck. Truth comes as light, honey, and a way out: "*Now* I see a much better way to understand myself. *This* really makes sense, whereas those other labels just left me feeling stuck and even more hopeless. Yes, the pattern of my flesh *is* my problem. And Jesus died for me and ever lives to intercede for and help me."

So Lois is not a codependent with low self-esteem who needs to learn to love herself because of the deep wounds to her inner child. She is a rather ordinary sinner, not all that different from you, the counselor (1 Corinthians 10:12f.). But Jesus is a rather extraordinary Savior of this sort of person, to the praise of His glorious grace!

In your endeavor to persuade a person with biblical truth and expose erroneous thinking, don't expect instant results. The persuasion process in counseling is not easy or automatic. The entire Bible supposes a conflict between truth and error, true prophecy and false, the Holy Spirit and Satan. You will find counselees and counselors who are suspicious and resistant, who create disgusting caricatures of what the Bible says in order to justify opposing it. They really believe what they believe.

Don't become discouraged, however. God promises to renew minds progressively when the truth is spoken in love and applied accurately to persons and situations. The savor of life and death will bring life to many a Lois and many a confused counselor. Some Loises and counselors will choose the darkness of competing, godless explanations. But one of the repeated joys of ministry is that many choose the light.

The counselor who works wisely stands able to help confused and wandering people renew their minds, repent, and find the light of truth, love, and life. Through Lois' example, we have seen how we can polish the arrows of truth, aim them into *her* individual life, stand her current understandings on their head, and open the door for the gospel of Jesus Christ to enter. The general foundational truths have been worked and applied to bring about specific conviction of lies believed, lusts pursued, and sins committed.

The goal of biblically reinterpreting human experiences—whether described by a counselee or a psychologist—is not fundamentally "look how much we can learn from them." Of course, with biblical eyes, we can learn something from anything, even if what we learn is simply how error works. But the real goal is the ministry of the Word that converts the soul. In our culture, that soul is often a psychologized soul. Psychology is to our society as Islam is to Morocco. Therefore, we must use God's truth to liberate psychologized people from the tyranny of untruth.

TRUE CHANGE, TRUE FREEDOM

Scripture is sufficient for my discipline. I hope I have demonstrated that sentence to be more than conservative Christian rhetoric. I hope I have demonstrated clearly that the hundreds of schools of psychological theory and therapy must bow the knee and confess sinful error against the Wonderful Counselor. He alone makes deep and satisfying sense of human life; He alone can truly reorient and refashion human life. I hope I have shown that biblical counseling is not obscurantist: we stand for spreading, not hindering, the truth about people. I hope I have shown that biblical counseling is not triumphalist: we have not "arrived" at the fullness of wisdom, but have received a standpoint for the lifelong acquisition of true wisdom. I hope I have contributed a small piece to that growing wisdom for each of my readers. I hope I will even convince integrationist Christians to take a fresh look at the Bible and at the purposes for which God has tailored His revelation. Perhaps even the occasional non-Christian will look into what has been said and see the light of God in the face of Jesus Christ!

The Scripture is *about* what counseling is about. God speaks about people whose lives are twisted away from the image of God. And God empowers true change into the image of the Lord of glory, Jesus Christ. That is what truly biblical counseling is all about! It is not Bible-banging counselees into submission to our view of Christian maturity. Rather, it is helping them find the only true freedom that can be found—the truth that sets them free!

TOTALLY
SUFFICIENT

4

TRUE CONFESSIONS OF A PROFESSIONAL PSYCHOLOGIST

Chris Thurman, Ph.D.

P ain is a reality of life! There are many hurting people in this world, and most of them are looking for help. Some struggle with feelings of depression and hopelessness that make each day seem futile. Some battle with chronic anxiety, or the perception that everything in life appears to be an overwhelming threat. Still others struggle with pervasive feelings of worthlessness that make them feel the world would be better off without them. Whatever it is that troubles a person, the pain is quite real and the solutions often seem far off or unreachable.

There appear to be as many theories about why people develop these problems as there are people with problems. Hundreds of therapeutic approaches have been put into the counseling marketplace, each seeming to offer that long-awaited cure that hurting people so desperately want. It is no wonder that many people in need of help are confused about what type of counseling can actually help them.

My own experience as a psychologist indicates that many of the psychological "cures" being offered today are as destructive as the original "disease" they were designed to help. Many people have been more harmed by them than helped. I know how broad and sweeping that statement is, but I believe it to be true! Much of the counseling done today is based on the humanistic assumptions that people are basically good, that people have the answers to their problems inside themselves, and that everyone has the personal power to solve any problem he or she faces. These ideas are not only wrong, but dangerous. They lead people further into the self-centered abyss of "looking out for number one," "pulling your own strings," "being your own best friend," "awakening the giant within," and "winning through intimidation."

THE ONE TRUE CURE

I believe that there is only one true cure for what ails people: an intimate relationship with the God of the universe. Anything short of that is a mere Band-Aid placed over a deep wound that requires major surgery. The current plethora of psychotherapeutic approaches can offer temporary relief from emotional pain, but they can never meet the deepest need of the human heart. Therefore, all secular counseling approaches fall short of truly meeting a hurting person at the deepest level of their need for God. Secular approaches cannot meet sacred needs.

Simply put, God created us, and there is no one who knows us better than He does. His understanding of who we are and how we are to live goes so far beyond what any human theory could generate as to not even be a fair comparison. God knows what our deepest needs are and has very lovingly and powerfully acted to meet each of them. Any effort on our part to meet our own needs and have emotional and spiritual health apart from Him is in vain.

Not only did God make us, but He also wrote the "owner's manual" for how we can live our lives to the fullest. It's the most widely sold but least read or understood book on the planet—the Bible! The Holy Scriptures are the source we can look to if we want to understand God and ourselves. In the most straightforward way possible, God told us how He views the Bible's role in our lives when he prompted Paul to write these words to Timothy: "All Scripture is God-breathed and is useful for teaching, rebuking, correcting and training in righteousness, so that the man of God may be thoroughly equipped for every good work" (2 Timothy 3:16).

The Word of God is the word of life. In it are the truths that we need in order to be set free from emotional and spiritual destruction. It is more than adequate in addressing the major issues in our lives. Scripture helps protect us from sin (Psalm 119:11), provides enlightenment (Psalm 119:18), counsels us (Psalm 119:45-46), comforts us (Psalm 119:52), offers hope (Psalm 119:74), gives wisdom (Psalm 119:98-100), guides us through life (Psalm 119:105), and provides inner peace (Psalm 119:165).

Most secular counselors completely ignore God's Word as the authoritative handbook on who we are and how to live life. Sadly, many who take the title "Christian counselor" are lacking in a basic understanding of what the Bible has to say about people and the solutions to their problems. I have made my own considerable contribution to this problem. For most of my 17 years as a counselor, I was a Bible illiterate who relied more on secular psychology than biblical theology for my understanding of people and their problems. I thank God that He was patient with me and has lovingly brought me back to Himself and His Word as the foundation of my efforts as a psychologist.

The bottom line is this: Scripture is the authoritative Word of God about who He is, who we are, and what it takes for us to live an abundant life. It meets each person at the very heart of where they hurt and gives them the truth they need. Truly wise people rely on biblical truth for their own lives and for the counsel they provide to others. When I hear someone say that Scripture is not sufficient to help hurting people, I cannot help but wonder how sufficient their understanding of Scripture is.

HOW SCRIPTURE MEETS OUR NEEDS

I want to demonstrate the sufficiency of Scripture in handling three of the most important areas of need that people have: love and intimacy, purpose and competency, and identity and worth. It is one thing to say that Scripture is sufficient, yet another to prove it. Let's see if we can demonstrate Scripture's sufficiency in the pages to come.

The Sufficiency of Scripture: Love and Intimacy

God created us for love and intimacy. We were, from the very start, meant to be intimately involved with Him and other human beings. God is love (1 John 4:8), and when He created us in His image, we were created to deeply thirst for love and intimacy. I believe that is why loneliness is so devastating. It flies in the face of our deep thirst for closeness. Our desire for intimacy with God and significant others is why self-sufficiency is such a problem. It leaves God and others out of the picture when they are meant to be at the very center of the picture.

Scripture clearly says that one of our deepest desires is for intimate connectedness with God and others. Having put that desire in us, God meets it by offering us perfect love. Love that has no strings attached. Love that cannot be earned. Love that cannot be made stronger or weaker. Love that, like the father looking for the return of the prodigal son, yearns for reconciliation with the person whose sin has damaged the relationship. God's love is freely given so that we can freely accept it, and freely pass it on.

Not only does God love us directly as His children, but He also works through other people to show us His love as well. God will work through our spouse, friends, family, and even strangers to reach us with a kind word, a supportive statement, a hug of acceptance, a truth we need to hear, a challenge to keep pressing on when things seem hopeless, and even needed correction. It is part of God's character to love us. He doesn't have to put on an act or find the strength to love us. He loves us because He is love.

The boldest expression of God's love for us, of course, is that He sent His Son to die for our sins while we were still in rebellion against Him (John 3:16). We were at odds with God and He still sent His Son to die for us. God's love took action on the cross. His aim was to reunite us with Him in an intimate relationship. And His love for us was not determined by how we were acting at the time. If God's love depended on how we behaved, He would have never come to earth, much less die for our sins.

The Bible's teachings on our need for love and how God meets it have staggering implications for my work as a psychologist. Most, if not all, of my clients have been rejected in one way or another throughout their lives. Many of them were abused as children—the most serious form of rejection a person can encounter as a child. The wounds created by rejection during early childhood and later in adolescence are extremely painful, and many choose to cope by either withdrawing into their own self-protective world or latching on to whomever comes along that seems to offer the faintest hope of acceptance. Unfortunately, further injury often results.

God offers love that doesn't injure us. It is pure and is motivated by a desire to help us, not harm us. In counseling, if I can help a person understand that this is the kind of heavenly Father they have, it makes all the difference in the world. When abused clients allow God to be who He really is (rather than some distorted version of an earthly person who abused them), they can draw toward Him rather than run from Him. And they can have their needs for love and intimacy met at the deepest level possible. Yes, this is easier said than done, given the wounds that most clients are dealing with. Yet, no matter how large the wound of rejection may be for someone,

God can heal it with a love than none of us can truly fathom.

Do we have a deep thirst for love and intimacy with God and others? Yes, absolutely! Who can meet that thirst completely? Only God! Secular counselors do not offer God to their clients. They offer only the encouragement to love oneself and seek love from others. But apart from God, how can we properly love ourselves or avoid selfishly taking from others? Secular counseling puts people in a closed system, encouraging them to give and receive "love" that is finite, often self-centered, and usually conditional. That isn't love at all, and it will not solve people's deepest thirst for intimacy with God.

Secular counseling shortchanges clients of the very thing they need to be truly healed and set free from the wounds of the past—the pure love of God and its power to heal. Scripture understands only too well what the love of God is all about, and its pages are full of descriptions of that love. For those who care to study what the Word of God has to say about His love for us and how to really love our neighbors and ourselves, it is theirs for the taking.

The Sufficiency of Scripture: Purpose and Competency

All of us, at one time or another, have asked the question, "Why am I here?" That question addresses another basic need I believe we all have: a need for purpose in life. We all want to be involved in purposeful activity, meaningful work, and something that is larger than ourselves. When that desire is not met, a host of emotional symptoms often appear, such as frustration, worry, anger, and resentment.

God created people to have meaning and purpose in life, and He gives men and women the necessary skills, abilities, and gifts to carry out their unique calling (1 Corinthians 12). For starters, we as God's creatures were given the responsibility of taking care of the earth (Genesis 1:26). What an incredibly important responsibility!

This earth is God's creation, and each person has the job of looking after it.

Another amazing job that God has given us that has ultimate meaning and purpose is the Great Commission. When Christ told His disciples to "go . . . and make disciples of all the nations" (Matthew 28:19), He was telling all of us that we are part of the most important mission the world has ever known. Every Christian has a crucial role to play in being used by God to bring others to Christ and help them mature in their walk with Him.

Scripture teaches that we are here on earth for the ultimate purpose of bringing glory to God (Isaiah 43:7; Ephesians 1:11-12). The *Westminster Larger Catechism* is correct when it says, "Man's chief and higher end is to glorify God, and fully enjoy Him forever." In all that we do, we are to seek to glorify God (1 Corinthians 10:31). Our main purpose in life, then, is to fulfill the reason God created us: to glorify Him. That is what makes our lives truly significant.

Meaning and purpose in life—as defined by Scripture—have incredibly important implications for my work as a psychologist. Many of the people who come to me have placed the meaning of their lives in the hands of how successful they are at work, or at raising kids, or at looking fit, or at having the nicest home on the block. In other words, they have mistakenly trusted in earthly things to find meaning and purpose in life when only heavenly things can provide that.

When a counselee says, "I no longer have a reason to live since my boyfriend left me" or, "There has been no purpose in my life since I lost my job," I know that the Bible would want that person to understand otherwise. The Bible would remind him or her that losing a relationship, a job, a home, or anything else is not the determining factor in whether or not our lives have meaning. According to the Bible, even if we lost everything here on earth our lives would still have significant meaning and purpose because we are to have dominion over the earth, help bring others into the fellowship of believers, and glorify God with our lives.

Please don't misinterpret me to be suggesting that significant losses here on earth shouldn't bother us. Anyone who loses a valued relationship, job, or whatever will naturally feel sad and grieve over their loss. But even in the midst of the losses we suffer during life, we never lose our meaning or purpose in life because that is always secure.

In a world that seems bent on finding purpose and meaning in money, power, and instant gratification, what I am saying here can be an extremely hard sell. Try to get even Christians facing great difficulties convinced that their primary purpose in life is to glorify God, and they will often shrug and walk off in disbelief. How many times, though, do we put other gods before God in our efforts to find meaning in life, only to have those gods fail us time and time again? It is a hard lesson to learn—one that even wise old Solomon got burned on when all his earthly riches and power didn't prove enough to keep him from crying out, "When I surveyed all that my hands had done and what I had toiled to achieve, everything was meaningless, a chasing after the wind; nothing was gained under the sun" (Ecclesiastes 2:11 NIV).

Do we need meaning and purpose in life? Yes, absolutely! Who can provide the meaning and purpose in life that will truly satisfy our souls? Only God! Do we need to have skills, abilities, and gifts to carry out the purpose of our lives? Yes. Who is the source of those? Only God! That is why we are supposed to boast in God whenever we do something well because the ability really came from Him.

Secular psychology acknowledges the importance of meaning and purpose in life but often instructs each person to find their own. It also knows about the importance of personal competency but encourages each person to find it in themselves. By contrast, God instructs us to take hold of the meaning and purpose we already have in Him by being His children. We don't have to go out looking for it. It is already here for the taking. He has also equipped us to play our part in the body of Christ through various gifts and abilities. They are to be appreciated as coming from Him and we are to be good stewards of their use.

Scripture is sufficient in telling us our main purpose on earth and the means by which we can competently carry it out. The Bible meets us at one of the most important areas of need and does so with great success. For those with ears to hear, the Bible offers much encouragement about why we are here and how we can be powerful for God. For those who seek meaning in earthly things and try to be successful via personal power apart from God, they have Solomon's lament to sing and disappointment to face.

The Sufficiency of Scripture: Identity and Worth

Another basic need that many of us have is reflected in the questions, "Who am I?" and, "Do I have any value?" From the crib on, we are forming a sense of identity and worth that is critical to how our lives turn out. Once established, our identity and sense of value are very hard to let go of.

Most of the counselees I see have negative views of themselves, such as "I'm just a loser," "I've always been stupid," or, "I have nothing to offer." Accompanying these various negative views is a sense of worthlessness—a feeling that it wouldn't really matter if one's life ended. I have heard people say, "Everyone would be a lot better off if I wasn't around" or, "No one would miss me if I died."

We all want to know who we are and that we matter. The Scriptures meet both of these challenges head-on, leaving us with a true picture of our identity and worth.

If a person isn't a Christian, then his identity is actually tied to Satan. He is of Satan's family tree, not God's. This can be and should be frightening. To have your identity linked with Satan is to be tied to the same end result that Satan faces—eternal separation from God. So, as tough as it is to do so, I try to show hurting counselees who are unbelievers that unless they become Christians, their identity rests with Satan.

For those in Christ, the news is much better. Every believer is given a new identity—one that is linked with Jesus Christ. Once reborn, Christ is in us and we are in Christ. We are in Christ's family tree, and we face the same end result that He faces—eternal life in heaven. If you are a Christian, you have been given a whole new identity. According to Scripture, you are now:

- justified and redeemed (Romans 3:24)
- sanctified (1 Corinthians 1:2)
- set free from the law of sin and death (Romans 8:2)
- sealed with the Holy Spirit (Ephesians 1:13)
- given access to God (Ephesians 3:12)
- made complete (Colossians 2:10)
- accepted (Romans 15:7)
- forgiven (Ephesians 1:7)
- liberated (Galatians 2:4)

A great deal changes when a person becomes a Christian. He or she goes from being in Satan's family tree to being in God's family tree. From being a sinner to a saint. From a dark future to a bright one. His or her identity couldn't be in better shape!

Yet, a Christian can have a completely new identity in Christ and still walk around feeling worthless as if nothing has changed. That seems to be the state of many believers. They are born again but still hanging on to their old identity as a sinner and feeling worthless. The challenge here is for them to go back to what their true identity is until it begins to take root in the deepest recesses of their soul. This often takes a great amount of time and patience.

The Bible teaches that whatever worth we have is because God made us in His image. In other words, we have great worth, but it is a function of God having made us, not anything we did. We can neither lower nor raise our objective "worth" because it is totally unrelated to us. We may subjectively feel more or less worthwhile at times (based on how we look, how well we perform at work, how nice our material possessions are, and so on). But then we'd be succumbing to the world's definition of worth. In the world, worth comes from good looks, performance, or material prosperity.

The matter of worth is of monumental importance in counseling. As I have already mentioned, so many people who seek counseling have such distorted identities and low feelings of worth that it would break your heart. They desperately need to know that the Bible says they are fearfully and wonderfully made (Psalm 139:14), made a little lower than the angels (Psalm 8:5a), crowned with glory and honor (Psalm 8:5b), and made in the image of almighty God (Genesis 1:27). They need to know they have no *self*-worth, but complete and unchangeable *God*-worth that they can enjoy as a gift from their loving heavenly Father. They need to see, as clearly as possible, that seeking worth the way the world does— through beauty, money, or power—won't bring true fulfillment or meaning to life.

Do we need to know our identity and have an appropriate sense of worth? Yes. Who can provide this? Only God. This is yet another area in which secular psychology comes up short; all it can offer is that you have worth because you exist, and if you want to raise your self-esteem, you need to make positive changes in your life. By contrast, God's desire is that believers make positive changes in their lives as a way of showing their appreciation for the identity and worth they already have as His children.

APPLYING SCRIPTURE TO OUR NEEDS

Judy, a 35-year-old homemaker, came for counseling related to the recent unexpected death of her husband. She reported feeling depressed, anxious, and confused, and was experiencing some mild sleep and appetite difficulties. She also reported that she did not feel like being with other people and had withdrawn from many of the activities that she normally participated in (Bible study, exercise class, social club). Judy was left with sufficient life insurance to live comfortably for a period of two years, but after that she would have to find a job in order to provide for herself and her three young children. Judy's DSM IV diagnosis was 309.40, Adjustment Disorder with Mixed Emotional Features.

I operate from the perspective that *counseling is a three-stage process.* The first stage is *exploration,* which involves having the counselee tell his or her story. During this phase, I attempt to learn as much as I can about who my counselee is, what experiences have shaped his or her life, and what feelings he or she has about these experiences. I try to "walk in the counselee's shoes" and see life from his or her perspective.

The second phase is *insight,* which involves helping counselees to better understand the truth about their situation and their style of handling it. And the third stage is *action,* which involves counselees putting into practice their new insights so as to "mature in Christ" and handle the problems they face in a healthy, God-honoring way.

My first few sessions with Judy were spent exploring the circumstances surrounding the death of her husband and giving her the freedom to express her feelings. Following the biblical guideline to "mourn with those who mourn" (Romans 12:15 NIV), I attempted to grieve with her over the loss of her husband as well as explore any fears or concerns his death had triggered off for her. We also spent time during these initial sessions discussing other losses she had experienced in her life.

In discussing these other losses, Judy told me that her parents had divorced when she was seven and that her father moved away and remarried. She experienced this as the "death" of her relationship with her father, and this earlier-life experience accentuated her sadness over the death of her husband. Thus I attempted to help Judy grieve the loss of her father from years ago, something no one had ever done with her.

As we explored Judy's current situation and experiences from the past that were similar, we worked on deriving a better understanding of who she is and how she copes with life. In keeping with the biblical teaching that God wants us to have "truth in the inner parts" (Psalm 51:6 NIV), we focused on how her husband's death and the divorce of her parents had triggered feelings of abandonment, mistrust of people, and insecurities about whether or not she could cope. As a child Judy had withdrawn from people when her father left, and she was doing the same thing now that her husband had died. We discussed how withdrawing from people made it difficult for God to meet her emotional needs for comfort and security during her time of mourning.

It was also during the exploration and insight stages that we discussed Judy's feelings about God. She had come to mistrust God over the years, seeing Him as someone who wasn't really there for her when she needed Him most. She was angry that God had allowed her parents to divorce and her father to leave, and she had become angry at God again for allowing her husband to be killed in a car accident. I encouraged her to freely express her feelings in our sessions, yet I also encouraged her to examine her view of God more closely.

Specifically, I attempted to help Judy see that she viewed God as distant and uncaring and that she had also come to see God as someone who was supposed to protect her from all of life's painful realities. We explored certain Bible teachings related to her situation: that God loves her deeply (John 3:16), is good (Psalm 86:5), and makes all things work for good (Romans 8:28), has plans to help her, not harm her (Jeremiah 29:11), and allowed even His own Son to suffer horribly at the hands of men (Isaiah 53:3). Judy came to realize that she didn't see God as good or having her best interest in mind, and that her parents' divorce and husband's death had surfaced those feelings. She also realized that she had been expecting God to protect her from experiencing painful circumstances in life.

A final matter that we worked on together was her habit of withdrawing from people in times of emotional pain. She felt she really couldn't depend on anyone else, so she had decided over the years to depend on herself. We explored how God really did want to meet her needs and that He often uses other people in the body of Christ to do so. God is "the God of all comfort" (2 Corinthians 1:3 NIV) and He enables people in the body of Christ to comfort each other, like He did when He sent people to comfort Mary and Martha when their brother, Lazarus, died (John 11:19). We all have needs for comfort, encouragement, support, and security, and God constantly uses individuals within the body of Christ to meet those needs. Thus Judy came to an understanding of the fact that God wants to comfort us when we are hurting, and that isolating ourselves from other believers interferes with Him doing so.

With these and other insights in hand, we moved into the action phase of our work together. This stage involved Judy committing to doing various things, such as memorizing and meditating on specific Scriptures in order to overcome erroneous views of God, herself, and others; meeting with close friends on a regular basis for the purpose of sharing her feelings and being comforted (as well as doing the same for them); and meeting with a vocational counselor to determine how she could best use her interests and abilities in the work world when the time came for her to work.

Counseling with Judy, then, was successful in that she was able to properly mourn the death of her husband and loss of her father, see God more accurately, and develop greater intimacy than she had ever experienced before with God and others.

TRUSTING SCRIPTURE'S SUFFICIENCY

I have attempted to emphasize why Scripture is sufficient for the work that I do as a psychologist. I have mentioned that God Himself views His Word that way (2 Timothy 3:16-17) and that the person who meditates on God's Word day and night is promised many positive results (Psalm 119).

In relation to my method of counseling, I've shared about three areas of need that many people struggle with and how the Bible could be used to address these needs. We all have a need for love and intimacy, and God meets that need by loving us with a perfect love. God made us for intimacy with Himself and with others. And He desires to help us have both in the fullest way possible. We have a need for purpose and competency in life, which God has met by giving us dominion over the earth; including us in the Great Commission; putting us here to glorify Him; and providing us with the necessary skills, abilities, and gifts for getting the job done. Finally, we have a need for a clear sense of personal identity and worth, and God has met that need by creating us in His image and identifying us with Christ at the moment of salvation. In the truly essential issues of life, then, God's Word reveals the answers we need.

It seems to me that any serious student of the Bible will come to recognize how wonderfully sufficient the Bible is for answering the most basic questions of life. At the same time, I do not believe that the Bible presumes to answer *every* question that can be asked related to a person's problems. As much as the Bible does say, we often face questions for which the Bible offers no direct answer. We need to pray about such questions and seek the counsel of others. Where the Bible directly speaks to an issue, we need to obey it. Where it does not, we need to be guided by the basic truths of Scripture and the power of the Holy Spirit to help us discern His will for our lives.

When a hurting person walks into my office, I know that I have the answers to all the main questions he or she can ask. Why? Because the Bible has those answers and I, as a member of the royal priesthood of believers (1 Peter 2:9), have access to the truths of the Bible. Beyond the basic issues that all of us deal with, I trust God to guide the counselees and me into specific answers based on that fact that God is the author of truth and His desire is for people to be set free by the truth. My biggest concern in counseling is not that God won't guide us into truth, but that either I or the counselee will get in His way through rigidity, pride, blind spots, defensiveness, and the like.

Satan is fighting against every Christian counselor's efforts every day. Satan is the father of lies, and he is very good at getting people to believe distorted thoughts about God, themselves, others, and life. It is really no contest, though, because Satan was defeated 2,000 years ago by a carpenter from Galilee, and he has been on the run every since. When God is on our side, who can stand against us?

Yes, the Bible is quite sufficient for the work that I do. Pray for me that I will grow in my understanding of Scripture so that God may use me even more to help those whose problems and hurts make their lives unbearable and put them in emotional and spiritual bondage. Christ came to set us free, and I pray that all of us in the body of believers will become serious students of God's Word and be powerfully used by God to defeat Satan and the stranglehold he has on many people's lives.

TOTALLY SUFFICIENT

5

IS THERE A PSYCHIATRIST IN THE HOUSE?

Gary L. Almy, M.D.

A married 43-year-old woman and mother of teenage sons arrived 30 minutes early for her appointment to be seen by a psychiatrist. She is sitting alone in the waiting room nervously paging through popular magazines. She wonders whether she should have agreed to this consultation, but is sure that her Christian counselor knows best. When she, some months before, had revealed to her pastor mounting difficulties with insomnia, anxiety attacks, and fears of leaving her home, she could not have anticipated the possibility of actually being mentally ill or having a mental disease.

During the ten minutes the psychiatrist allows himself between patients, he reviews the consultation letter for his next patient:

> Forty-three-year-old hysterical and narcissistic female, apparent panic attacks . . . agoraphobia . . . three years' duration . . . worsening . . . insomnia . . . . marital disharmony . . . dysfunctional family . . . low self-esteem . . . massive repression with neurotic

defenses, not too productive in therapy . . . request consultation for medication management to facilitate therapy process.

To this first session the physician/psychiatrist brings knowledge, experience, fact, and opinion to aid the patient in the discovery of symptoms, signs, disorder, and perhaps a disease.

The *physician* approaches his patients using the medical model that was set before him during his training. The medical (or disease) model is his way of understanding any deviation from good health. This model is comprehensive and governs how he conceptualizes illness, what questions he will ask, what measurable data he will collect, what alternative explanations he must rule out, and finally, the explanation he deduces, or the final diagnosis: the "disease" causing the illness.

Medicine is the search for true and treatable diseases. This is so because of what the very concept of "disease" entails: A disease is an entity that impairs the delicate balance of human function with resultant distress or disability. It is an illness. More importantly, disease is a concept which by its very definition, includes a specifically observable etiology. Disease produces a resultant pathophysiologic or unhealthy body process that results in a typical presentation of physically measurable signs as well as felt and describable "symptoms," all of which are abnormal.

To the physician, a "course of illness" is predictable and recognizable because such disease-specific presenting signs and symptoms proceed and develop. In addition, a true disease is an entity which, when exposed to a logical and rational treatment, will lead to an outcome of either cure or some improvement that is predictable. Thus the goal of a physician is to logically and carefully discover the disease behind the illness. This is true because, in so doing, the cause, course of illness, treatment, and expected outcome will also be discovered. In this way a rational and specific treatment can be selected for that specific disease in the hopes of bringing about a cure. This, simply speaking, is the goal of medicine.

THE LIMITATIONS OF PSYCHIATRY

Psychiatry, on the other hand, has not progressed beyond a syndromal or disorder concept of diagnosis, nor does it seem inclined to do so. Syndromes or disorders, as the terms are used in psychiatry, are collections of subjectively experienced *symptoms* with or without objectively measurable *signs*. These symptoms and signs are grouped together as packages in the endeavor to understand the illness, disorder, or disability based on the experience, theory, or notion that they belong or fit together. In psychiatry syndromes and disorders are entities which cause dysfunction or disability and which have supposed (but as of yet not observed or proven) pathophysiology. This concept of diagnosis does not have a proven cause, a predictable course of illness, a specific and reliable treatment, or a typical response or outcome from that treatment.

One aspect of the syndrome and disorder concept of diagnosis used in psychiatry is the continuous revision of just what criteria differentiate one syndrome or disorder from another. Without objective data, or known etiology, the definitions or "diagnostic criteria" change merely on the basis of differences in experience. Such diagnostic criteria also change with new or different hypothetical explanations or guesses as to supposed cause. One of several results of this constant change is that the *Diagnostic and Statistical Manual of Mental Disorders* (Syndromes) is now entering its fourth revision.[1] Other results of this constant change include defective communication, imprecise definition, inadequate criteria for labeling individual patient symptoms and signs, sub-rational treatment, and an inability to regularly and predictably "cure" patients. These results have become the characteristics of psychiatry as a medical specialty.

What's even more worrisome is that the syndromal approach and its loose definitions have a disabling effect on research in psychiatry. It is much more difficult to test a treatment, measure an outcome, or search for a predictable course of illness when researchers cannot be sure that they are reliably able to separate apples from oranges, or for that matter, identify and agree upon just which is the apple in the first place!

Because of his medical training, the psychiatrist will seek from his new patient a full description of her subjective symptoms. He may ask about attendant physical changes or objective signs of illness. He will gather history about the onset of his client's illness. In so doing he will also explore alternative explanations (the differential diagnosis) before he settles in his mind on a diagnosis or best "educated guess" as to what process is at work in this patient's body and mind which will explain all the available information about her complaints. Along the way he may request some additional measurable information (psychological testing, tests for diabetes or thyroid disorder, and so on). However, his goal is medical; he wants to determine the disease and then apply a treatment that either eliminates the underlying disease process itself (as penicillin will kill pneumococci, which cause pneumonia) or at least blunts or blocks its effect on the sufferer's health (as aspirin will reduce fever from pneumonia).

For much of the practice of psychiatry, the search for true diseases has been unsuccessful. The physically based or "organic" mental diseases represent the only diagnoses of psychiatry that have "advanced from mere syndromal diagnosis to disease diagnosis and a comprehensive understanding of pathophysiology."[2] The use of objective measurements of brain structure and function has allowed entities like neurosyphilis, vitamin deficiencies, and alcoholic encephalopathy to be, for the most part, understood in accordance with what constitutes the concept of a true disease. There simply are no examples in traditional psychiatry—outside of the organic mental or brain diseases— where a distinct, measurable, observable alteration in brain structure or function has been discovered such that the concept of disease can be fully and honestly applied.

Diagnoses such as Passive–Aggressive Personality, Hysterical Personality, and narcissism, while discussed as if they were true diseases, in no way fulfill the definitional criteria for inclusion in any listing of true diseases. In cases where distinct measurable and observable alterations in brain structure or function have been found at the root of a patient's mental illness, the patient is subjected to the domain of neurologists, and internists or specialists in mental retardation.

Subjectivity v. Objectivity

Because psychiatric diagnoses are based, for the most part, upon subjectively described symptoms rather than objectively measurable signs, the reliability of two different psychiatrists labeling the same patient with the same diagnosis is quite low.[3] This "inter-rater reliability" is high only when psychiatrists are dealing with the true diseases of psychiatry (such as Korsakoff's Psychosis, Vitamin B12 deficiency dementia, mental retardation, and the other established organic diseases). When psychiatrists deal with diagnoses for which no physical basis has been demonstrated (the so-called "functional" as opposed to "organic" disorders), their inter-rater reliability plummets.[4] Such is the case for diagnoses such as schizophrenia, Dysthymic Disorder, anxiety disorders, and especially the various personality disorders.

Some efforts have been made over the years to utilize a so-called phenomenological method of diagnosis in psychiatry. This represents an attempt to apply the same sort of objective, empirical, and observational methods in the description of mental signs and symptoms that a person would utilize in any other kind of scientific observation. The goal of such an approach is to find certain observable signs that exist aside from any theory that might predict or explain them.

The *phenomenological approach* to diagnosis rests on three fundamental bases:

1. *Objective observation* uncontaminated by theory or interpretation.

2. The *use of terminology* that is as precise as can be used.

3. An emphasis on *recognizing the form* of what is observed rather than only the content.

Most of the observations recorded by modern psychiatrists are actually interpretations of what they see and hear rather than precise, objective descriptions. The set of "observations" about the patient at the opening of this chapter were actually psychoanalytic interpretations of the content of her complaints rather than careful, nontheoretical descriptions of her "illness."

Objective observation and evaluation requires precision of language and definition. This task is more readily accomplished in the description of behaviors that can actually be seen, measured, and easily described by different observers. Interpretive words like *regressed, narcissistic, oedipal conflict,* and *neurotic* are products of a theory. As such they are inherently speculative and are used in various ways by different examiners. As might be expected, "such terms have no demonstrated reliability, often substitute for objective observation and should not be used in clinical diagnosis."[5]

The *psychoanalyst* who believes in the theory of repression also believes that its existence is evidenced by the intrusion of "repressed" content into the dreams of the individual undergoing psychoanalysis. When the analyst observes what he believes he ought to observe, then he is confirmed in his belief. Such is the circular logic of psychoanalytic theory and any other philosophy and hypothesis that is based upon entirely subjective data.

A *phenomenologist* will search among similar individual patients for bits of observable and measurable data that need no theory to predict or explain them. He will search for data or signs that lend themselves to easy recognition, measurability, simplicity, and which would be recognized by multiple observers with a high degree of inter-rater reliability. Two problems that lend themselves well with this approach to psychiatric observation are *early morning awakening* and *phonemes.*[6]

Patients who have experienced *early morning awakening* (ema) find themselves spontaneously aroused from sleep early in the morning, at about 3:00 or 4:00, and find themselves unable to fall back asleep. This particular problem or sign is easily observed and completely atheoretical in its understanding. This sign, however, when observed with several other objective signs among a population of people who are described as very depressed, seems to select out those who have the very worst cases of depression. At the same time, the presence of this objective sign selects out those cases who usually have the most decisive-appearing responses to antidepressant medication or electroshock therapy.[7] This is not to say that the existence of ema means that depression is a true disease but rather, I simply give this example to demonstrate the application of the phenomenological method.

Phonemes are hallucinatory voices that are heard while the person is in a clear state of consciousness and are distinct, clear, seem loud to the hearer, are believed to come from "outside" the patient, and are alien to his own self.[8] This sign, when observed with several other such signs in individuals known to be free of demonstrable organic brain disease, seems to select out the worst cases of so-called schizophrenia with the very highest degrees of inter-rater reliability.[9]

Even though the phenomenological method of diagnosis is interesting and much more rigorous from a scientific viewpoint, it still has not afforded to psychiatry the elucidation of fully formed true diseases beyond those organic mental or brain diseases that have been long known and already established.

Problems of Research

The principal benefit of a rigorous approach to data collection or objective method of diagnosis might be the real ability to separate the apples from the oranges. To be more specific, it might cull out from a host of people who claim to be depressed those few who might have the true disease of depression. Toward this end, numerous lists of *research diagnostic criteria* for depression and a panoply of other supposed mental diseases have been proposed.[10] To date, however, none of these efforts seem to be heading in the direction of success. Instead of discovering true diseases, modern psychiatry seems only to be able to invent ever more elaborate lists of criteria. The criteria in these lists are used to label the customers of psychiatry with the resultant tendency of such "scientific" labels to be thought of as true diseases. This, in part, is allowed to take place because a truly objective and scientific method of observing and describing and testing is not mandated by leaders in the field. Thus confusion reigns as the field continues in relativism, speculation, and theory in an attempt to lend meaning and importance to the labels that are used.

A second benefit of rigorous, objective atheoretical or phenomenological diagnosis might be the ability to select out a *group of individuals* for whom a choice of treatment might lead to a desired outcome. This is, by the way, one of the historically verified pathways to the discovery of true diseases. Medical history is replete with examples of someone observing a connection between objective signs of illness and a seemingly inexplicable but successful treatment and using this connection to discover the ultimate cause, course, and concept of a disease. Modern psychiatry has not availed itself of this potential benefit. Trial and error remains the principle method of treatment selection in psychiatry. This is true not only because accepted methods of science are simply not used, but also because the overriding goal of psychiatry is to make any patient "feel" better as quickly as possible.

Making an Educated Guess

Because a psychiatrist lacks the full complement of information to honestly apply the medical or disease model, he utilizes hypotheses from psychology or psychodynamic theory to explain to himself the underlying cause of his patient's discomfort. In so doing, he believes that he has discovered a *pathophysiology* (an explanation) such that he can feel comfortable in his understanding and treatment of the patient. Lacking an objectively measurable pathology, he utilizes a hypothesis or a theory to fill in the gaps in his medical (or disease) model. Thereby, he can approach his patient in a "scientific" and authoritative manner and prescribe a "disease-specific cure." In this way, he can satisfy the basic motivation of every physician: to discover the disease behind the illness.

When the patient described at the beginning of this chapter first came to visit the psychiatrist, she assumed that a single session would be sufficient. Instead, the one visit became three more visits with the psychiatrist, one more visit to a psychologist for testing, and a visit to her internist for lab work.

One month later, she sits in the now-familiar book-lined office awaiting her "final diagnosis." She has developed respect and a kind of affection for this caring psychiatrist, and speaks highly of him to her regular counselor. After the usual pleasantries, the psychiatrist begins his explanation of her illness, her disease. "You have a classic case of Panic Disorder with agoraphobic features." Her hearing dulls as he reassuredly imparts to her the nature, frequency, projected treatment, and likely outcome. She is considerably more attentive to his explanations of "course...deep seated...stress...repression...neurotic defense mechanisms...breaking through." Now thoroughly "diseased," she is only mildly shaken when he says that she needs long-term psychotherapy and, of course, medication.

After she leaves, the psychiatrist basks in the glow of a job well done. Using his professional powers, he has once again deduced the "disease" causing a patient's discomfort. He had determined the workings of the disease, "knew" its cause (even though psychological and vague), and was sure the treatment would relieve her of her suffering. "After all, isn't that the bottom line?" he tells himself.

Even though the psychiatrist could not point to any ultimate disease-causing agent under a microscope or inside a test tube, he is confident that "complex unconscious processes" (even though they were never strictly observable) were at work as the causative agents. He "knew" this because the theories he relied upon had been discovered by "experts" and were "scientific." They seemed to adequately explain his patient. And the treatment based on these theories seemed to work—at least some of the time. Everything fit the satisfactory tests of truth for the psychiatrist, which are authority, plausibility, expediency, and outcome.

The next Sunday, the patient makes her way to church. The morning is beautiful. The service is uplifting and she is eager to speak with her pastor during the fellowship hour.

"My psychiatrist has cured me," she says breathlessly. "No anxiety, no insomnia, I went to the mall this week, I am back on top of the world!"

Her pastor listens attentively as she recounts her experiences with *her* psychiatrist, *her* diagnoses, and *her* medication, and its positive effect. She is delighted to say, "I am a Panic Disorder Sufferer. There are many people like me out there; I think I may join a PDA (Panic Disordered Anonymous) Survivor group at the community center. I am considering in-depth psychoanalysis to really get the bottom of my problems and turn my life around!"

Concern shapes the pastor's countenance as he asks, "Are you still seeing the Christian counselor I referred you to?"

Somewhat startled and not a little uncomfortable, she replies, "Oh there's no need for that now!" Then she turns her attention to someone in the crowded room.

The pastor briefly thought over her words. *That physician—does he have any real understanding of illness or suffering? That psychiatrist—does he have any real understanding of the human mind?* The pastor knew about this woman's life, her family, and her faith, and he wondered, *Has the doctor really helped her?*

This pastor had a deep and thorough understanding of theology and of what the revealed Word of God said. He knew that the Bible is not and does not pretend to be an exhaustive textbook of medicine. He did know, however, that the Bible is a sufficient and authoritative guide to the practice of medicine by physicians just as it is to the experience of illness and suffering. He also knew that only Scripture provides the key to understanding the human heart and mind. He too was a "professional" in the truest sense of the term.

WHAT IS MISSING?

In the introduction of an authoritative textbook on medicine, I found some statements about what a physician is taught to believe about the meaning and purpose of his chosen profession. However, these sage statements, no matter how noble, are peripheral to the real meaning and purpose of the "learned profession of medicine." They ignore the meaning and purpose of life itself. Here are a few examples:

> Medicine is not a science but a learned profession, deeply rooted in a number of sciences and charged with the obligation to apply them for man's benefit.[11]

> The goals of medicine are usually described as preservation of health, the cure of disease and the amelioration of suffering.[12]

> The practice of medicine rests firmly upon a foundation of biologic and behavioral sciences . . . . The physician must acquire both an extensive knowledge base in science and a comfortable familiarity with the ways of science.[13]

> The responsibilities of medicine are threefold: to generate scientific knowledge and to teach it to others; to use the knowledge for the health of an individual or a whole community; and to judge the moral and ethical propriety of each medical act that directly affects another human being.[14]

Resting on the sufficiency and authority of Scripture and its presuppositions in all aspects of human life, the pastor/theologian recognizes that there was a time on this created planet when there was no illness or suffering. Only after the fall of man did illness and mortality enter our lives. The pastor, then, understands that the ultimate cause of all human illness and suffering is the sin of Adam. In the same way, illness and suffering can and do result from our own individual sin. Additionally, we may suffer illness or injury at the hands of another sinner or because of another person's sinful behavior. The pastor/theologian understands that illness and suffering exist as part of the created order—an order sustained by a God who is all-sovereign, holy, and just.

The pastor regularly hears medical scientists reporting on ever more minute and complex discoveries about the healthy and unhealthy human organism. Regular features in the media document the relentless progress of medicine in its efforts to help man improve what is known as "the quality of life." The amelioration of suffering remains the obvious and seemingly sufficient goal of medicine and medical research.

All this raises an important question: Did the psychiatrist who counseled the 43-year-old woman have any real understanding of the purposes of a sovereign, holy God? A God who has revealed himself in Scripture and, through His Spirit, mediated actions consistent with that Word in people's lives? Did it occur to the psychiatrist that this patient's illness might have a purpose? Might God be using it as a means to prevent pride?[15] Could her illness be used to further her spiritual growth?[16] Might her illness be the wages of sin, a chastisement?[17] Could her body be responding to a spiritual problem that needs desperately to be discovered, confronted, and taken to her Lord and Savior? Might her illness and her response to it be an opportunity to glorify God and serve Him more fully?[18]

We who are Christians—including pastors—should be concerned when we see that a person's opportunities for growth and maturing in the faith have been bypassed by a quick, easy diagnosis and "successful" elimination of his or her symptoms of discomfort. In such circumstances, an opportunity has been lost. The physician may believe he helped his patient in accordance with the guidelines and ethics of his profession, but has he really helped at all?

THE BIBLICAL VIEW OF MAN

Scripture speaks of the complexities involved in the fact that man was created in the image of God.[19] Unlike animals, or other created living things, man is unique in this respect. The most important manifestation of man being created in God's image is the spiritual aspect of his being. It is this spiritual aspect that allows man to have any relationship with God. Our outward or physical aspect is temporal and may suffer illness, but our inward aspect is renewed day by day.[20] While our physical aspect is temporary, our unseen spirit is eternal.[21] Our bodies may suffer and die, but not so our spirits.[22] Ultimately this spiritual aspect may be absent from our body for a time, but it is eternal, and eventually it will inhabit either heaven or hell.

The sage statements quoted earlier from the textbook on medicine are conspicuous in their *neglect of this spiritual aspect of man.* They evidence a lack of understanding related to purpose in the suffering of man. Nowhere is this neglect more evident or more far-ranging in its disastrous effect than in the medical specialty known as psychiatry. The theories, practices, and research of modern American psychiatry refuse to accept the supernatural aspect of man and his mind as the very seat of the spirit of man as well as the potential physical home of the indwelling Spirit of God.

Recognizing the supernatural aspect of the human mind is of fundamental importance to any theory or practice of psychiatry, psychotherapy, or counseling. This concept, and its acceptance, or denial, lies at the heart of the differences between biblical counseling and all other forms of counseling.

If we accept the reality that the human mind is not just an exquisitely complex physical cybernetic organ but also one that is indwelt with and controlled by a supernatural spirit, then we can understand that man can never fully know or comprehend the total *how* or *why* of his mind.[23] He will never be able to reliably predict his behavior. He will never have all the answers. In the same manner that believers cannot fully comprehend the nature of the incomprehensible God, no man can fully know his own inner nature.

THE SECULAR VIEW OF MAN

Those who deny the spiritual aspect of the human mind believe just the opposite. They believe that, given enough time and equipment, man will be able to fully know how the brain works. They believe a day will come when all the factors will be known and measurable. Life will become controllable, predictable, remediable. Man will then become a perfect man—"like a God."[24]

Natural man has always sought to understand his mind via the use of whatever happens to be the latest tools of knowledge, philosophy, and science. In this century, we've come to see the mind understood in *psychodynamic* terms, and more recently, in *cybernetic* terms. These "scientific" disciplines and their constructs, metaphors, and vocabulary are the means by which man attempts to know his mind.

These secular models attempt to explain and understand the human mind as a storehouse of information available to its possessor. Both models emphasize access to this storehouse as being important because of what it contains. The psychodynamic model postulates an unconscious and a variety of processes related to its operation. Cybernetics emphasizes access, storage, retrieval, and capacity. Both models understand the mind as an endless videotape recorder archiving with total accuracy a vast storehouse of recorded information. The recorded information is entered into this supposedly limitless storehouse from the womb onward through life.

Both models conceptualize the recording of information to be total in scope and essentially totally retrievable.

Both models postulate that this content wages control over the thoughts, feelings, and behaviors of man. Psychodynamics especially emphasizes the importance of the content of the storehouse and the fundamental importance of fully knowing that content, the "story."

Freud's lasting contribution to the "science" of psychotherapy is based on the above-noted concept of the vast influential unconscious. From his perspective, to understand this unconscious is to control it. To control it is to control the self. When a person is able to control his self, he can achieve his goal to feel good and be his own god. This kind of understanding is said to be available only to those who come to know their unconscious. This is achieved by "remembering, repeating and working through" one's unconscious mind with the help of a skilled guide, therapist, or psychoanalyst.[25]

A biblical counselor, by contrast, typically emphasizes more objective, measurable, verifiable aspects of the human mind. Perhaps without even knowing why, he looks to the current operations of the mind, including its day-to-day productions of speech, feeling, and behavior. He is interested in some of the memory content of the storehouse (past history, previously related experiences, family structure, beliefs, and so on) but only to the degree that it allows him to understand and respond to the current behavior that is of concern to him and the counselee.

The biblical counselor is almost instinctively disinclined to delve into the mind's storehouse or its operations on a "fishing" kind of expedition. Rather, he is careful to keep his information search specific to current mind issues. He understands that the mind of man, his "heart," is not to be trusted, and thus avoids general information retrieval, which tends to provide subjective and introspective information.[26]

The psychodynamically inclined counselor, however, is very much inclined to open-ended exploration. The more content that can be retrieved, the more the client can know (and thus supposedly control) his own mind. As might be expected, the exploration is boundless and endless. There are no limits that the subjective introspective method of inquiry can explore on the mental terrain.

WHO'S TO BLAME?

Another issue dividing biblical counselors from all other counselors is their philosophy of *responsibility and accountability*. For the biblical counselor, the client alone is responsible.[27] For the psychoanalyst or the typical psychotherapist, the client is the passive recipient (or *victim*) of input from his genes, parents, rearing, shaping, trauma, and love-insufficiency. The unconscious of the client is the storehouse of all such experiences and thus is the source of the resultant unhealthy influences on his daily life. Therefore the client's responsibility for his day-to-day mental functions are not emphasized; instead, the focus is on the content of the storehouse—content that was placed there by the victimizing, outside world. The fault, the accountability, and the problem lies with the outside world.

For the biblical counselor, however, there is the certainty that the client alone is responsible for his thoughts, feelings, and behaviors.[28] He understands that man is proscribed from blaming his parents or anyone or anything else for his own sinful thoughts, feelings, and behaviors.[29] This completely different view of accountability is not simply a tradition or a theory, but rather is the expected outworking of an understanding of man which rests upon the full authority of the revealed Word of God.

The other view of man (that he is a victim) is also the expected outworking of another understanding of man. That understanding was first invented in the Garden of Eden when Eve blamed the serpent and Adam blamed Eve. Ages later, it was more fully conceptualized and turned into a practice of healing by Freud. This view of man's problems and his lack of responsibility for them was further elaborated by the various followers of Freud and continues to flourish even to this day.

Growing out of this divergent understanding of man is an aberrant expectation of healing. For the biblical counselor, the hope is that 1) the counselee will be convicted of his sins; 2) he will accept the free gift of salvation through the completed atonement of Jesus Christ; 3) his human spirit will be indwelt by the Holy Spirit; and 4) that he, through exposure to and use of the authoritative and sufficient Word of God, will put off the life of darkness and walk in the light.[30]

For the psychoanalyst or the psychotherapist, the expectation never goes beyond the use of self-understanding (*insight*) in order to bring about correction in the counselee's life. In therapy, self-introspection leads to self-understanding, which leads to self-control, which leads to self-actualization, which leads to self-esteem. Since most people are ill-equipped to do all this by themselves, a therapist with skill, secret knowledge, and experience is required to achieve the self cure.

THE UNIQUENESS OF MAN

Of all the living beings created by God, man alone has within him a spirit that can have a relationship with God.[31] Additionally, only man can become indwelt by the Holy Spirit. These spiritual capabilities separate man from all other creatures. He has a physical body endowed with wondrous God-created complexities. He also has a non-physical spirit;[32] the body of man is not alive without its spirit.[33] The Bible is replete with references that help us to understand that the mind of man is the seat of his spirit.[34] This mind has its physical home in the brain, and works its effects through the rest of the physical structure of our body. The spirit/brain is the "heart" of man, or his "mind." No other creature has such a mind; other creatures merely have brains. They are not created in the image of God, nor can they comprehend the mind of the Spirit.

There exists a systematic relationship between the spirit of man and his brain as well as a part of his body. One aspect does not exist in this life apart from the other. Our spirit controls our body via the brain. With its attributes and its frailties, our body may serve or hinder, and

in some rare cases, overpower our spirit. As fallen creatures, our spirits are weak,[35] and our bodies and brains
are subject to defects, diseases, injury, and misuse.[36] The
two aspects interact together, each having an effect on the
other.

Because the brain is a physical human organ, it is
subject to injury, disease, defects, and misuse. According
to the dictates of legitimate science, some true diseases of
the brain are known to exist. Many other so-called "diseases" of the brain, however, are mere human specula-
tions. The brain cannot be diseased or defective without
some kind of systematic effect on the spirit. To attempt to
understand "mental illness" (brain disease) aside from a
scriptural understanding of the mind is folly, and to expect to completely understand the mind of man is also
hopeless.[37]

THE CURE OF SOULS

To assume that we can achieve a vast understanding
of the mind and its relationship to our spiritual and
physical aspects is to step outside scriptural truth and
into the arenas of human wisdom, philosophy, and the
traditions of man.[38] One example of this is the popular
concept of the term *mental illness*. This term and its related terms, *dysfunction* and *disorder*, should be stricken
from the vocabulary of any Christian. We should make
every effort to use terms that are precise and truthful. On
the one hand, there are a number of true brain diseases;
several are listed in this chapter. These fulfill every requirement of the disease concept. On the other hand,
there are spiritual problems as well as problems of sin
and human responsibility. In the midst of these is the systematic interaction between the physical body and the
immaterial spirit—the soul. No matter where the
problem lies, the approach must be the same: honest, precise, objective assessment measured against established
truth. For physical malfunctions, the truth can be discovered in the laboratory. For spiritual problems, the bench-
mark is Scripture.

When we use terms *mental illness, disorder,* and *dysfunction,* we convey the implication that true diseases are in view when, in fact, they are not. In addition, these terms assume that suffering, including misbehavior "caused by a disease," renders the sufferer no longer personally responsible for his behavior: "I am not committing the sin of drunkenness; I am an Alcohol Dependence 303.90. I have a disease. I am a victim. I am not responsible. I am definitely not a sinner. I need support and affirmation. I have rights. I need a therapist, not a Savior!"

Man today seems to have solved the profundities of the long-debated mind-body problem and his responsibility for sin: all are victims, none are responsible. In a headlong flight from the conviction of sin and the need for a Savior, modern man seems determined to be oppressed, victimized, disordered, dysfunctional and diseased—all for the justification of irresponsibility. There are true brain diseases that can overpower the human spirit and give rise to behaviors which can be injurious to ones self and others; Temporal Lobe Epilepsy is one such disease. Such diseases, however, are quite rare. Most can be controlled by medication. They account for an incredibly small portion of the vast panoply of behaviors for which no man has a real excuse.

We should use our God-given minds to conduct truly scientific inquiry as to whether this or that "disorder" ordained by *DSM III* (revised edition) actually represents a true disease with all that is entailed by such a concept, or whether the illness, dysfunction, or disorder is just another *relativistic, subjective label* produced by the philosophies and traditions of men.

History of Mental Illness

Throughout recorded history, man has attempted to attain a kind of understanding of his mind that only God possesses. Rather than relying on the revealed Word of God for answers, man has always sought to know and control his own mind, and thus, to be his own god. The history of psychiatry is a history of such an effort.

The historians of psychiatry, especially those of the twentieth century, want to weave a rich and colorful tapestry of psychiatry as old as recorded history itself.[39] They seek to include the most ancient concepts of mental illness and its treatment under the rubric of psychiatry and thereby establish a robust and authoritative history standing behind what today is known as the medical specialty of psychiatry.

The term *psychiatry*, however, is relatively new. It was actually first used at the dawn of the nineteenth century in Germany, where, at the same time (1805), the first professional journal of psychiatry was founded.

The history of the concepts and explanations of mental illness is a prime example of how man uses his available reasoning, experiences, and philosophy to explain the unknown. These concepts and explanations have included the magical influences of malevolent deities; improper mixtures of air, water, earth, and fire; "atoms" in motion; misbalance of humors; vital substances or "tendencies"; excesses of phlegm or black or yellow bile; passions and unsatisfied desires uncontrolled by the "soul"; and adverse external circumstances playing upon "predispositions."

These ancient views held sway in one form or another until the late 1400s. During the time of the Inquisition, witchcraft and demon possession became the most common "explanation" behind mental illness. Subsequent to that period the ancient views were again in use, especially the old views of Galen (A.D. 130–200), attributing mental illness to humoral and animal spirits. In the 1600s Animism supplanted Galenism and postulated that the *anima* (soul) held sway over the body (*soma*) and fueled speculation as to the "psychological" causation of mental illness. This was in addition to the already assumed physical, natural, or somatic causation of mental illness.

Thus was initiated the ongoing debate over the concept of mental illness. Is it psychic or somatic? Is it of the *soul* mind (reason, intellect), or of the *body* (the tissue, the chemistry)? Should the search for explanations be *psychic* or *somatic*?

The Somatic School

The postulation of specific "diseases" with required signs and symptoms first flourished during the rationalistic period of the Enlightenment. This was so even without any notion or evidence of fundamental pathogenesis or cause. Mental illnesses were grouped into diseases with supposedly *objective anatomic causes*. For example, spasms or flaccidity of muscles and vessels influenced by a brain in unequal states of excitement or collapse were believed to cause neuroses. Theories based on unequal distributions of the bodily fluid, "animal magnetism," malshaped brain structures and related functions were concocted in association with the phrenologic mapping of the skull. By 1845, when Wilhelm Greisinger published his textbook, the Somatic School had reached its fullest flower.[40] Greisinger and his followers asserted that all mental illness was of objective physical causation and that there was no need for psychological explanations. With Greisinger's book, psychiatry became acknowledged as a medical specialty. It was one field with neurology, and Greisinger was named the first professor of neurology and psychiatry at the University of Berlin.

By the end of the nineteenth century, the Somatic School affirmed by Greisinger had lost favor among people. Up to that time, much work had been done in proposing sites of disease within the brain to account for the recognizable "diseases," and many refined definitions of these mental diseases were codified. In the later years of the nineteenth century the diagnoses schizophrenia, Manic-Depressive psychosis, Paraphrenia, Alzheimer's disease, and General Paresis were established in accordance with the disease concept. As such, they were seen as having recognized and typical onset, presentations, course, and outcome, even though their causes were unknown.

The fact that these causes were unknown, along with the lack of available scientific methodology to make the causes known, led to the withering of the influence of the Somatic School of psychiatry. Without an objective cause (observable and demonstrable), the loop of the disease concept (cause and specific cause-related treatment) could not be closed. The Somatic School lost influence and was replaced by the Psychic School of thought.

During the flowering of the Somatic School, people who were interested in mental illness took the initiative to develop ideas about the psychic causes of mental illness. They traced their roots to the ideas of animism and were strengthened in their notions of psychic causation by the apparent success of psychic treatment. The Romantic philosophical movement (which arose after the Enlightenment)—and its emphasis on subjective experience, introspection, and self-awareness—thoroughly facilitated the rise of the Psychic view over the Somatic.[41]

The Psychic School

Throughout the nineteenth century there developed several significant improvements in the treatment of mentally ill patients in asylums. Kind treatment, exercise, activity, entertainment, good food, pleasant environs, conversations, education, reason, and persuasion replaced dungeons, chains, and beatings. These new treatments and their humane "successes" fostered psychological explanations of the mental illnesses they seemed to be treating. The growing psychic school of psychiatry argued for different diagnoses like *neuroses* and *Neurasthenia*, which were postulated as having no somatic or organic bases. The Psychic School, however, had a deficiency similar to the Somatic School—*no* idea as to causation.

Into this arena came Sigmund Freud. *Neuropsychiatry* was established as a respectable medical specialty. The physicians who practiced it were respected and were viewed as valuable and successful, especially so in the asylums. A plausible and acceptable system of diagnosis had been established. The Somatic School was floundering and the Psychic School, while seemingly effective, was still in its infancy.

Sigmund Freud was a neurologist and a member of the so-called Somatic School. He was trained by its chief theoreticians. Being of a scientific bent, he sought explanations for people's mental problems. Being unable to observe or discover any explanation using the available scientific methodology of his day, he adopted psychic views from various sources as well as paradigms from hydrostatics and the field of hydraulics to propose an entirely new concept of the working of the human mind. His concept of the *unconscious*, its effect on a person's daily life, the means of its exploration, and the possibility of its correction were bold new theories for the time. His grand theory was highly acceptable to the Romanticized culture of his day.[42] He and his followers solidly established the Psychic School of psychiatry. This predominance holds to this present time.

Only in the last 15 years has the long-dormant Somatic School of psychiatry been reawakened. In recent years there has been an infusion of interest in the "organic" or Somatic bases of mental illness. This, for the most part, has been supported by the apparent successes of somatic therapy (drugs, electroshock) and the availability of scientific methods of measurement and observation never before available. This line of inquiry, even though exciting to its adherents, has not yet provided any real closure of the disease-concept loop. No specific pathogenesis has yet been found for the so-called "functional" illnesses—schizophrenia, Manic-Depressive Illness, neuroses, and so on.

The Psychotherapeutic Lifestyle

Long-term insight-oriented psychotherapy, ongoing medication management, and outpatient group support have become the typical prescription of modern American psychiatry. The methods of modern American psychiatry involve collecting subjective symptoms, categorizing them according to the latest theory-based diagnostic manual, and long-term follow-up. The lifestyle of the modern American psychiatric patient involves being labeled as a *disease sufferer*, recognizing one's *victim* status, attributing the blame and responsibility to the *perpetrators*, searching for self-*affirmation*, focusing on the inner child, an endless quest for *deeper insights*, and the fortification of *self-esteem*.

The patient whom we met at the opening of this chapter, like so many others in our society, has embarked on the psychotherapeutic lifestyle. She will invest much time and money examining and revealing her innermost thoughts, feelings, and recollections. She will be encouraged to "remember, repeat, and work through" her past for the purpose of obtaining "insight." From this personal understanding, she will be expected to somehow derive the strength and ability to change herself, make herself happy, make herself "well." She will visit her therapist often and consume various medications. Sometimes she will feel better ("it's working"), sometimes she will feel worse ("I need more therapy"). She will attend groups where similarly afflicted people tell similar stories over and over in an effort to "support" each other. Her relationships will center on group, therapist, and self. When asked, "Is it working?" she will provide abundant (though difficult for the uninitiated to comprehend) testimony as to how she "has changed." Along the way, relationships that are or were "destructive, codependent, non-affirming" will be jettisoned. "Unsatisfactory" traits will be replaced with "adaptive" skills: self-esteem, assertiveness, forcefulness, independence. Through self-actualization via therapy, our subject is promised that she can become a "modern woman" ready for life on her own terms, at her own pace, in her own way.

In the therapeutic lifestyle there is no room for the real Jesus. He is simply unnecessary for self-affirming people. Biblical concepts of how life ought to be lived are neglected, avoided, and often rejected. Christian beliefs, values, and morals are replaced by the secular jargon conveniently adapted to the counselee's mind-set.

IS THERE A BETTER MODEL?

What would have happened if the psychiatrist had adhered to a biblical concept of the human mind and a biblically tested concept of his role as a physician? What would he have done differently?

A married 43-year-old woman and mother of teenage sons arrived 30 minutes early for her appointment to be seen by a psychiatrist. She is sitting alone in the waiting room nervously paging through popular magazines. She was assured by her biblical counselor that this visit and evaluation was a part of his plan to understand her problem in both spiritual and physical terms so that he might be better equipped to assist her in the goal of more fully serving and glorifying God.

During the ten minutes the psychiatrist allows himself between patients, he reviews the consultation referral letter for his next patient. He is pleased that the letter is from a counselor he knows and with whom he has worked many times in the past. He considers this counselor not just a source of professional business but a partner with him in his effort to achieve his goals as a physician, a psychiatrist, and a Christian. With his Christian counterpart, he shares a biblical understanding of illness and of the spiritual challenges and opportunities that illness presents to the sufferer. To his partner he provides expertise which he has in the physical aspects of the human body. He knows how, as a fallen entity, it is defective, can be diseased, injured, and misused. He also knows how the body can create signs and symptoms in its physical responses to spiritual problems, thus complicating those problems.

The letter reads:

Forty-three-year old female, apparent panic attacks . . . agoraphobic . . . three years' duration . . . worsening. Obvious spiritual problems manifest in marital disharmony and problems with sons. Believes she is failing and unable to do what she knows is right. Is preoccupied with anxiety, fears, and insomnia, and is unable to really concentrate on spiritual things, homework, or follow through. Request evaluation and recommendations.

To *this* first session comes a *Christian/physician/psychiatrist* and a patient: spiritual wisdom and established science to the aid of symptoms, signs, disorder, and perhaps a disease.

This physician, with prayer, will approach this patient from not only a *medical model* but also a *spiritual.* He will seek from his patient the fullest possible range of physical and objective historical information that he believes might have some bearing on her current state. In addition to assessing the likelihood of any medical illnesses that could have contributed to her distressing symptoms, he will look for any ways that her body's response to her underlying spiritual difficulties might be worsening her overall situation.

A Thorough Medical Examination

Along the way this physician will pay special attention to the *functioning of his patient's brain.* He knows that there is a supernatural unity of physical brain and immaterial spirit, and thus he understands the importance of assessing the functioning of the physical aspect of the whole. As a result, he will specifically examine and test specific mental functions that have been proven to be measures of physical or "organic" brain function. He will specifically examine consciousness, ability to pay attention, and the power of concentration. He will observe and test the language abilities of his patient. He will test her memory functions and her ability to answer abstract or thought-provoking questions. He will ask her to do some simple calculations and perform some commanded actions. He will document all of the test results in her record. He will perform a physical and neurological examination and carry out a screening test of cognitive functions, such as the Mini-Mental State Exam,[43] or perhaps an Electroencephalogram.

If the physician does all the above and finds nothing abnormal, he can assure himself and his patient that she does *not* suffer a brain disease like delirium, dementia, mental retardation, or some other disease with a known physical, structural, or organic cause.

This physician's next line of inquiry would focus on the remainder of a *mental status examination*. In this examination he is most interested in specific phenomena of mental functioning, which are examined by asking questions and observing the patient. This psychiatrist is, however, not so interested in the *content* of the answers but the *process* of those answers. (Not the subjective but the objective.) He has a phenomenological understanding of the mental status examination; he is looking for objective or measurable things rather than "felt" things and meaning in symbols. Rather than just ask what a hallucinated voice is saying, he will ask, "How loud is the voice, where does it come from, is it clear, and is it you or something outside of you?"

A phenomenological examination lends itself to an empirical, objective measurement of the symptoms, while a psychological examination is inherently speculative, subjective, and on a "feeling" level. To the extent that psychiatry will ever (and it has not) find true diseases that might be known as depression or schizophrenia, those diseases will be marked by phenomenological symptoms that all examiners can agree upon, observe, measure, document, test, prove true or false, and establish as part of a true disease.

At this point in the history of the re-emerging somatic or "biologic" school of psychiatry, the elucidation of diseases known as depression, schizophrenia, and the like remains unsuccessful. Presently, the best any somatic or biologic psychiatrist can do is examine the mental status of his patient for a set of phenomenological signs that, by experience, has been shown to be associated with a good response to some type of medication. This is still only the syndromal approach to diagnosis. Treatment is directed toward the amelioration of symptoms rather than towards the rational application of some disease-specific regimen proven to attack the underlying patho-physiology responsible for the illness itself. No wonder, then, that there is little assurance of effect, reliability of prediction, or certainty of outcome in much of the practice of psychiatry! Worse yet, few psychiatrists even care about a phenomenological mental examination as opposed to a "feelings" examination.

Spiritual Hope and Help

One week later our patient sits in the now-familiar office, awaiting the results of her evaluation. She was pleasantly surprised by the thorough, meticulous questioning of this caring psychiatrist and spoke highly of him to her biblical counselor. She was surprised at his invitation to pray with her that she might understand her illness and through it be more able to glorify God in her life. She was surprised at the lack of Freudian-type questions about her self-concept, early memories, or sexual fantasies.

After opening with prayer, the psychiatrist spoke with her concerning her difficulties: "You do not have a medical or physical problem or brain disease that can explain all of your felt discomforts. You clearly have some important issues, *spiritual issues*, with which you need help—sound biblical help." She became more alert as she listened to his teaching. He went on to explain to her that the symptoms of anxiety were to be expected and that she should not see them as "the problem"—the disease—but more as an indicator of her need to participate in and eagerly submit to biblical counseling. He went on to assure her that her symptoms would abate as she worked with her counselor and expected that with the help of the Holy Spirit she would be more and more able to put off the wrong and put on the right in her goal to serve and glorify God.

The psychiatrist then pointed out that some patients like her do benefit from medication, but only those whose physical responses to their own spiritual problems are so extreme as to become an impairment to their progress while receiving biblical counseling. Even in those cases, he added, once the counselee has stabilized, the medications are reduced with time and discontinued as quickly as possible. He went on to assure her that he had spoken to her biblical counselor and that together they agreed on a specific plan and would remain in contact to monitor the progress they believed she would enjoy.

As the patient leaves the office, she wishes she could do more to express her gratitude. She is deeply grateful for this psychiatrist's help and advice and his plan to maintain contact with her biblical counselor. Only later, on the way home, does it come to her mind that she is *not* suffering from a mental illness. There is no disease controlling her. She is not a victim. The kind of hope and understanding she was given is the best that can come from the medical profession today.

"With the Lord's help, I am doing better," she excitedly told her pastor. "I still get anxious and sometimes I can't sleep, but the truth will set me free. I am more able to get out and take on responsibility, and I am actually able to do my counseling homework."

Her pastor listened attentively after he asked her how she was doing in the counseling he had arranged. (He knew of her progress, for he was a partner in it as well). She was delighted to relate how much she had grown during her time of difficulty and how much her perseverance and growth was proving to be a witness to those around her.

Physician-Counselor Partnerships

Are there psychiatrists out there like the one depicted above? Are there psychiatrists who approach their specialty from biblical presuppositions? Are there psychiatrists who are in eager partnership with a biblical counselor? Unfortunately, the answer is that they are few in number. I have attempted to describe ideally how a truly biblical psychiatrist might think and behave, but I have rarely seen such. The individual physicians who elect to specialize in psychiatry and the kind of training they receive do not promote anything approaching a biblical view in the assessment, conceptualization, and treatment of human mental suffering.

The biblical counselor, however, needs to have a *physician-partner*. That's because some clients will have significant medical or physical problems. Some may need brief hospitalization to prevent suicide or destructive behavior. Others may have physically mediated symptoms of such intensity that short-term medication control is needed for effective biblical counseling to begin and continue.

Two suggestions are offered for the biblical counselor who desires to form such a partnership. The first would be to seek out and cultivate a physician who is knowledgeable in general internal medicine, family medicine, general practice, or perhaps emergency medicine. The goal should be to enlist the interest of such a physician in biblical counseling in general and in your practice of it specifically. Efforts should be made to educate this physician in the presuppositions and practices of biblical counseling as well as to demonstrate to him its outcomes.

A relationship with an interested physician can be cultivated into a true biblical counseling partnership by referring, consulting, sharing, and fellowshiping over time. To hasten this development, you might acquaint such a physician with some of the meetings held specifically for this purpose by groups dedicated to the advancement of biblical counseling.[44] Attendance at such meetings can be an eye-opening experience for the uninitiated, as they offer not only training, but also the opportunity to fellowship with other similarly interested professionals.

The second suggestion, frankly, is more risky. This involves finding a psychiatrist who, by virtue of his personal inclination and his training, might be known as a biological psychiatrist. When asked the question, "Are you a biological psychiatrist?" every psychiatrist should understand your meaning. Those who answer in the affirmative will have trained in one of the several centers across the country that have become well known for their emphasis on biological psychiatry. Such a psychiatrist will likely have a practice marked by a dearth of psychotherapy patients and a wealth of hospitalized, acutely ill patients who manifest more serious forms of mental illnesses. Such a psychiatrist will have a strong interest in objective and more meticulous methods of diagnosis. He will also be more capable of and accustomed to teasing out any physical basis for his patients' complaints.

Though uncommon, such psychiatrists are often willing to work in partnership with counselors who refer cases for assistance with diagnosis and medication management. To make this kind of partnership work, the biblical counselor needs to establish an agreement with the psychiatrist that he limit his involvement with the patient to diagnosis, evaluation for possible medication management, and follow-up. The biblical counselor would be well advised to educate this psychiatrist as to the presuppositions, practices, and especially the outcomes of biblical counseling. Biological psychiatrists as a group tend to be impressed with objective measures of patient outcome rather than anecdotal reports of subjective psychological improvement, which are the watchword of secular psychotherapy.

THE BEGINNING OF ALL WISDOM

It is my hope that this may offer to you a better understanding of psychiatry, its history, and the base for its method of diagnosis and treatment. Psychiatrists and the other practitioners in the American psychotherapy industry have basically become a pagan priesthood in our society. They purvey a tantalizing and thoroughly false gospel—sadly without challenge by most in the modern church.

Be strong and of good courage.[45] Remember that the fear of the Lord is the beginning of wisdom and the knowledge of the holy gives understanding.[46] In all your ways, acknowledge Him and He will direct your paths.[47]

TOTALLY
SUFFICIENT

6

WHAT'S THE BRAIN GOT
TO DO WITH IT?

Edward T. Welch, Ph.D.

Today we have unprecedented windows to the brain! In generations past, philosophers and amateur scientists speculated about the function of the brain, but technological limitations kept research from progressing beyond what is now considered to be a very primitive level. Now, with new chemical-labeling techniques and brain-imaging devices, brain research has peered into the genetic underpinnings of brain cells and is deciphering the scores of chemical patterns that maintain the brain's communication network. An increasingly solid foundation of pure research will most likely result in lifesaving advances in diseases such as Parkinson's and Alzheimer's. For brain researchers these are, indeed, "heady" times.

Such scientific sophistication may seem far removed from the lofty though simple teachings of Scripture. In fact, some Christians have separate categories for the two: neurons belong to the "book of nature" or general revelation; redemption belongs to Scripture or the book of special revelation. The distinction is understandable if you try to do a biblical study of the brain. For example, no concordance will have entries under *brain*, *neurotransmitters*, or *serotonin*. Yet even though it may appear right to separate general and special revelation, most Christians realize that to do so is to create a false dichotomy. In actuality, Scripture is a lens through which we can see everything, including the brain sciences.

The problem is that when we ask Scripture to demonstrate its sufficiency in the brain sciences, it seems less than muscular. It says that God created all things, so we know that God created the brain. It adds that God has created an orderly world, so we know that His creation, including the brain, can be studied and partially known. And because Scripture indicates that we should be people of integrity, we know that when scientists report their findings, they should be careful not to fabricate data or skew results to suit their private agendas. This, at first glance, is the extent of what we can know in regard to the theology of the brain. To ask Scripture to speak any further to this technical discipline might result in eisegesis rather than exegesis. The result of this apparent poverty of relevant biblical data is that in theory we place the Bible over the brain sciences, but in practice we allow Scripture to have very little functional control in the interpretation of neuroscientific data. The Bible becomes a head of state that has no actual power, a puppet king at best.

As a result, some people have suggested that the Bible is pre-scientific in some of its formulations and that we should limit its use to statements about God, and nothing more. In the place of biblical presuppositions, alternative systems have gradually won large-scale acceptance. One of the most popular of these ruling models is the proposition that all that exists is matter. In other words, the brain alone is the ultimate cause of human behavior. All our actions, thoughts, and intents are rooted in material substance. Not only are language problems, problem-solving abilities, and our ability to know left from right the results of brain activity, but heavy drinking, homosexuality, fear, anger, sexual lust, and stealing are also caused by brain problems. Those who adhere to such thinking say that Scripture is not only insufficient for understanding the brain, it is also insufficient for dealing with commonplace moral problems that have been considered a part of its turf for centuries. In their bifurcated world of the book of nature and the book of Scripture, the book of nature continues to be given more and more credence while Scripture is given less and less. The consequence has been a gradual erosion of biblical confidence that will severely limit the scope of scriptural sufficiency for the next generation. The Christian's task, then, is to show that the matter of biblical sufficiency is more than just a theory, and to develop biblical categories that actively inform and functionally control the neurosciences.

UNDERSTANDING THE MAKEUP OF MAN

Standing behind much of the discussion in brain research are questions that are very familiar to the Scripture: Who are we? Are we monistic or dualistic? Are we best understood as one substance or more than one? The biblical answers to these questions have been available for centuries. To date, however, the implications of these answers for brain research have rarely been discussed.

Two Substances in One

The clear teaching of Scripture is that we are embodied souls. We comprised of at least two substances in one person. We are material body and immaterial soul or spirit. Well-known church documents have consistently affirmed this distinction. For example, the first answer to the questions of the *Heidelberg Catechism* is "I belong—body and soul, in life and in death— to my faithful Savior Jesus Christ." Later, the catechism continues this distinction by saying that "my soul will be taken immediately after this life to Christ and that my very flesh, raised by the power of Christ, will be reunited with my soul." The *Westminster Confession* agrees: "The bodies of men, after death, return to the dust, and see corruption; but their souls (which neither sleep nor die), having immortal substance, immediately return to God who gave it."

This duality is not to be confused with Greek dualism, which suggested that the soul is heavenly while the body is earthly and less noble than the soul. Scripture indicates that the body, like the soul, is meant for the Lord (1 Corinthians 6:19) and is essential to our humanness. The body is our means of concrete service in the created world. If there is a distinction between body and soul, it is a distinction of function, not value.

Distinctions Between Body and Spirit

It is certainly awkward to talk about the body as separate from the spirit or soul because the body and the spirit belong together. They are, however, two distinct substances. In fact, they are even capable of being separated at death. Given that our beings are a unity of two substances, it follows that these two substances or structures can be distinguished at the level of their function, and this, indeed, is the case. Although clearly interdependent, body and soul have different "responsibilities." The body provides the soul with a vehicle for concrete living in a material world. It is the soul's "equipment." As this equipment, the body is never called sinful. Instead, it is called weak or strong—adjectives that intuitively make sense. For example, Matthew 26:41 tells us, "The spirit is willing, but the flesh is weak." Elsewhere we learn that the body fades like grass (1 Peter 1:24); it wastes away (2 Corinthians 4:16). The body can contribute to temptations in the sense that its desire for food can dominate the undisciplined soul. Or, its desire for rest, when coupled with the tendencies of the sinful nature, can turn into laziness. But the body itself is strong or weak. It is never the locus of sin. The body is not the moral helmsman; rather, the body carries out the moral intents of the soul.

These features of the body, minus the spiritual references, are commonly accepted within the philosophy of the neurosciences. What is absent in the neuroscience's understanding of the person is the soul or spirit. "There is no longer any need for the spirit," said a prominent brain scientist, "it is enough that we are neuronal man."[1] The logic is simple: Why do we need to posit the existence of a soul when we have been able to find everything we consider to be distinctly human in the brain? Memory, cognitive abilities, and language have all been found to emerge from different areas of the brain. But does that mean the soul has finally been located in the body? Are those who study the brain missing an essential element of the person? To answer these questions, we should consider what Scripture attributes to the spirit or soul and what it does not.

First, the spirit is not intelligence. When Scripture uses the term "mind" (for example, Romans 12:2), it is referring to the person-before-God, the person as one-who-is-to-be-holy. A renewed mind has nothing to do with an improved IQ score. It is distinct from intelligence which is better understood as embedded in the brain. Certainly intelligence is a gift from God that gives us the capacity to subdue our world for His glory, but it is best attributed to the material substance of the body. For example, Alzheimer's disease is debilitating and lethal. As this disease worsens, the affected person's intellect declines. The decline, however, is not a decline of spiritual vitality. Those who are afflicted retain faith and the ability to know right and wrong. They can still know about God's will for them, yet perhaps in a less sophisticated, more childlike way. What declines are brain functions such as memory, the ability to think abstractly, basic academic skills, and even speech. But these people do not lose their capacity to respond to God in trust and obedience.

The spirit is also not personality. Personality, or our tendency to demonstrate some stable relational traits over time, is best understood as a function of the brain. We often hear comments about how some child's personality seems to duplicate that of one of the biological parents, and it appears that certain personal characteristics seem to be more than just the result of simple imitation. Furthermore, it is well known that a person's personality can be dramatically altered by brain injury. This is typically the major complaint of families in which one member has sustained brain injury. For example, wives have frequently said, "My husband is completely different; I feel like I am living with a stranger."

If our understanding of the soul or spirit consists of intellectual abilities or personality, then the brain sciences are correct to say that we no longer have any need for the spirit. Yet the spirit or soul *does* exist. It is a biblical concept; it overlaps and is interchangeable with other words such as *heart*, *inner person*, and *mind*. The spirit or soul is the seat of all that we would call moral or ethical. In our spirit (hearts, souls) we know God and His law (Romans 1–2). By our spirit we know right and wrong, and we live in either obedience or disobedience. The spirit is the ever-awake moral helmsman who is constantly faced with the decision to either fear God or worship idols. At its best, it might be called pure, soft, righteous, undivided, and clean. At its worst, it may be called rocky, hard, divided, and filled with lust and pride.

On a theoretical level, the dominant voices within the neurosciences deny the existence of the spirit. They say that the spirit—the person-who-lives-before-God or even the person-as-moral—does not exist. They have no lenses that allow them to see this most central aspect of our being. But they also see something that cannot be completely understood from a monistic position. For example, Jerome Kagan, a well-respected secular psychologist, has stated that the person-as-moral is central to understanding people. He further suggests that such behavior can not be explained biologically:

> I side with the majority of moral philosophers and some psychologists in suggesting that one of the unique qualities of *Homo sapiens* is the continual disposition to apply a symbolic good-bad evaluation to

most events. . . . Humans are the only species that evaluate symbolically their acts, ideas, and feelings with a moral gloss and are motivated to regard themselves as good. . . . The receptors and the neural circuits that mediate sweet tastes and soft textures are known to a large degree, but those that mediate pride or guilt remain mysterious.[2]

The Bible is unequivocal in its distinction between physical weakness and moral behavior. The heart of man is the seat of both sin and faith and it is sinful or righteous; the body is the material substance of the person that is either strong or weak. Sin proceeds from the heart; broken legs or brain dysfunction proceeds from the body, and is never called sinful in itself. Furthermore, this biblical distinction fits the facts. Notice how Scripture captures the data around us. It allows us to see that a certain mentally retarded adult may have the cognitive abilities of a three-year-old but at the same time demonstrate moral maturity that is exemplary. It reveals that judgments of right and wrong are universal. It explains that whenever we are angry, we are revealing some of the "oughts" in our hearts.

Notice too that many who might claim to be monistic in their view of the person are inconsistent with that in practice. For example, many seasoned clinicians will say that dementia, schizophrenia, depression, or hyperactivity in children—all allegedly physical problems—should never be an excuse for "bad" behavior. By saying that, they are implicitly recognizing that biology alone does not capture the whole person. Our righteousness and sin might be *represented* on a biological level, but a biochemical *accompaniment* to moral thoughts does not imply a biological cause for those thoughts.

In these two categories—inner person and outer person—the Bible demonstrates its competency even in areas that are modern and technical. Of course, this does not mean that we should ignore the observations of the brain sciences. No indeed; Scripture teaches us just the opposite. We should carefully observe and understand our world. At the same time, we should recognize that there is no nook or cranny where Scripture doesn't provide the contours for theory and practice.

Key Principles About Our Nature

There are numerous principles that follow from a biblical understanding of the two-in-one nature of human beings. For the purpose of thinking biblically in the brain sciences, these two principles are the most relevant:

1. The body never makes us sin. Weakness in the body can diminish intellectual capacity and leave us with fewer options in our concrete service to God (for example, a 70-year-old man cannot serve God in Olympic track and field or a Down-syndrome girl cannot be a scholar. But neither physical weakness nor physical strength can render us less morally competent or less useful in God's kingdom.

2. The physical body always gives shape to the responses of the inner person. We are creatures in the context of physical bodies, so everything we do will have the stamp of bodily strengths and weaknesses. The brain sciences can be very helpful in helping us learn more about the consequences of bodily strengths and weaknesses.

UNDERSTANDING BIBLICAL SUFFICIENCY

A Closer Look at Prozac

A recent book from the applied brain sciences is the best-seller *Listening to Prozac*.[3] Because of the immense popularity of Prozac, the book has captured the attention of laymen and professionals. While some critics have suggested that the book seems like a drug company advertisement, the book actually is provocative and philosophically astute. Yet it raises questions that might encourage people toward a deeper commitment to the view that we are just body, not body and soul. The book consists of a series of case studies as a backdrop for musings about human nature. Let's consider just two brief but representative case studies.

Sam was an architect, nearly 40 years old, who came for psychiatric care because he was depressed. The ostensible triggers seemed to be difficulties he was experiencing in his business and the deaths of his parents. Also noteworthy were his history of fighting with his parents (fights that were without reconciliation), and his habit of indulging in pornography. In fact, his interest in hardcore sex films, which he insisted his wife watch with him, was a central conflict in his marriage.

Talk therapy had given Sam some insight into the circumstances surrounding his depression, but insight did little to dislodge his deep sadness. After an unhelpful trial with one type of antidepressant medication, Sam was given Prozac. The change, apparently, was remarkable. Sam not only was rid of his depression; he claimed to be "better than well." He reported that he was more optimistic, more efficient at work, and more mentally agile.

From a biblical perspective, there is nothing unexpected so far. If drugs can manipulate the brain environment, then drugs can potentially affect functions that are directly mediated by brain activity. The changes Sam experienced were all changes that the Scripture would subsume under the heading of the body: improved mood and improved mental alertness. There was one change, however, that cast doubt on Scripture's ability to stand over the brain sciences: Though Sam enjoyed sex as much as ever, he no longer had any interest in pornography.

Prozac took away Sam's appetite for sin! Can you see the dominos starting to fall with this apparent change? If we were Sam's counselor, perhaps we would be happy for Sam's wife. But what about other Christian brothers who struggle with pornography and are challenged to repent and follow Christ in faith and obedience? Should we call them to take Prozac rather than repent? Does this mean the Bible is insufficient for some modern problems? Is the Bible out of date? What other areas of life might the Scripture not be able to speak on? Clearly, the short vignette about Sam is potentially lethal data that could be used against affirmations for the sufficiency of Scripture. How can we demonstrate that biblical categories reign over even the data in Sam's case study?

There are a host of possible biblical explanations. One possible though improbable explanation is that the vignette isn't true. There is no Sam except in the imagination of the author. Our culture tends to be lulled into the myth that researchers are impartial, objective, and nearly infallible in their observations. The truth is that researchers can skew their data to fit their hypotheses. In an age where the publication of important results can mean tenure or substantial grant money, researchers can be tempted to publish spurious results.

Another explanation is that we cannot conclude anything on the basis of Sam alone. Cause-and-effect relationships (cause=Prozac, effect=loss of interest in pornography) are never established on the basis of one case study regardless of the abilities and ethical standards of the researcher. There may have been other reasons for Sam's decreased interest in pornography—reasons that had nothing to do with Prozac.

But let's assume that there *was* a Sam who indulged in pornography at one time, then later he became uninterested in pornography, and Prozac was the difference. Did the Prozac actually change his heart? The following story may help us answer that question. The dynamics are the same, but the illustration is less technical.

Let's say Mary lives with her argumentative sister. One day Mary decides that the way to deal with her sister is to argue better and louder than her. After a few years of practice, she succeeds. By this time Mary is ready to fight with her sister without provocation. Mary's sinful pattern of quarreling continues until her sister finally moves out. Now, amazingly enough, Mary isn't quarreling anymore. Why did Mary stop quarreling? The answer: Mary's sister moved out. What was the cause of her quarreling? The answer *seems* obvious: her sister. If you put her sister into the house, Mary will quarrel. Take her sister out and the quarreling stops. This is a natural conclusion, but it is natural only if we ignore Mary's heart (spirit, or soul).

Biblically, however, Mary quarreled because of her own sin. She wanted her own desires, not God's (James 4:1-3). The fact that her sister's presence went hand-in-hand with the arguments simply means that Mary needed certain situations to help expose the true state of her heart. Mary's demanding and selfish heart might not be exposed when she is surrounded by friends who are always kind to her, but mix her sister's argumentative style along with the privacy she is seeking in her home, and the result is that Mary's heart is exposed. The circumstances didn't cause her to sin; they simply were the occasion for it.

In a similar way, Sam, like Mary, had difficult circumstances: depression, a sense of gloom at work, the sense that there was no spark in his life. Pornography became the vehicle through which he attempted to deal with his circumstances. Perhaps it added a perceived spark to his life that allowed Sam to temporarily escape his depression. When Prozac was introduced as a different kind of spark, the purpose of the pornography was no longer there. He felt better without using the pornography. Had his heart changed? Not at all. Given the right circumstances, Sam's selfish desires will be exposed again. Even without the right circumstances Sam's sinful desires will continue to be expressed, but they might not be expressed in the use of pornography. Instead, they may be expressed in the form of neglecting his wife because he works too much. Therefore, there is no reason to believe that Prozac is the treatment for pornography. Prozac, at most, can alter *bodily* symptoms and emotions that can be uncomfortable or painful. But Prozac did not change Sam's sinful struggle with pornography any more than the leaving of Mary's sister produced spiritual fruit in Mary's life. Sam and Mary's hearts remained unchanged.

Pornography is not the only symptom that some people are attempting to treat with Prozac. The book *Listening to Prozac* suggests that the new "cosmetic psychopharmacology" can effectively relieve many symptoms that were once considered to have a spiritual cause. For example, sensitivity to rejection has always been considered to be a nonmedical symptom. Biblically, it is a modern version of the ever-present tendency to fear man rather than fear God. Gail, however, dealt with her "rejection-sensitivity" by taking Prozac.

Gail had become a physician before it was common for women to go into medicine. She had married her teenage sweetheart, also a physician, and successfully raised twin daughters. But her marriage gradually became unsatisfying, so when her husband was offered a job some hours away she chose not to relocate, thus seeing her husband only on weekends. Interestingly, Gail preferred this arrangement because it left her with more control around the house and away from her husband's sharp tongue, which she felt had dominated her for years. In therapy, her competent exterior belied a woman who "found little pleasure in life and was very vulnerable to attacks on her self-esteem."

After taking Prozac, Gail soon noticed that she seemed more self-assured, less critical of herself, and able to handle perceived rejection and disappointment. When she contemplated applying for a new job, she took even more Prozac to help her handle the blow that her self-esteem might receive if she was rejected. She subsequently applied and was rejected, but the boost from the extra Prozac helped her to take the rejection in stride.

This again raises questions about the sufficiency of Scripture. Perhaps people in the pre-Prozac era could deal with the fear of man by learning the fear of the Lord and knowing their duty before God, but today's generation has found it more effective to just get a prescription.

These new drugs seem to work magic, but that shouldn't surprise anyone. For example, alcohol has been used by people all through history to deal with rejection-sensitivity. And it is unlikely that Prozac could temporarily dissolve rejection-sensitivity better than cocaine or other stimulant drugs. In fact, most mind-altering drugs, prescription and illicit, will typically diminish rejection-sensitivity.

How do these drugs perform their magic? Is a fear of man caused by the brain rather than the spirit? To answer these questions we must understand that emotions are bodily experiences that can be caused by a person's spirit, his body, or both. But regardless of their ultimate cause, emotions are physical phenomena. You can *feel* them. As a result, we would expect that by manipulating the brain's chemical milieu it is possible to provoke certain emotions. Medicine cannot make you love more, but it might change some of your feelings. For example, depression is a notorious side-effect of certain drugs, and it accompanies various diseases that affect brain function. The physical jitteriness associated with anxiety can also be easily provoked by chemical changes in the brain. And what about when we feel "great" after a good night's sleep or we win a prize of some kind? Can the body be tricked into experiencing such feelings even though the inner person has not really changed? Yes, it can.

Prozac, for some people, can produce a physical experience that mimics contentment. That is not to say that the heart is any better equipped to deal with the cruel comments of other people. But it does mean that Prozac can cause intense emotional reactions to diminish, giving people the impression that they feel more capable of dealing with the stresses of this world.

Drugs such as Prozac can have a surprising influence on people, but this can be quickly understood when traditional biblical categories are given full reign to demonstrate their competencies. In that context, we find that the complexities of psychopharmacology do not evade the categories of Scripture. In fact, the Scripture's doctrine of the person has a depth that is unfathomable to the brain sciences. While the brain sciences may provide illustrations for the biblical category of the body, the brain sciences will never uncover the mysteries of the human soul.

A Closer Look at Homosexuality

A second area in which the brain sciences have entered the mainstream of American thought is that of homosexuality, and they have entered our corporate consciousness with some force. Whereas the research on psychoactive medications has offered subtle challenges to the sufficiency of Scripture, the research into the biological basis for homosexuality has been used as an overt attack. The *interpretation* of this research states that the biological causes of homosexuality are well established, and any person who suggests that homosexuality is a moral problem is either a bigot or a fool. Three studies in particular are being cited as evidence for this claim.

Perhaps the most well-known study appeared in the periodical *Science*.[4] The lead researcher, Simon LeVay, conducted postmortem examinations on the brains of 19 homosexuals who died from AIDS and 16 presumed heterosexuals, six of whom died of AIDS. His results suggested that the brains of the homosexual men consistently had fewer brain cells in the specific area of the brain that had to do with sexual behavior. The conclusion LeVay reached is that homosexuality is caused by specific conditions in the brain.

Is it biblically possible that homosexuality is caused by a unique brain configuration? It would be possible if homosexuality was described as a strength or weakness. Scripture, however, is unequivocal. Homosexuality, in thought or action, is sin. To suggest that the biblical prohibitions against homosexuality were temporary cultural guidelines would be to jeopardize Scripture's entire moral code. The prohibitions against homosexuality are as clear as the prohibitions against idolatry. Therefore, we will not find evidence that the brain irresistibly causes homosexuality. We may find homosexuality represented by a pattern of brain activity, but we cannot say that the brain activity is the ultimate cause of the sinful behavior.

On closer inspection, LeVay's observations are consistent with Scripture. LeVay himself recognizes the limitations of his study, suggesting that it is little more than an invitation to further research by others. He knows that his observations are very tentative until corroborated by other researchers, and this corroboration has not as yet been forthcoming. But even if there is research that supports his study, LeVay acknowledges that "the results do not allow one to decide if the size of INAH 3 in an individual is the cause or the consequence of that individual's sexual orientation." In other words, it is just as likely that the possible brain differences are a *result* of homosexuality as they are a cause.

Another approach to studying whether there is a genetic basis for homosexuality is to observe the occurrence of homosexuality in families and twins. A frequently cited example of this kind of research was done by Michael Bailey and Richard Pillard.[5] This study reported that of 56 homosexuals who were identical twins, 52 percent (29) had a twin brother who was also homosexual. Among non-identical twins the rate was 22 percent, and among related siblings the rate was 9 percent. This is what you would expect if homosexuality was genetically shaped: the closer the genetic relationship, the higher the rate of shared homosexuality.

The researchers are aware, however, that the only thing these figures really prove is that homosexuality is *not* solely caused by genetics. If genetics was the only contributor to homosexual activity, then the concordance rate in identical twins would be 100 percent. Since the statistic is much lower than that, homosexuality cannot be a straightforward genetic trait. Apart from that, the study is inconclusive. Along with problems in the way that the study was structured, we have to keep in mind that identical twins share an environment that is more similar than that of other siblings. Therefore, it is not unusual for them to share in the same sins. The only way to strengthen this particular vein of research would be to study twins who were separated at birth.

Let's suppose for a moment that this research was done on twins who were separated at birth and raised in different environments. This has not been done yet, but what if such research were to find that identical twins more frequently share homosexuality even when they have no contact with each other? Even if such a finding did emerge, it would still illustrate biblical truth. First, there will never be a 100 percent concordance rate. Second, a principle of Scripture is that the context for our lives is the physical body, and we should expect that the physical body (the brain, in this case) would have some way to biologically represent the intents of the heart. It is even possible that a certain brain type is necessary to express homosexual intent. This brain type or genetic hardware is not sufficient to cause homosexuality, but it may be necessary. Or, to put it another way, a certain *genetic predisposition may be necessary for homosexual intent, but it is not determinative.* An analogy is that if I am going to wash my car, a pail of water might be necessary. However, that pail of soapy water is neither sufficient to cause me to wash my car, nor is it determinative in that it irresistibly forces me to wash it. The sufficient condition for me to wash the car is that I must have the intention or motivation to wash it. In the case of homosexuality, moral intent is a function of the heart, and the heart is always morally responsible before God.

A third type of research on the biological basis of homosexuality also focuses on genetic data, but instead of looking for it in large populations, it looks for it at the microscopic level, on the gene itself. Dean Hammer and his team at the National Institute of Health have taken the lead in this work.[6] This highly technical research is in its infancy, but neither its youth nor sophistication should keep Christians from asserting the functional authority of Scripture over the data.

When this genetic research is viewed through the lens of Scripture, it has the logical flaws of its predecessors. First, it has not been duplicated, so there is really very little that must be said at this point. Second, even if practicing homosexuals were consistently genetically distinct from heterosexuals, this would not make homosexuality a biologically based behavior for which people are not morally responsible. A sinful heart is the only sufficient cause for homosexuality.[7]

SCRIPTURE AND THE BRAIN SCIENCES

The fact that we are a unity of two substances, body and spirit, has two important implications: 1) the body cannot cause sin, and 2) the body shapes, influences, and limits the expression of the spirit. Of these two implications, the focus has been on the principle that our bodies can never make us sin. This is an inviolable principle that can bring increased clarity to brain research. We have not discussed the principle that we live a body/brain existence, and further study of the brain will only help our understanding of people. From this perspective, brain research provides important descriptions and illustrations of bodily weakness. For example, it can help us understand the world of the brain-injured people and can guide our efforts to maximize their cognitive strengths.

When the brain sciences sit under the categories of Scripture, they can be a blessing to us. We must be alert, however, to the growing suspicions that Scripture and the brain sciences are two different books of truth. The brain sciences are part of God's world, and God has given us the principles that mark the contours of this burgeoning and exciting area.

7

WHAT ABOUT BIOMEDICAL RESEARCH?

Paul Madtes, Jr., Ph.D., and Arnold Hyndman, Ph.D.

During the last century, the world has under-
gone tremendous change. Many of those
changes have been brought about through
scientific exploration. Science has grown and developed
into a powerful discipline that influences everyone's life
in one form or another. In previous centuries, a significant portion of a person's typical day was spent working
to sustain life by doing tasks such as planting seeds, har-
vesting crops, and feeding the family. Today, many of
these tasks can be accomplished by fewer people in
fewer hours, leaving time for other pursuits.

It is now possible to sit in your home and experience
the activities of other people all around the world
through the media of television and radio. Technological
advancements allow us to communicate with people
globally by using telephones. Not only is voice communication possible, but documents and images can also be
transmitted by telephone lines. We can use these lines to
fax documents to each other. In fact, with cellular phones,
a person can create a document, make a copy, send it

nearly anywhere in the world, and receive a reply all while traveling down the highway in an automobile.

Scientific discoveries have not only changed the way people live at home, they have also changed the home itself. The equipment and materials used to build today's homes allows people to maintain a constant temperature indoors all throughout the year. In the kitchen, meals can be prepared in mere minutes, and the leftovers can be stored easily. In fact, those leftovers can be warmed later by using a microwave oven to reheat the meal so it can be enjoyed just as much as it was the first time around. Outside the house, we now have lawnmowers that allow us not only to maintain beautiful yards, but also to recycle the cuttings so the grass is constantly being nourished.

The list of areas in which science has had a significant influence on people is extensive. Indeed, scientific findings have fundamentally changed the lives of everyone. And the future promises even more change as a result of scientific investigation.

THE BIOMEDICAL CHALLENGE

While the entire realm of science has influenced many facets of society, one area in particular has seen dramatic changes that have altered the quality of life: biomedical science. Biomedical research has made many advances that are of significant benefit to mankind. This area of research has made possible things that 50 years ago could hardly be imagined. Scientific advances in the world of medicine have changed life greatly due to improvements in health care, such as the treatment of diseases and disorders. For example, surgery is now possible for many physical conditions that previously were fatal, such as heart defects, cancer, and kidney failure. The discovery of new drugs has enabled people with otherwise fatal disorders to live a normal life. Consequently, it is not unreasonable to expect people to live well into their seventies or even their eighties.

The medical alteration of life before birth is now a reality. It is now possible to clinically determine the health state of a developing fetus while it is in the uterus of a woman. In the event that the fetus has a physical defect, *in utero* surgery can be performed in an effort to correct the problem. Many children who at one time would not have made it to birth now have the possibility of being brought to term and living a normal life. In addition, recent technological advances have saved the lives of significantly premature babies and enabled them to live a full, normal life.

Scientific progress has also performed wonders for people with cardiovascular problems. For example, children who come down with rheumatic fever usually suffer from damaged heart valves. Not too long ago, this kind of damage would have resulted in death at a young age. Today, however, faulty valves can be replaced with either a natural one from an animal such as a pig, or with an artificial, mechanical valve that enables the recipient to live many additional years.

Similarly, a person with arteriosclerosis (a condition in which the diameter of the blood vessels narrows, often caused by a buildup of plaque, which comes from having a high level of cholesterol in the bloodstream) is faced with a potentially fatal situation. However, advances in the recent decades have enabled doctors to perform surgery to replace the affected blood vessels with new ones. These coronary bypasses are allowing people to live many years longer. Furthermore, technology has also made it possible, in certain situations, for heart patients to forego a coronary bypass. Instead, an angioplasty can be performed. In this procedure, a balloon is inserted into the damaged area and inflated. This breaks the blockage into smaller pieces that are reabsorbed, thus freeing the blood vessel for normal blood flow again. This approach to reopening clogged blood vessels has been expanded recently into a procedure somewhat like that of using a corkscrew to drill through the blockage to insert a screen beyond the blockage. This screen captures any pieces that break free and prevents them from causing damage at blockages farther along the vessel. As a result, patients with extremely serious cardiovascular conditions are now living longer, healthier lives.

One of the most dramatic examples of how biomedical research is improving human health is in the area of genetics—in particular, *gene therapy*. Each person is born with a specific set of genes that determine the characteristics of that individual. In some instances, a person might be born without a specific gene, or with a defective one, so that a necessary gene product is missing. In some cases, a person can be given regular oral administration of the missing biological product and thus live a normal life. Cystic fibrosis (CF) is a disease in which a defective gene results in the absence of a molecule whose presence normally allows fluid levels in the lungs to remain low. If this molecule is missing, then excessively thick mucous is produced, allowing fluid to accumulate in the lungs. As a result, the patient dies, literally drowning in his own fluids.

Recent strides in genetic engineering has enabled researchers to deactivate the cold virus of its ability to cause a cold, yet render the virus useful for attaching itself and inserting genetic material (DNA) into the cells in the respiratory tract. The cold-virus DNA can then be altered so that it contains the gene that replaces the molecule that is missing in CF patients. When inhaled, the cold virus enters the respiratory tract and attaches itself to the cells lining it, where, in turn, the DNA is inserted and incorporated into the respiratory cell's DNA. Here, normal function allows expression of the new DNA, resulting in the synthesis and secretion of the missing molecule. It is hoped that this development will help relieve CF patients of their respiratory symptoms and thus lengthen their life greatly.

There's another type of alternate-gene therapy treatment that involves introducing normal genes for defective ones. This was used to help individuals who had a defective immune system. Instead of producing the correct molecules to aid in fighting infection (antibodies), this person's B-lymphocytes did not respond. He was given gene therapy that temporarily corrected his problem. While the direct correction of a defective gene is not yet possible, recent advances suggest that this kind of treatment may soon become a reality.

Every one of the advances I've cited were the result of many basic and applied research investigations. Biomedical scientists—both those involved in studying how the body functions and how to correct defects in normal function—are unlocking the mysteries of the human body. These discoveries prove very valuable to mankind, but it's also possible for them to be misused. In addition, many findings in biomedical research are applied without a frame of reference concerning their overall impact on humanity. Both Christians and non-Christians often lack adequate perspective for deciding what should be permitted in terms of the approved use of scientific information and technology. Should limits be placed on scientific investigation? If so, at what stage of scientific research should limits be considered? What about applying the new knowledge and understanding to humanity—who should determine the guidelines for using such information?

Before we can answer those questions, clear standards must be established and agreed upon. The failure to have standards can have a tremendously negative impact on society and social order. For example, in the first half of the twentieth century, a significant amount of work done under the guise of science was actually designed to annihilate a particular group of people. Adolph Hitler attempted to use scientific information as a basis to destroy the Jewish people and create a "master race." This example represents an extreme case of the misuse of science. However, it illustrates well why standards must be established—standards that deal with both limitations on research and the application of findings.

DOES SCIENCE HAVE ALL THE ANSWERS?

The general public seems to believe that science, given enough time and money, could solve all the questions of life. Dr. Victor H. Fiddes addressed this: "The more rapidly the human situation deteriorates, the stronger man's reliance upon his technological resource-fulness seems to be."[1] However, it could be detrimental if science continues to function without the proper frame-work for conducting research and applying the findings. Yet scientists continue to work in their laboratories, often without regard for any social or moral framework. Presently, they are responsible for establishing their own guidelines and restrictions, and, in general, this approach has been adequate. Historically, science has sought to govern itself. This worked well in the past because many scientists were devout Christians who worked from the perspective that God's creation would reveal God Him-self. Thus, the application of their findings would include biblical principles.

Today, however, many scientists interpret their find-ings with little or no regard for any biblical framework. The standards they use may originate from their personal values or views, or from those of the source that is paying for the research. In the latter case, a conflict of interest can arise, thus creating a barrier to doing research without an ulterior motive. The basis for study, then, becomes one of personal benefit, not a search for truth. In addition, the pressure to generate data and publish those results has led some scientists to falsify their research papers. This type of behavior in science was unheard of until recently, and these are but two small aspects of the problem of doing scientific investigation without a frame of reference. Be-cause of the need for integrity in science, it is imperative that the proper framework for both conducting research and applying the finding be established—one that in-cludes a biblical perspective. Professor T.F. Torrance of Ed-inburgh has said, "Natural science through its remarkable intelligibility cries out for a proper doctrine of creation."[2] Many science organizations and research funding agen-cies are being forced to address this issue; they are looking to scientists, politicians, and others to help develop a con-science for creating a framework for approaching scientific research. However, such a framework already exists; it is the Word of God as found in the Scriptures.

What we know about the universe comes from God's revelation to us, both in nature and in Scripture. Nature reveals God's greatness, whereas Scripture reveals God's grace.[3] Through God and the Scriptures, Christianity alone has the resources to properly inspire and transform the world. The question is whether we will use what God has given us to do so.[4] Christians cannot live by eternal principles without reference to the real world.[5] This chapter addresses the issue of the relationship between the sufficiency of Scripture and biomedical research, proposing that the Bible be used as the foundation upon which all scientific research is conducted and applied.

Since we are writing as scientists and not as philosophers, this chapter is not an in-depth discussion of the philosophy of science. We will concentrate on science more than theology. While biomedical research is our area of expertise and the focus of our discussion, the issues raised in this chapter could be raised for other disciplines in science as well. With these things in mind, it is our purpose to show 1) that Scripture provides a basis for both doing biomedical research and applying it to mankind, and 2) that science in general can adhere to biblical principles.

WHAT IS SCIENCE?

Science can be defined in many ways. J.P. Moreland has discussed this issue extensively in his book *Christianity and the Nature of Science.*[6] While his perspective is that of a philosopher, he does accurately portray the difficulty of describing both what science is and what it is not. For our purposes, science will be defined in the traditional sense, as taught by scientists to their students.

> Science is concerned with the material universe, seeking to discover facts about it and to fit those facts into conceptual schemes, called theories or laws, that will clarify the relations among them. Science must therefore begin with observations of objects or events in the physical universe.[7]

... [science] seeks to understand the world of reality in terms of basic general principles ... involving observation, intuition, experimentation, debate, and reformulation.[8]

To put it simply, *science is the search for truth and an explanation of that truth.* It uses what is termed the scientific method, in which the investigator observes, hypothesizes, and tests that hypothesis until a valid interpretation results. This conclusion, a theory, is continually subject to verification and modification through further experimentation until the scientific community is convinced that no major or contradicting exceptions have been or are likely to be discovered. Then the theory is given the status of being a law of science. An example would be Newton's Law of Gravity.

In today's society, science has been elevated to an uncritically prominent status. People glibly accept scientific theories with little or no regard for the evidence required to support those theories. The word of the scientific expert is taken as absolute. This unfortunately leads people to respond to new information in a manner that can be inappropriate or unfounded because the scientific process has not yet been completed. In fact, most recent scientific findings have not reached the final stage of the scientific method—the law of science. Rather, they are at the earlier stages of hypothesis or theory. Unfortunately, these unproven findings are often presented as fact.

Science is a dynamic discipline. While scientists endeavor to formulate scientific theories and laws, science is far from being absolute. Much of what is done in scientific studies is based on basic assumptions. For example, chemistry is based upon the atomic theory—everything is made of atoms. While the evidence clearly supports this theory, the theory itself is based upon many assumptions. The validity of the theory is dependent on the assumptions being true. It's possible for scientific principles that are based on a set of assumptions to change as a result of further testing, including the testing of the assumptions on which those scientific principles are based.

WHY STUDY SCIENCE?

Two questions arise from the issue of studying science. The first is, What conclusions and principles come from studying the evidence of the world around us? Romans 1:18-20 states:

> The wrath of God is being revealed from heaven against all the godlessness and wickedness of men who suppress the truth by their wickedness, since what may be known about God is plain to them, because God has made it plain to them. For since the creation of the world God's invisible qualities—his eternal power and divine nature—have been clearly seen, being understood from what has been made, so that men are without excuse (NIV).

Scripture was given to reveal the God who created the world, and nature reveals many aspects of that Creator. Science, then, in examining the universe reveals God's wonder and power. When a scientific law is established (e.g., the law of gravity), it often is referred to as a law of nature. But it may be more appropriate to refer to it as a law of God because it reflects the plan and design of God as Creator.

Although Scripture is primarily a message of grace and redemption, it does speak on scientific issues. Today, however, biblical wisdom related to the sciences is often ignored by the scientific community in favor of other views. This multiplicity of views can easily result in conflict among scientists because they do not have a common framework for addressing the outcomes, interpretations, and implications of scientific research.[9]

Scientists spend a great deal of time studying nature and commenting on their observations. Many of those ideas have been discussed in both private and public arenas, and some of them appear in *Cosmos, Bios, Theos: Scientists Reflect on Science, God, and the Origins of the Universe, Life, and Homo Sapiens* (edited by Henry Margenau and Roy Abraham Varghese).[10] This book is a compilation of the thoughts of many prominent scientists, some

174 • TOTALLY SUFFICIENT

Christian and some not, concerning the relationship between science and God. We've placed here some noteworthy excerpts from the book.

Professor Thomas C. Emmel (professor of zoology and director of Lepidoptera Research at the University of Florida) states,

> To me, the concept of God is a logical outcome of the study of the immense universe around us. My readings in science and my professional pursuit of science have simply confirmed further to me that there are ultimate questions that we as scientists cannot answer, but yet these questions exist and it is silly at best, and unscientific at worst, to ignore them. . . . To me, God exists as the Supreme Being who started this creation that we call the universe, and he was responsible in a very real sense for the development of life on earth. . . . The evidence is all-too-pervasive for me to think otherwise. I do not pretend to believe that I will ever know the ultimate mysteries of this Supreme Being. . . .[11]

Professor Ulrich J. Becker (professor of physics at the Massachusetts Institute of Technology and member of the Research Council of Europe in Geneva, Switzerland) states,

> How can I exist without a creator? I am not aware of any compelling answer ever given. The eighteenth- and nineteenth-century determinism (including my dearest Immanuel Kant) tried a universe running down like a clock with a "departed" watchmaker. How naive can one get to use a time-argument (departed) for the creator of space-time![12]

Albert Einstein (Nobel laureate in physics), quoted by Professor Margenau (emeritus professor of Physics and Natural Philosophy at Yale University), commented,

> The discovery of a fundamental, verified law of nature is an inspiration of God.[13]

Professor Sir Nevill Mott (Nobel laureate in physics) wrote,

> I knew, of course, that all scientific theories are provisional and may be changed, but that, on the whole, they are accepted from Washington to Moscow because of their practical success. Where religion has opposed the findings of science, it has almost always had to retreat. I thought then, and still do, that science can have a purifying effect on religion, freeing it from beliefs from a pre-scientific age and helping us to a true conception of God. At the same time, I am far from believing that science will ever give us the answers to all our questions.[14]

Professor Robert A. Naumann (professor of chemistry and physics at Princeton University) answered,

> The existence of the universe requires me to conclude that God exists.[15]

Thus, intense study of the world God created *can* logically lead to the conclusion that God exists and has created the world around us. (One could also conclude that there is no conflict between belief in God and science.) Science, therefore, can be a means for learning about God by studying His creation. The scientist, knowingly or unwillingly, is attempting to discover God's beauty, simplicity, and creativity by learning about the universe.[16]

The second question that arises from the issue of studying science is, What motivations are there for Christians to study science? Robert Chasnov, in his chapter on "Natural Sciences" in W. David Beck's book *Opening the American Mind*, describes three reasons for "doing science": 1) a love for God, 2) a love for God's creation, and 3) a love for other human beings.[17]

Many scientists throughout history have become involved in science for at least one of those three reasons. For example, James Clerk Maxwell, the noted physicist of the nineteenth century who described light as magnetic and electric waves, was a devout Christian. Maxwell reasoned that since the world somehow reflects its Creator, who is Triune in nature, then one can derive from theology a metaphysical picture of reality wherein relations among the part of wholes, relations between wholes, and the wholes themselves are just as fundamental as are atomistic parts of those wholes. Thus, light should be viewed as a continuous field, a unity with different aspects (magnetic and electric) in relation.[18] Thus, we can see that science and faith can be mutually supportive and enhance each other. While the natural scientist might not be "seeking to ascertain the will of God through the leading of the Holy Spirit, if there is unity in nature he has the right to expect that a search for understanding will have its faith reward."[19]

When choosing a standard by which all scientific investigation is to be conducted, it is important to test that standard for accuracy and reliability. The Bible is clearly not a book of science. However, it does make scientific statements that can be tested (Dr. S.I. McMillen discussed this in his book *None of These Diseases*).[20] In the Old Testament, we are given many commandments for the people of Israel to obey. Moses recorded most of these in his writings in Exodus, Leviticus, and Deuteronomy. Since we also know Moses "was educated in all the wisdom of the Egyptians" (Acts 7:22), we must determine whether the accuracy of Scripture was from God or the Egyptians. The *Ebers Papyrus* is the Egyptian medical textbook written about 1522 B.C. It records many treatments for diseases and health conditions, using such items as animal parts, "sacred" oils, dung, and so on. The death rate of those who subjected themselves to these treatments was very great, which is not surprising when we consider that the cures (e.g., dung) often contained bacteria that caused diseases.

In contrast, at the same time, Moses recorded that God commanded eating regulations, sanitation, and sterilization. Some of the techniques implemented by God have been "discovered" by the scientific community only in the past 150 years. For example, God directed the people of Israel to wash themselves before eating and when dealing with diseases or dealing with the dead. Even as recently as the 1840s, Dr. Ignaz Semmelweis was ridiculed for training hospital staff to wash their hands before dealing with patients. Today, hand-washing is a standard practice because it helps to avoid the spread of disease. In this case, the Bible was not only scientifically accurate, but predated scientific understanding by a few thousand years.

BIOMEDICAL RESEARCH: THE TWO ASPECTS

Basic Research

Biomedical research can be divided into two aspects: *basic* and *applied*. Basic research refers to studies that are concerned with the normal structure and function of a living organism, and the possible pathological states that accompany impaired structure or function. Experiments are conducted to explore the basic or foundational principles by which living organisms function. While research is generally done with the hope that the information will lead to betterment of mankind, the application of the findings is not of primary concern. Rather, the emphasis is on the pursuit of new knowledge and understanding about biological systems and how they function.

On the other hand, applied research refers to that aspect of biomedical research in which the foundational information and principles are utilized in improving the quality of life for mankind. For example, basic research has determined that failure of the kidneys to properly filter the blood will result in poisoning throughout the body. If left unchecked, the individual will die. Technological advances in applied research have enabled scientists to design dialysis machines that can be used, either in the hospital or at home, to act as artificial kidneys and prolong a person's life for as long as several years.

In order to conduct basic scientific investigations, several requirements must be met. The primary requirement is the consistency of nature. While unique events may be of interest, it is the fact that nature is constant which enables researchers to conduct experiments on a day-to-day basis.

Scripture attests to the consistency we see in nature:

God said, "Let there be lights in the expanse of the sky to separate the day from the night, and let them serve as signs to mark seasons and days and years" (Genesis 1:14 NIV).

I will send you rain in its season, and the ground will yield its crops and the trees of the field their fruit (Leviticus 26:4 NIV).

He is like a tree planted by streams of water, which yields its fruit in season and whose leaf does not wither (Psalm 1:3a NIV).

What has been will be again, what has been done will be done again; there is nothing new under the sun. Is there anything of which one can say, "Look! This is something new"? It was here already, long ago; it was here before our time (Ecclesiastes 1:9-10 NIV).

These are promises from God that nature is and will be *consistent*. This consistency allows scientists to practice the scientific method of making observations, forming hypotheses to explain those observations, and then performing experiments that test those hypotheses. If an investigator finds a particular molecule in the brain on Monday, God has promised in the consistency of nature that, when the exact same experiment is repeated on Tuesday, the same observation will be made. Biomedical research, then, can be repeated and verified, allowing understanding of how an organism works.

Biblical principles can assist us in determining the types of experiments that should be conducted. The use of animals is fundamental to biomedical research. But what about people? Scripture teaches that man was made in the image of God (Genesis 1:26-27). Furthermore, man alone received the breath of life (Genesis 2:7).

Finally, Jesus Christ died on the cross so that man alone could regain a relationship with God (Romans 5–6). The sanctity-of-life principle—the principle that man alone is of infinite value to God and his life of infinite worth— is the reason humans are treated with special dignity far beyond all other forms of life. For example, medical students learn human anatomy using cadavers. The sanctity-of-life principle is so highly regarded among medical institutions that no parts of the body can be randomly discarded. All parts are disposed of using special precautions and containers. Most medical schools even conduct a special service at the conclusion of the use of the cadavers in memory of those who donated their bodies.

No such dignity is, or needs to be, given to animals. God established that man alone was created in His image and, therefore, deserves this lofty form of respect. However, God also commanded man to take care of His creation, and that includes taking proper care of animals (Genesis 2:15). This principle is clarified in Genesis 9:2-6, where God reinforced the distinction between man and animals in that, while man is to care for animals, it is only the shedding of the blood of man for which man must give an accounting. Biblical principles, then, can and should be instrumental in establishing policies regarding the appropriateness of animal use in basic research and the quality of care that the animals used in research should receive.

Not only does the Bible provide principles by which scientific investigation can be carried out, it also contains *information that is scientifically correct* and useful for directing some lines of scientific investigations. Some of these were mentioned previously when we compared the *Ebers Papyrus* with some of the Old Testament commandments.

When we visit a doctor, he or she will usually check our eyes. The doctor uses a light source to study the retina at the back of each eye. This is done to check for abnormalities that might be present. For example, diabetic retinopathy occurs because of a high level of glucose, which results from a lack of insulin or the presence of factors that oppose the action of insulin.[21] The physical changes that accompany this include microvascular occlusion, microvascular leakage, microaneurysms, hemorrhages, hard exudates, and retinal edema. These changes can be readily observed by studying the retinal surface. Thus, conditions such as diabetes mellitus can be discovered by a simple eye examination. The Bible makes the following simple statement concerning this: "The eye is the [light] of the body" (Matthew 6:22-23 NIV; *see also* Luke 11:33-36). Other disorders and diseases that can be found by examining the eye include hypertensive retinopathy, arteriosclerosis, sickle-cell retinopathy,[22] congenital heart disease with cyanosis, Sturge-Weber syndrome, hypertension, anemia, polycythemia, leukemia, myelomatosis, collagen diseases, and multiple sclerosis.[23] Clearly, an examination of the eye can give a great deal of information about the health of the entire body. Indeed, "the eye is the [light] of the body" and the Bible's accuracy is again demonstrated to be perfect.

In Numbers 19, God commanded the Israelites to make a "water of cleansing" in order to become pure again after touching the dead. A red heifer without defect or blemish was to be burned. The ashes were to be placed in fresh water and used to wash the person. Biochemically, the reactions that occurred in this process were converting the triacylglycerols in the beef tallow into potassium salts, which today is commonly called lye soap, which acted as a disinfectant, and glycerol, which has been viewed as a medicine since ancient times.[24] Therefore, God's directive is the first record of proper cleansing using a disinfectant to remove the bacterial contamination often found on dead or decaying organisms.[25]

It was a reading of Psalm 8:8 (NIV)—which says in part "all that swim the paths of the seas"—that caused Matthew Maury to search for and describe in detail the ocean currents, including the Gulf Stream. This is yet another example that demonstrates the accuracy of the

]Bible when it broaches scientific subject matter. Today, with the help of supercomputers, the information gleaned about ocean currents and eddys hold great promise of benefit to mankind.

Proverbs 14:30, 16:24, and 17:22 all clearly link a positive mental attitude with healthy bones. This is very possibly a reference to the relationship between the psychological state of an individual and the function of his or her bone marrow, which is extremely important in the production of blood cells, including the immune cells B-lymphocytes. It also is possible these Scripture references apply to the body in general. For example, there is evidence that stress and anguish can lead to an increase in the number of health problems, whereas a positive mental attitude leads to more rapid healing and recovery from sickness.

One additional example of scientific accuracy in the Bible is found in Genesis 17:12. Here God directed Abraham, "For the generations to come every male among you who is eight days old must be circumcised." This directive has been found to result in lower rates of penile problems, urinary tract infections, sexually transmitted diseases, and cancers in both males (penile) and females (cervical).[26] Furthermore, the level of prothrombin (a component essential for blood-clotting) is at 119 percent of the adult level on the eighth day after birth, making this day the safest time ever for a circumcision to be performed on a male.[27] Thus, God's directive in Scripture fits perfectly with medical concerns related to hygiene and safety.

Many other examples can be given which support the contention that the Bible is accurate in its scientific statements and references. These give us the assurance that both the principles and the facts found in the Bible can be used as a foundation for basic research.

Applied Research

While there are clearly a vast number of examples of how basic research has been utilized to benefit mankind, the application of basic research leads to many questions about issues that must be addressed. One issue is that the application of basic research often involves a significant financial burden for both individuals and society. For example, life-support systems can be used to enable individuals to live longer. However, the expense incurred can be so extreme that families are unable to recover financially from the experience. The practical question that arises, then, is this: What will be the basis for determining which individuals receive the treatment, since the cost will not permit everyone to be treated? A second question deals with the fundamental issue of ethics and morality: Which research applications are within the framework of improving the quality of life, and which are beyond that realm and deal with matters that ought to be left in God's hands? Let's consider three examples that show that there are ethical considerations for which Scripture alone can provide guidance.

The Ethical Considerations

Genetic Engineering/Gene Therapy

Scientific advances in the realm of genetics have gone far beyond the simple conclusions of Gregor Mendel in the middle 1800s. Molecular biology has progressed so rapidly that we now are in the process of locating and identifying every gene in the human genome. Techniques are now available that allow us to place any gene in any position on a chromosome. This offers the potential of being able to remove a defective gene and replacing it with a normal one. For example, a genetic disorder called phenylketonuria (PKU) results from the absence of a normal gene that produces an enzyme responsible for breaking down the amino acid phenylalanine. High phenylalanine levels in the blood then results in damage to the brain, which often leads to mental retardation, and eventually, death.

Up to now, the typical treatment has been to alter a person's diet so that low levels of phenylalanine are present. With the advances in molecular biology, however, it is theoretically possible to replace the defective gene with a normal one. Obviously, since this alleviates human pain and suffering, this technology would be viewed as beneficial to mankind and ought to be pursued. Studies are currently being conducted to determine how to accomplish this form of gene therapy, replacing defective genes with normal ones in a mature individual, as was previously described for cystic fibrosis.

However, with the advances in technology come ethical questions that must be addressed. The same technology that allows for the replacement of *defective genes* also allows for the replacement of *undesired genes*. Initially we might think that the ability to replace undesired genes would be beneficial to our world. However, we have to define what we mean when we refer to undesired genes.

Suppose two parents wish to have a normal child. What is the standard by which "normal" is to be defined? Advances in molecular biology now allow for the creation of any gene desired. With this technology, and with the complete human genome mapped, parents could actually select the combination of genes—and therefore characteristics—they would like to see in each child. Random gene combinations, which occur during normal processes, could be avoided. Using this technology to produce children with no genetic defects certainly sounds appealing. But what about those parents who desire to control every facet of their child's makeup? They could use the technology to choose only children whose intellect would be superior, or athletic abilities would be exceptional. What basis do we have for determining the limits of the application of this technology or even the research being done to improve this technology?

The issue becomes even more difficult in light of the recent advancement in *cloning research*—namely, the cloning of a human embryo. We are within reach of being able to take a single cell and produce a normal human. What should we do with this type of knowledge? Will we allow a clone of a child to be made—a clone that is fully human—and store that clone until needed?

Here's another example: Suppose we have a child who has a defective heart valve. Within a few years, that child's heart valve will need to be replaced. Knowing that, we could implant the clone into a surrogate mother and bring it to maturity. Since the genetic composition of the clone would be identical to that of the original child, we know that a transplant would be accepted by the original child. So do we sacrifice the life of one child for another? This possibility is now being discussed by many in the medical community and elsewhere.

Prenatal Testing (Abortion)

Significant progress has been made in the area of child development. One area that recently has been the center of attention is prenatal development. As mentioned previously, technology today allows for the correction of defects in a fetus while it is still *in utero*. These defects can be determined primarily in two ways: 1) genetic screening of tissue samples taken using a method like amniocentesis, and 2) spectroscopy. The major question that arises is the issue of the options generated by the results of prenatal testing. For example, recently my wife and I (Paul) visited her obstetrician/gynecologist when she became pregnant. At the first meeting we were informed that genetic counseling is now strongly recommended for patients and their families. *Amniocentesis* would be performed and a complete *genetic testing* would be done to determine whether the fetus had any defective genes. Based on those results, we would be given the option of maintaining the pregnancy or aborting the baby. Whatever decision we made, it had to be immediate. That situation is one example of many which deal with the fundamental question associated with all applied research: On what basis will we use the available technology for mankind? Thus, it is clear that guidelines for scientific investigations, discoveries, and technology must be established and put into place.

Aging/Euthanasia

Biomedical research has enabled physicians to prolong people's lives through the use of machines that can support body functions, sometimes indefinitely. For example, during open heart surgery, patients can be placed on a life support system that both circulates their blood and ventilates the respiratory system. This allows them to undergo lifesaving surgery.

Sometimes accident victims are placed on similar machines to save their life. Clearly, this aspect of technology is beneficial to mankind. However, there is a movement in today's society to allow "death with dignity." People can sign documents that will permit physicians to terminate their life in the event that the only means of remaining alive would be through a life-support system. In addition, a prominent physician in the Great Lakes region of the United States is actually helping his patients to terminate their lives. The concept being proposed today is that it's not right to be a burden to others through expensive hospital treatment. The "death with dignity" proponents say it is actually better to offer oneself for others by ending or taking one's life. This directly opposes the traditional, biblical concept of the infinite value of human life.

A person's view on the issue of terminating life—either by direct action or by indirect action—reflects his or her view of man. Physicians, family members, and friends can choose to assist an elderly person terminate his life by supplying the materials needed, such as drugs or poisons. It is not unusual to read newspaper stories of husbands "helping" wives who are suffering to become "free from pain" by giving them an overdose of medicine. Families are being asked to sign authorization forms that permit a physician to remove a patient from a life-support system when "there is no hope" for the patient to recover. Furthermore, parents are being given the opportunity to withhold approval for treatment of newborn children who have a particular defect. Thus, by not administering medical assistance, parents can "allow" a child to die without being held legally accountable. Clearly, society today is rapidly accepting the concept that quality of life is the basis by which all actions should be measured.

The Biblical Response

In contrast to this view stands the biblical principle of the sanctity of life—human life is of infinite value because man alone is created in God's image. Throughout the Bible, references are made that distinguish man from all other forms of life. To begin, a distinction is made between plants and animals. "Life" refers only to animals (Genesis 1:30; 9:1-6,12). As we've affirmed earlier, the fact that man alone is of infinite value to God and his life of infinite worth is the reason humans are to be treated with a special dignity far beyond that shown to all other forms of life (*see* Genesis 1:36-37; 2:7, 15; 9:2-6; Romans 5–6). Thus, the Bible is clear in its determination of value; animals have greater value than plants, and man has infinitely greater value than animals.

Given this foundation that man is unique in relationship to God, animals, and the rest of creation, how can we determine how we should respond to applying biomedical research? What will be our ethical standard? The Bible lays out additional guidance for these matters. For example, in Psalm 139:13-16 (NIV), David wrote,

> You created my inmost being; you knit me together in my mother's womb. I praise you because I am fearfully and wonderfully made; your works are wonderful, I know that full well. My frame was not hidden from you when I was made in the secret place. When I was woven together in the depths of the earth, your eyes saw my unformed body. All the days ordained for me were written in your book before one of them came to be.

Clearly, each child is not simply the result of the whims or pleasures of men and women. God has a design for each person—a design that goes beyond the framework of our concepts. Isaiah confirmed that God's plan and design are beyond our comprehension when he said,

> "For my thoughts are not your thoughts, neither are your ways my ways," declares the LORD. "As the heavens are higher than the earth, so are my ways higher than your ways and my thoughts than your thoughts" (Isaiah 55:8-9 NIV).

Also, Jeremiah wrote,

> "I know the plans I have for you," declares the LORD, "plans to prosper you and not to harm you, plans to give you a hope and a future" (Jeremiah 29:11 NIV).

God's plan for each person in this world simply cannot be treated as insignificant. When individuals—whether physicians, family, or friends—are faced with making a decision concerning the fate of a person, his or her worth in God's eyes must be considered.

Let's look now at three hypothetical situations that are now possible as a result of scientific advances. We'll use these as illustrations of how biblical principles can be used to deal with the ethical considerations that arise in relation to applying current biomedical technology.

Situation 1

The parents of an unborn child are informed their child has a slight defect in the wall of the heart, which separates the two ventricles. This can be repaired *in utero*. A decision must be rendered. Biblical principles reveal that life begins at conception. Therefore, we are dealing with an individual whose life has infinite value. Furthermore, we are admonished to be stewards of God's creation. Thus, we should seek to restore that creation (i.e., the birth of a child) whenever possible. Our conclusion would be to save that life, if possible. A surgical procedure could be that means.

Situation 2

A young pregnant woman is informed that her child has an abnormal chromosome pattern for chromosome #21. This means her child will be a Down syndrome baby. The intelligence level of that child will likely be limited, possibly never going beyond that of a four-year-old child. She is given the option of terminating the pregnancy by having an abortion immediately. Again, biblical principles reveal that 1) human life, in any form, is of infinite value, and 2) restoration should be sought. Therefore, terminating that life for reasons based on a human standard— that a child with less-than-normal mental levels ought not to live—violates those principles and should not be done.

Situation 3

A man in his late seventies suffers a stroke which paralyzes him. He is no longer capable of taking care of himself and must receive help 24 hours a day. Since he has been an avid hunter and fisherman all his life, being forced to remain indoors is extremely difficult for him; he is in emotional turmoil. It also is difficult for his family to watch him suffer so much. An opportunity arises for him to terminate his own life, ending his own suffering and alleviating that of his family. Biblical principles again help us understand that God sees life as having value, even when man claims it no longer does, and we should restore it. The termination of any life, regardless of the invalid appeal to being humane, violates this principle and must be avoided.

While these illustrations clearly do not cover all the situations that could possibly arise, it is clear that the Bible has principles that can guide us in the matter of how we should or should not apply scientific technology. By using the Bible's standard, it is possible for us to know the correct way to handle each of life's situations.

THE VALUE OF A BIBLICAL PERSPECTIVE

The question of the relationship between science and biblical principles is of fundamental importance to society. The issue at stake is the frame of reference from which the question will be answered. For example, one controversial topic, both within and outside science, is that of origins. Usually, each side approaches the topic from their own perspective, using a frame of reference that attempts to both confirm one's own position and refute the other. However, an attempt to place the question within biblical principles is often ignored. The Bible is a presentation of the principles of stewardship and restoration, not primarily a focus on creation. God reveals Himself to us as Creator, and our responsibility is to be stewards and restorers of God's creation. Therefore, when we attempt to discern the correct approach to take in dealing with the ethical issues associated with applied biomedical research, we must remember God's directive to restore His creation. We have never been given the authority or responsibility to alter God's design. Thus, our efforts to create new plants, animals, or even people are outside our realm. We must help people become whole, not something outside God's design.

When God finished His creation, He "saw all that he had made, and it was very good" (Genesis 1:31 NIV). God's creation is already the way He intended it to be; our "improvements" are not from an eternal or omniscient perspective. Throughout Genesis 3–11, man's attitude said, "God's creation is good, but we can make it better." With that attitude, man attempted to find an alternative to restoring the creation and restoring his relationship with God. Even today, people are attempting to find alternative ways to God and avoid the penalty of sin. God revealed Himself as both our Creator and our Savior. Consequently, we are to respect His authority and use biblical principles in both our stewardship and restorative actions.

We propose that a biblical perspective can serve as 1) the *foundation* for directing scientific research and 2) a *frame of reference* by which guidelines can be established for the application of new knowledge in the biomedical field. Biblical principles can serve as a consistent standard that gives direction to scientists, physicians, patients, and family members on a wide variety of issues. Issues such as genetic engineering, responses to prenatal testing, and euthanasia can be addressed from the consistency of Scripture.

Furthermore, it is our conviction that the wisdom of Scripture can provide direction for future biomedical issues that will arise as our scientific knowledge continues to increase.

> The Christian who believes this way and for whom faith is the substance of his hope will not expect the scientific community to embrace this understanding simply because he says so, or because the Bible says so, or because the community of faith says so. The tragic fact is that the Christian community itself is too compromised by the world to make a convincing argument for faith. What the believer can do is to invite science to put this Christian understanding to the heuristic test which science itself recognizes as essential for establishing the truth of evidence.[28]

David, in his prayer in Psalm 25:4-5, gave an all-encompassing model for finding direction in every issue we face in life:

> Show me your ways, O LORD, teach me your paths; guide me in your truth and teach me, for you are God my Savior, and my hope is in you all day long (NIV).

TOTALLY SUFFICIENT

8

MARRIAGE AND FAMILY COUNSELING

Ronald E. Hawkins, Ed.D.

When Robert Bellah surveyed middle-class Americans in 1985, he found that they seek personal advancement from work, personal development from marriage, and personal fulfillment from church.[1] A decade later, little has changed. Americans, he discovered, are basically utilitarian: They measure the value of things by what they will personally gain through their interaction with those things. Concern for the needs of others is clearly secondary for Americans, who are given to what Bellah has labeled "radical individualism."

Paul Vitz and William Kilpatrick have also written about the impact of this cultic affection for self-fulfillment. In *Psychological Seduction*, Kilpatrick forces us to examine the "disturbing characteristics of a society seduced by the claims of psychiatry."[2] Vitz concurs and issues the powerful indictment that much of contemporary psychological teaching has given birth to a cultic affection for self-worship.

Yankelovich also laments this vigorous self-absorption. He particularly attacks the theories and practices of self-psychology that have promoted the idea that "sacredness" lies within the self. Yankelovich believes that the impact of the "duty to self" ethic has led to the development of selfish and hedonistic values.[3] He calls Americans away from this hedonism and urges them to embrace an "ethic of commitment." Related to the matter of commitment, Aaron Beck wrote of the need for marital fidelity in his recent book *Love Is Never Enough*.[4] He said that fidelity to the marital covenant is a necessary prerequisite for a successful marriage. The ability to meet this requirement will always elude those who are traveling up the "Maslovian Escalator" and make the highest goal of life "duty to self."

THE SPIRIT OF THE TIMES

Minimal reflection on the spirit of our times would seem to warrant some degree of pessimism regarding the future of America's marriages and families. Given such a bleak picture, and the sense of urgency that accompanies it, counselors and other students of human behavior are often tempted to sail full-force into the treatment of symptoms. Christian counselors would do well to pause before responding to these alarming symptoms. We must recognize that beneath the readily seen symptoms are deeper problems that often escape our attention. The average American Christian has no clear commitment to the absolute authority of Scripture, or for that matter, the absolute authority of anyone or anything but self. American Christians frequently profess an allegiance to Scripture but then make choices that clearly indicate allegiance to "the duty to self ethic." We give lip service to the "lordship of Christ" and the authority of Scripture and then choose the path that promises the greatest comfort and personal gain.

Every pastor and Christian counselor has seen the impact of this "bits and pieces" approach to the development of a life- and worldview. Call such a person to obey the clear teaching of Scripture, and you will find in his or her chosen response a commitment to a belief or value that is absolutely contrary to the teaching of Scripture. Such people often admit to this dichotomy in their thinking but still feel compelled to hold to what they believe is a wisdom beyond that of Scripture. In their allegiance, they join a vast number of other people—from generations past and present—whom Paul was quick to label as fools (Romans 1:16-22).

People have a set of lenses through which they view their world. Partners differ from one another in the way they view sports, politics, education, marriage, standards of right and wrong, news events, mental illness, and a host of other issues, including religion. These variant opinions help to explain a significant portion of the conflicts that couples experience. These lenses are what we would call a *worldview*.

Ron Nash has suggested that "a worldview deals with at least five major topics: what we believe about God, the universe, knowledge, right and wrong, and the nature of human beings."[5] The lack of unity that characterizes many couples is not surprising when we listen to their differing views on the topics suggested by Nash. Each element in the partners' worldview should be carefully assessed, then, before marriage counseling begins. The problems couples experience are frequently rooted in a worldview that's riddled with error and markedly deficient to that advanced by Scripture. People who hold to such errors are awash in a sea of subjectivity and relativism. Unless this deficiency is remedied, all attempts at counseling are like putting a band-aid on a mortal bullet wound.

THE ISSUE OF AUTHORITY

The Source of Marital Guidance

Marriage counseling that is Christian must first resolve the issue of authority. What gives the counselor the right to expect certain behaviors from a husband, wife, son, or daughter? To what standard should counselors appeal when they assess the rightness or wrongness of a particular behavior or worldview? These are important questions that do much more than simply ask what we might do for couples to help provide relief for a current crisis.

Again and again in marital counseling we come to a fork in the road: Couples want to act on the basis of what some current writer says, what they have heard from a friend or parent, what they have heard from a pastor, or what they feel in their "inner self." Counselees frequently seek to resolve issues in their marriages by appealing to extrabiblical sources.

What is it that individuals must steadfastly obey if they want their personal and marital relationships to be perfected and matured? Paul answered that question without hesitation: He exhorted Timothy to remember that it is God's Word that demands our allegiance and obedience (2 Timothy 1:13; 2:15; 3:15-17). Solomon and Paul stated that God's Word is truth (Ecclesiastes 12:10; 2 Timothy 2:15), and all who follow Jehovah and Jesus Christ must bring every thought and behavior into conformity with the truth of Scripture. The critical issue is always that of yielding to the instruction of Scripture and making ourselves bondservants to obedience (Exodus 21:1-6; Romans 6:11-23). Bondservants forsake the appeal of personal freedom (Exodus 21:5-6), follow the motivation of love, bear their responsibilities even if it means great pain, and commit themselves without reservation to the care of those with whom they have made a covenant. The challenge in biblical marriage counseling is to get couples to appreciate their need to look to the Lord for the spiritual empowerment that will enable them to imitate the way of the bondservant (Galatians 5:13-26). The goal of biblical counselors is to foster in counselees a willingness to bring every thought into captivity and conform every idea to the truth of God's Word (1 Peter 1:13).

The power for healing in a relationship becomes available to us when we submit to the Word of truth. The power is Holy-Spirit power (Ephesians 3:16-19). It is the power of the indwelling Christ that renders the power of the flesh inoperative in relationships. Wonderful blessings flow from the filling of the Holy Spirit. Singing, submission, and thankfulness flow from the life where the Spirit dwells in fullness (Ephesians 5:16-21). We find identical characteristics flowing from the life of the person in whom the Word of Christ dwells richly (Colossians 3:14-18). Both spiritual empowerment and letting God's Word dwell in you are inextricably woven together in these parallel texts. The powerful combination of the Word and the Spirit produces a relational environment that makes involvement a source of enrichment and edification for the participants (Galatians 5:22-26).

Paul is on the same track when he implores the brethren to present their bodies as living sacrifices and avoid conformity to the world while pursuing transformation through the renewal of their minds (Romans 12:1-2). The ability to achieve a personal transformation that breaks with the patterns of the old life is tied to a renewing of the mind. This renewal is possible only for those who consistently enjoy a rich and obedient relationship with the Spirit of God through the Word of God.

Many marriage counselors who call themselves Christian do not appreciate the power that Scripture has to transform people's lives; nor do they bow to the authority of Scripture. They fail to see the overwhelming impact that salvation and sanctification can have in transforming marital relationships. These counselors fail to recognize the unparalleled resource of the Holy Spirit, His relationship to the Scriptures, and the power that these two resources offer to people who desire to change for the better. They underestimate sin's power to destroy people and the destructive influence of the deceitful human heart (Jeremiah 17:9).

The Source of Truth and Wisdom

Solomon clearly saw the gravity of man's condition. In the book of Ecclesiastes he described the danger of life under the sun (10:1-11). In the first nine chapters of Ecclesiastes, Solomon wrestled with the vanity of life under the sun. He spoke for all mankind when in essence he asked, "Where do we find meaning (profit) in a world where all things vanish (Hebrew, *hebel*) like steam rising from a teakettle?" (*see* Ecclesiastes 1:2-3). Wisdom alone provides direction in the midst of such peril (Ecclesiastes 10:10b).

The questions people ask about direction and profit transcend time and culture and find their answers in God's Word. What's tragic is that few Christians today realize just how timeless Scripture is. The Spirit spoke through the inerrant and inspired Word and addressed issues of significance to generations past, and the Spirit continues to speak to every kind of person and every culture today (Psalm 19:7-11; Isaiah 8:19-20; 2 Peter 1:3). A truly biblical counselor will seek out and set in order the proverbs of Scripture and fit their message to the needs of people (Ecclesiastes 12:9-10). Scripture contains goads and nails (Ecclesiastes 12:11); some Scripture is designed to help correct, reprove, and exhort people, while other passages offer security and encouragement (2 Timothy 3:16-17). The process of sanctification is directly related to giving counsel (Romans 15:14; Hebrews 10:23-25), and giving counsel is directly related to the Scriptures, or the Word of truth.

Wise counselors will utilize God's Word to correct, reprove, and instruct those in need of guidance. They will use Scripture to teach doctrine to those who seek a foundation upon which they can build securely with the confidence that they are laying a lasting foundation. Those who build their lives on the foundation of doctrine will know a wonderful freedom that fosters spontaneity and intimacy. This freedom is rooted in the joy that comes from having an unwavering commitment to obeying the teachings of God's Word (John 8:31-32).

Truth and wisdom are found in the Son and in the Scriptures. Paul reminds us in 1 Corinthians 1:30 that Christ "became to us wisdom from God, and righteousness and sanctification and redemption." Direction and profit in this world are found only in the One who said, "I am the way, and the truth, and the life" (John 14:6). Wisdom is also a spiritual gift (1 Corinthians 12:8) and is given to us when we diligently seek it in prayer (James 1:5). In a world of conflicting views, Christians are obliged to bring every element of their worldview under the illuminating lens of Scripture. When Scripture exposes errors in our belief and practice, we must repent and bend our wills to conform with God's divine standards. Only then will we experience joy—a joy that is founded on the knowledge that we have chosen the path of submission and obedience to truth rather than the call of the world, the flesh, and the devil.

A SCRIPTURAL WORLDVIEW FOR CHRISTIAN MARRIAGES

Believers who are committed to the authority of Scripture will confess allegiance to a core set of beliefs. These core beliefs provide a common foundation that enriches and structures our fellowship with others and is essential to the success of our relationships with God and others. More specifically, these core beliefs are vital for couples who want to know the fulfillment God designed for them to enjoy in the marital relationship. Couples who fail to submit to these scriptural truths will find themselves robbed of much of the power God makes available for building strong marriages. Let's turn our attention now to these core truths.

Scripture affirms the reality of a sovereign Creator (Genesis 50:20; Ecclesiastes 3:11; Romans 8:28). God has absolute authority and rules benevolently over His creation; there are no accidents in a believer's life (Psalm 115:3). Husbands and wives who do not understand God's sovereignty believe in a God who is too small to sustain them through the trials of life. This belief in a "small god" will leave its adherents cowering in anxious fear before the ups and downs associated with the challenges of marriage.

The Creator designed the marital team to play a vital role in His purposes (Genesis 1:26-28; 2:18-25). Male and female together form a dynamic dyad. Each draws his or her completion from his or her spouse (Genesis 2:18; 23-25). The divine intention for the marital team can be realized only as each person participates fully in his or her allotted place beside the other (Genesis 1:26-28). Alone, neither person can experience the reward that is only within the grasp of the team (Ecclesiastes 4:8-12).

As individuals, Adam and Eve were deeply loved. Each possessed great value and was wonderfully constituted by their Creator Father (Psalm 139:13-16) and provisioned with mandate, with law, and with purpose. Their lives were to be lived out within the context of these provisions. But the team rebelled! Their relationship with God was cast in an oppressive light by Satan (Genesis 3:5). The woman believed the lie and the man followed (Genesis 3:6), and devastating consequences followed their abandonment of truth (Genesis 3:7-13,14-19).

One tragic result of this rebellion was that a wedge was driven between man and woman (Genesis 3:16). This wedge symbolized the commencement of the war between the sexes. Themes like desire and power have since marred the relational terrain between the sexes, and only the Lord Jesus Christ has the power to remove the wedge and restore the team. The world in which we live has been turned inside out as a result of this tragic war; as couples, our experience in the universe is marked with pathos and vanity (Genesis 3; Ecclesiastes 11–12; and Romans 8:18-27).

After the rebellion, the sovereign Creator did not abandon His creatures. He sought them out (Genesis 3:8-9). He moved immediately to reconcile fallen humanity and accomplished that reconciliation through the Son, the Spirit, the Scriptures, and His suffering servants (*see* Hebrews 1:1-3). The cost to our God was high; this work of reconciliation involved Him in the experiences of personal suffering (Hosea 11:7-8; Luke 19:41-44; Hebrews 12:2). God not only teaches about loving servanthood in Scripture; He modeled it in His pursuit of restoring relations with His created human family (Philippians 2:5-11).

People who view God, themselves, the world, truth, and morality through the lenses of these core beliefs are radically different from those whose worldview does not contain an emphasis on divine sovereignty, human rebellion, divine revelation, and human/divine reconciliation and restoration. These beliefs compel a person to depend upon whom they realize is a gracious God and openly confess their need for divine guidance. God grants that guidance to those of us who ask for it, and calls us away from vain attempts to anesthetize our frustration with things, and leads us to pursue the rewards found in relationships, worship, and labor (Ecclesiastes 2–6). There is a better way, and the Scripture consistently directs us to the profit found therein.

Few experiences introduce us to our human limitations faster than marriage. We who are counselors would do well to caution couples who feel an unwarranted exuberance over "their abilities" to produce good marriages. Solomon confessed his need for help when he ascended the throne of Israel, and God gave him wisdom and understanding (1 Kings 3:5-13). A biblical worldview will compel Christian counselors and couples to make the same confession and petition. And we can be confident that God's response to us will be as gracious as His response to Solomon. In His Scriptures, His Son, His Spirit, and through spiritual gifts, He gives us wisdom for the purpose of directing and enriching our lives (Ecclesiastes 12:1-10; 1 Corinthians 1:30; 12; 2 Timothy 3:15-17; James 1:5).

Christian counselors are called to define marriage within the biblical paradigm; however, a biblical worldview does not disallow the helpfulness of knowledge from sources outside the Bible. Clearly, Scripture is sufficient to deal with all issues that are *central* to the building of a quality marriage. At the same time, sources viewed as secondary and passed prayerfully through the grid of God's Word may provide some valuable insights for assessing problem areas and structuring efficient intervention. A problem develops only when we attempt an integration that holds all sources to be equal.[6] This approach we must reject. All our beliefs and actions must be in total conformity with scriptural teaching if we want to help couples achieve a great marriage. Integration of Scripture with the data of scholarship may prove helpful only if we are tenacious in our commitment to and practice of the primacy of Scripture.

Wisdom, as we know it from the Bible, counsels us to develop a worldview in which God is seen as the author of marriage and the architect of its place within His divine program. Fallen inventive man, of course, will not readily bow to such a worldview. In Adam and in sin, these people seek marriages and relationships that do not conform to the divine plan (Romans 1:18-21). In contrast, those who choose to enact God's plan within their relationships will know incredible peace.

Even with positive choices we make, the number of things that are wrong in any situation is so great they can't be added up (Ecclesiastes 1:13). This reality must be faced in all of our relationships, and particularly in our marriages. We can be confident that God's truth will give us direction and God's sovereignty will allow us experiences of gain and loss that ultimately work out for our best. However, there is no safe place to hide from the consequences of sin.[7] Satan is active on our planet; in Christ alone we find the power to overcome Satan's subtleties, sufficient grace to bring about forgiveness, and reconciliation with an offended Creator. In Him we are enabled to survive a very bumpy ride.

A worldview drawn from Scripture provides a comprehensive rationale for people's personal and marital dilemmas, points the way to deliverance from a life of meaninglessness, places people securely on the path to temporal and eternal profit, and provides sufficient direction for building a lasting and fulfilling marriage. Essential to sound marriages is the careful application of scriptural teaching on issues such as loving servanthood, commitment to the marriage covenant, healthy communication, controlling and enjoying sexuality, and companioning—all of which we will now examine. Couples who allow their lives to be shaped by Scripture's teaching will move to higher and higher levels of intimacy as they continue onward through the complex and demanding experiences of marital life.

The Scriptures on Love and Servanthood

Biblical counselors have the privilege of introducing couples to concepts that are foreign to the wisdom offered by their secular counterparts: servanthood, submission, and love. Paul reminds us in 1 Corinthians 13 that the three staples for enriching relationships are faith, hope, and love, and the greatest of these is love! The bondservant of Exodus 21 exemplifies love and presents us with a paradigm to be taken seriously by Christian couples. The bondservant is not motivated by the love of self, which is endemic to the unregenerate person. Rather, bondservants are motivated by love for their master, wife, and children—a love that enables them to transcend the desire for personal freedom and utter the self-denying assertion, "I will not go out as free man" (Exodus 21:5). The ability to love one's spouse in the same way that God loved Israel (Hosea 11:1-9), Christ loved the church (Ephesians 5:25-33), and a bondservant loved his master, wife, and children (Exodus 21:1-6) is a hollow dream unless a person experiences the reality of the Holy Spirit working progressively in his life.

The Shulammite maiden in the Song of Solomon understood well the unparalleled value of love (Song of Solomon 8:7). Husbands and wives who are partnered with spouses who do not appreciate the power of loving servanthood are often consumed with anger, resentment, and depression when they seek counseling. They come for counseling personally crushed or ready to crush mates who for years have been too busy to focus on serving and loving them in a meaningful way.

The central issue in all marriages is a joint commitment to serving. Jesus Himself placed a high value on serving (John 13:2-17). The environment generated through serving promotes greater trust. Servant spouses are free to make decisions that are in the best interest of their partners. This freedom fosters growth and security in relationships. Sin makes the achievement of such an environment impossible without God's intervention. This intervention became manifest in the person of Jesus Christ, and Jesus' submission even to the point of death represents the greatest act of servanthood ever known. It is truly the centerpiece of the greatest Christian story ever told (Philippians 2:5-11) and establishes the pattern for submissive servant relationships.

It is unfortunate that the doctrine of submission has so often been pitched only to the feminine gender. Christ was a man, and He modeled submission. Prior to Paul's instruction that wives submit to their husbands, we read that *all* believers are to submit one to another in the fear of the Lord (Ephesians 5:21). Such submission is possible because the ascended Christ has sent God the Holy Spirit to dwell in us (John 15:26-27; 16:12-15). It's the Spirit's power that enables us to overrule the flesh and live as servants and bear fruit that enhances and promotes relationships (Galatians 5:22-25). We cannot overestimate the important role that spiritual fruit has in building sound relationships. In relationships, this fruit is the forerunner to the development of trust. Without trust, all efforts at intimacy will crumble.

In the great drama of redemption, love, which is the centerpiece of God's fruit, is very much exhibited by God in response to fallen and backslidden people (Hosea 11:1-10; John 3:16-17). Love is to be the centerpiece of relationships between believing spouses as well (1 John 2:10; 3:11-18; 4:7-12). Those who are not believers—as well as Christians who fail to take seriously their need to progress in sanctification—will find it impossible to demonstrate this kind of love. Furthermore, it is extremely difficult to create any forward momentum in a counseling situation when we are dealing with people who daily witness the absence of spiritual fruit in their partner's lives. These unfortunate people are seized with anxiety at the very thought of trusting someone who has never been free to serve them in a way that meets the bondservant paradigm of Exodus 21. This freedom is only found in the Son and in the Spirit whom He sent (John 8:31-32; Romans 6:7,22; Galatians 5:24-25).

The Scriptures on Commitment

There is a dynamic link between love and commitment. A person who professes to love yet is not committed will reveal, through his actions, that his love is false. True love is rooted in a system of beliefs that compels the confessant to pursue a scripturally prescribed course of action (Luke 6:45-46).

Consider again Jehovah's confession of love for Israel in Hosea chapter 11. Hear the confession: "When Israel was a youth I loved him" (verse 1). This confession led Jehovah to teach, to draw, and to feed Israel (verse 4). It led Him to declare that He would not surrender Israel in spite of her backslidden condition. Love forced a commitment that drove Jehovah to act in a manner that held undeniable value for the object of His love (verses 8-9).

The Elements of Commitment

The Shulammite maiden in the Song of Solomon teaches us more about the relationship between love and commitment. We learn from her that when love is professed and commitment is lacking, a deadly process ensues. It is as cruel as the grave and is the experience of the jilted party (Song of Solomon 8:6). Commitment is vital for the stability and growth of a relationship.

Though this commitment is from the heart, it is supported by *external action*. The concept of commitment implies the "doing or practicing of something" and "delivering or entrusting something to a person." Commitment then involves the binding or pledging of oneself to a particular course of action. In Song of Solomon 8:6, we see commitment verified by an external seal that represents the external validation of an internal covenant.

Commitment implies a *choice* based on reason (Isaiah 1:18-19). The act of entrusting ourselves to another should be supported by sound reasoning. Commitment also involves volitional consent (Hosea 5:4,11; Romans 6:13). We will ourselves into relationships. The will to relate to another is supported by reason and strengthened by a pattern of decisions that are in concert with the covenant. A willingness to relate that is supported by sound reasoning and demonstrated through consistently loving behaviors makes for a secure relationship.

The Lord models this kind of commitment in His relationships with Israel and the church. Honoring a covenant, of course, is not a simple or easy matter. In Hosea 11:1-9 and Luke 22:39-46, our Lord demonstrated His willingness to maintain His covenant promise even in the midst of His own personal suffering. Our Lord showed and continues to model a commitment that is beyond the level of what we deserve. His commitment involves a resolve that will not surrender those whom His volition has moved Him to love. His commitment is unqualified and guarantees that He will always be there. He pursues the best for His own and guards all of His actions in the light of that commitment. That is the same kind of commitment we are called to within the context of marriage; we are called upon to imitate God (Ephesians 5:1-2).

Commitment *costs us something* (Hosea 11:8; Luke 14:28-35). Dependability has a price tag, but the reward is high (Ecclesiastes 4:9-12). Biblical counselors are to call people away from responses that do not demonstrate God's attitude and behaviors (Ephesians 5:1-17). The imitation of God's character is a serious calling for God's people; to misrepresent God by failing to live out the metaphor of Ephesians 5:22-33 is to do serious damage to the cause of evangelism and discipleship. Such a failure ultimately brings serious judgment upon our personal and ecclesiastical world. Thus it's important to counsel couples to encourage their partners, give the gift of sympathetic understanding, and say no to their selfish desires. Spouses are to organize their time, thoughts, and resources for the benefit of others.

Commitment requires *self-control* and a willingness to *compromise*. With the Holy Spirit's help, husbands and wives can surrender the desire for self-fulfillment and make choices that are in the best interests of their partner and family. He alone can empower couples to meet concrete needs in each other's life (1 Peter 3:1-7).

By contrast, selfish people do not consider their mate's needs. They are committed to themselves and their view of things (2 Corinthians 6–7). They are dominated by a previous commitment to their personal satisfaction and they seek to use other people as resources for meeting their personal needs. In bondage to their sin natures, particularly their ego-needs, selfish people are powerless to model the attributes of the bondservant. Such people are in deep need of repentance, which is the magic elixir that fosters the restoration of the believer's inner and outer worlds.

The only lasting cure for egoistic-selfishness that I know of is regeneration. The egomaniac is without resources to unshackle himself from his narcissistic covenant with self. Apart from regeneration, this person cannot be helped (Romans 8:5; 1 Corinthians 6:9-20). Only through obedience to the Holy Spirit, who is received in regeneration, will a person find the power to break the maniacal grip of selfishness and be set free to enter into a covenant with others that makes the meeting of their needs a priority. The fact that the pattern may have been learned in the family of origin only serves to heighten the need for the Spirit's power. By becoming part of a new family (the family of God), experiencing God's agape love, mobilizing the Spirit's power, and living in a context of accountability (Hebrews 10:25), a person can know the transformation that can lead to a truly fulfilling marriage that lasts.

The Hindrances to Commitment

An *unforgiving spirit* is a powerful roadblock to commitment. Holding grudges destroys intimacy. Forgiveness is essential if couples are to go on as marriage partners. Paul says in Ephesians 4:32, "Be kind to one another, tender-hearted, forgiving each other, just as God in Christ also has forgiven you."

Many people fail to forgive because they fear that they will be hurt again. However, forgiveness does not mean that we give another permission to hurt us in the same way over and over again. Often we cannot forgive because we lack confidence in our ability to stand against the assaults of another person. We see ourselves as weak. We do not recognize all the resources we have in ourselves, our God, and others.

In Christ, we can do all things (Philippians 4:13). We can stand before others in a position of strength with a willingness to forgive them. We are to forgive because God has commanded it (Matthew 6:12,14-15) and it is good for us (Hebrews 12:15). When we forgive others, we stop the potential for bitterness to defile us and those close to us. Another reason we are to forgive others is because we want them to see how God relates to people. We do not, as His ambassadors, want to misrepresent Him. We fear that (Ecclesiastes 12:13-14)!

The restoration of relationships is not based solely on our willingness to forgive. Those who injure us also have a responsibility. They must hear our rebuke and repent (Luke 17:3). Any absence of a willingness to receive the rebuke and repent should not alter our willingness to forgive them. In that case, we must wait patiently for their repentance before reconciliation can be experienced in a relationship. Hence forgiving is not really granting others permission to hurt us again, nor is it treating lightly their offense. Couples must learn to hang a "no fishing" sign over past failures and freely extend forgiveness to their mates.

Frequently we confuse forgiving and forgetting. Only God can forgive and forget. The human mind, however, generally doesn't forget offenses. Sometimes well-meaning believers try to forgive and forget, but assume that because they still remember a grievous wrong, they must have not forgiven it. It *is* possible to forgive someone and still remember the wrongdoing without any sense of anger or desire for retaliation. We *can* refuse to give power to our memories of past wrongs. Though we remember them by faith, we can reckon them to be past and not let them play a role in present decisions related to the relationship.

Unfaithfulness is another powerful roadblock to commitment. Unfaithfulness destroys the trust upon which any happy relationship must be founded. One reason the virtuous woman of Proverbs 31 is of such great value is because "the heart of her husband trusts in her" (Proverbs 31:11). It's difficult for a marriage when unfaithfulness is continuously present. In Matthew 19:3-9, Jesus affirmed the high biblical view that marriage is a permanent covenant, but He also indicated that persistent sexual immorality can do severe damage to the marital relationship.

A *lack of desire* to invest quality time in a relationship is another serious roadblock to the maintenance of commitment. Couples need to set aside time for themselves. Even with all our modern-day conveniences, people still seem to find themselves incredibly busy. That's why husbands and wives need to make an effort to budget time for themselves. In the family that has one or more children, such time doesn't happen accidentally. The Shulammite maiden reminded her fiance that she needed to hear his voice (Song of Solomon 8:13-14).

Biblical relationships are formed between persons who care about giving and are committed to the growth of their spouses. Professing Christians who lack such a commitment should examine the integrity of their relationship to salvation and sanctification for a person who has been changed on the inside by Christ will show that change in his or her actions. As for the person who makes his or her spouse a priority he or she will be the recipient of great pleasure, comfort, and satisfaction from his or her partner. Indeed, commitment is an investment that pays rich dividends.

The Scriptures on Communication

Communication is key to the development of any growing relationship. Poor communication between couples is the number-one reason for marital failure. Nothing that counselors can do holds more potential for enriching intimacy in marriage than taking the time to teach couples how to communicate in a manner that results in edification (Ephesians 4:29). The tongue can also be destructive; James reminds us of the power inherent in words when he says, "The tongue is a small part of the body, and yet it boasts of great things. Behold, how great a forest is set aflame by such a small fire!" (James 3:5).

The Supreme Example

As a communicator, the God of the universe is clearly head and shoulders above everyone who has ever spoken. He is a communicator (Hebrews 1:1-2) who consistently accepts the responsibility for initiating communication (Genesis 3:8-19; Luke 19:10). Prior to man's descent into sin, He spoke with Adam and Eve and blessed them with His speech and presence (Genesis 1:28-29). And after the Fall, God sought them. His desire for communication transcended the sin of His creatures.

God pursues those whom He loves and seeks to communicate with them. By contrast, sin produces within people a desire to disengage from the communication process—to go and hide (Genesis 3:8-10; Isaiah 1:18; Ecclesiastes 4:5). That, however, doesn't discourage God from seeking those distanced from His loving care (Luke 19:10). The Savior on the cross is the ultimate testimony to His commitment to the restoration of communication with His sinful, fallen creatures (John 3:16; 1 John 2:1-2).

God provides the lost with a covering for their sin that allows them to be reconciled to the Creator (Genesis 3:21; 1 John 2:1-2). When those whom He loves are confused and disengaged from the communication process, He provides them with that which is necessary to effect reconciliation. His love will not allow Him to stand against them without first seeking their restoration. Hosea captures this unfathomable love of God when he says, "How can I give you up, O Ephraim? How can I surrender you, O Israel? How can I make you like Admah? How can I treat you like Zeboiim? My heart is turned over within Me, all My compassions are kindled. I will not execute my fierce anger" (Hosea 11:8-9). In Romans 5:8, Paul captured the intensity of God's love—a love that overwhelms His enemies: "While we were yet sinners, Christ died for us."

History is a record of the actions of the God who has consistently sought to restore communication with His fallen creation. Paul focused on this action and stated, "God was in Christ reconciling the world to Himself, not counting their trespasses against them, and He has committed to us the word of reconciliation" (2 Corinthians 5:19).

The apostle John stated that the God of communication purposes that "you also may have fellowship with us" (1 John 1:3). A friend recently wrote and closed his letter with these words, "Yours because His." Therein lies the secret for marital communication: If we are His, then we seek to imitate His heart (Ephesians 5:1-2). We are absolutely committed to communicating with our mates because God is absolutely committed to communicating with us. The choice to communicate is not based on personal gain or pleasure; it is rooted in the conviction that we are called to implement in our relationships the same concern for ongoing communication that grips the heart of our God. A lack of enthusiasm for this replication can bring our prayer lives to a screeching halt (Luke 11:4, 1 Peter 3:7).

When Communication Breaks Down

No wonder Paul tells us that poor communication habits grieve God the Holy Spirit: "Let no unwholesome word proceed from your mouth, but only such a word as is good for edification, that it may minister grace unto the hearers. And grieve not the Holy Spirit of God" (Ephesians

4:29-30). We stand in the world as God's ambassadors (2 Corinthians 5:20). When we speak, we speak for God. This is not just true of what we say in the pulpit or the marketplace, but also what we say to our wives, husbands, children, and friends. When we as God's ambassadors wound a member of our family through cutting speech, we grieve God. Tragically, that may not be a cause of great upset to some. However, for a genuine believer, the thought of grieving God is cause for deep remorse.

Frequently we who are counselors approach communication problems with an arsenal of principles designed to help couples improve their communication. Although various principles sometimes prove helpful, they often are founded on a deficient view of the real problem: One or both partners really needs his or her attitude overhauled. New skills in the mind won't accomplish this; only a change of mind and heart can cure communication problems.

Resolving Communication Problems

It's interesting to note what Paul did when he faced a communication breakdown with the Corinthians believers. In 2 Corinthians 6:11-13, he wrote of his attempts to resolve the problem. Paul did several things to make reconciliation between himself and these believers possible.

First, he *clarified responsibilities*. When a communication breakdown occurs, all parties must be willing to examine themselves. Each must look for any contribution they might have made to the breakdown. Paul indicated that he had participated in such a self-examination and asked the Corinthian believers to do the same (2 Corinthians 6:11-13).

Second, Paul courageously and compassionately *identified the precise area* where the problem lay. He was willing to be the problem (and that's important), but in this case the problem was with the Corinthian believers. The constriction of emotions that was causing the communication breakdown was in the minds and hearts of the Corinthians. Paul was certain of that.

Third, Paul let them know that he was *totally committed to reconciliation*. He asked them to receive him (2 Corinthians 7:2). He let them know that his heart was always open to reconciliation. The shortage of initiative required for reconciliation was theirs, not Paul's.

Fourth, Paul *recommended a cure that was sufficient* in its strength to smash down the walls between them. Paul wanted love to flow between them again and knew that it could happen only if they fully participated in repentance. Paul did not believe that simply teaching new communication skills would resolve his problem with the Corinthian believers. He believed that only the spiritual power released through repentance could open the broken lines of communication between himself and the Corinthians.

Consider this illustration: Suppose I started to experience chest pains, went to the doctor, and the doctor told me that the arteries carrying blood to my heart were closing down. What if the doctor's sole recommendation for treatment were that I reduce the amount of sugar in my daily cup of coffee? I think I would quickly look for another doctor! The arteries must be opened; blood must reach the heart muscles to ensure that I will live. Technology is available to accomplish this, and the administration of that technology is not without pain and discomfort but it is often highly effective.

The Need for Repentance

Paul told the Corinthian believers that the treatment for their "heart condition" would not be without pain (2 Corinthians 7:8). He had mixed feelings over bringing them to experience sorrow (2 Corinthians 7:9). However, he believed in the absolute necessity of what he had done. He brought the Corinthians to a point of reality with reference to their sin and called them to godly sorrow over the negative beliefs that had produced the communication breakdown.

The good news is that the Corinthians listened to Paul and received the ministry of the Holy Spirit. They were willing to accept responsibility for and correct their sinful actions, identify and correct their sinful thoughts, and use the energy generated from repentance to open the lines of communication between Paul and themselves. No wonder Paul rejoiced (2 Corinthians 7:9)! He witnessed the transformation that is made possible through the miracle of repentance.

Repentance is in short supply in today's marriages. One reason for its scarcity is because counselors and preachers don't teach and preach the necessity of it. Frequently our counselees don't just need to learn how to communicate more effectively; they need to repent.

Certain characteristics are present in the life of people who have repented (2 Corinthians 7:11). There is a carefulness that characterizes their speech and conduct. They are deeply concerned about walking before God and others with a conscience that is clear of any known offense. They get angry with their own sin and the sin of others. They have a whole new respect and fear for the power of sin to deceive and ruin people's lives. They have a deep desire for the Word of God, for fellowship with the Spirit of God, and for fellowship with other believers. They manifest a zeal for the work of God. They believe in fasting and keeping their bodies and minds under the domination of God's truth and Spirit. They don't mind proving their sincerity. They believe what Paul says: "Let every man prove his own work, and then shall he have rejoicing in himself alone, and not in another" (Galatians 6:4 KJV).

Repentance needs to be mutual if people want to experience its full power to generate marital intimacy.[8] Paul and the Corinthians both needed to go through the examination process and stand ready to repent over identified sin. Marriages where lasting intimacy is a reality are made up of husbands and wives who are always open to repentance when they identify the need for dealing with sin.

Forgiveness, which is so essential for ongoing intimacy, cannot do its full work without clear evidence of repentance. Jesus said, "Be on your guard! If your brother sins, rebuke him; and if he repents, forgive him" (Luke 17:3). Forgiveness that is cheap (devoid of repentance in the sinner) is granted by persons who lack a biblical sense of personal worth and mission. Intimacy is impossible for such people.

A Key Responsibility

Believers have a responsibility to examine one another and provoke one another to love and good works (Hebrews 10:24). This responsibility should be taken seriously by mates, for no one is in a position to take us to greater heights of spiritual achievement than our mates. An attitude of love and mutual repentance over discovered sin will enable a couple to achieve levels of marital intimacy they never dreamed possible. Such attitudes, joined with the ministry of the Holy Spirit in our lives, will chip away coarse and hurtful words and cement us to a style of communication that edifies.

It is no accident that one of the greatest Bible passages on communication appears in the same area as a discussion about the filling of the Holy Spirit (Ephesians 4:29–5:18). All the characteristics we need for effective communication are the result of the Holy Spirit's ministry in our lives (Galatians 5:22). His fruit heals broken relationships. Consider this list of relationship enhancers: love, joy, peace, patience, kindness, gentleness, goodness, faithfulness, self-control. These allies of restoration and healing are not ours, they are His. They become ours when we become His. We desperately need the Holy Spirit in His fullness. We need for His fruit to be our daily offering to those around us. This can be true only if our minds are richly filled with God's Word (*see* Ephesians 5:18-33 and Colossians 3:12-25). Individuals who are committed to Him will be committed to each other (1 John 4:7-21). What passes between them will be His fruit, and it will fuel intimacy—not destroy it.

The Scriptures on Sexuality

The sexual relationship is a barometer by which a couple's overall level of intimacy may be assessed. Medical doctor Ed Wheat states:

> Your sexual relationship will always mirror the larger context of your life, revelating personal fears and tensions between you and your partner, which can fluctuate, depending on how well you are getting along in other areas of your marriage. Negative feelings in a marriage will often show up first in a couple's sex life.[9]

Sex is more than a thrilling event; sex communicates. Sex tells a person that he or she is loved and welcomed to the intimate world of another (Proverbs 5:18-20; Song of Solomon 2:1-17). Intimacy is impossible without sexual fidelity. People are left hollow through sexual betrayal, which will leave them struggling with anger, jealousy, and depression.

Terms are important when we speak of human sexuality. I do not use the words *sexuality* and *sex* interchangeably. The term *human sexuality* refers to everything we are in our maleness and femaleness. It is a much broader term than terms meant to specifically designate the sex act itself. It is meant to convey the joy of knowing someone who is different in gender, someone who complements and holds potential for completing another in an unparalleled manner. This experience can be highly positive and ought not to be viewed automatically in a negative light. The intensity, extent, and flow of the experience needs to be assessed to determine its normality or sinfulness. We experience our sexuality every day; sexuality sets the stage, but does not necessarily imply the necessity for the sexual act.

Understanding Sexual Desires

A Right Perspective

When God created us, He placed in us appetites that would ensure our personal preservation and the preservation of the human family. An example related to our personal preservation is hunger and thirst. We do not merely choose to eat or drink; hunger and thirst are a natural part of our life cycle and they demand attention. We can, however, live without sex. Yet compliance with the creation mandate and the extension of the human family makes sex necessary within the context of marriage (Genesis 1:28). God did not leave the fulfillment of the mandate to replenish the earth to chance. He placed in His creation a strong appetite that would ensure the fulfillment of the mandate (Genesis 2:21-24). The sexual appetite, then, is connected with a divine purpose, and therefore is good.

Occasionally we may hear someone say, "Sex should be done away with. The world would be a better place without it." They misunderstand the Scriptures and the importance of sexuality and sex in the divine program. The real issue with sexuality and sex is not extinction, but control (1 Corinthians 9:27; 1 Thessalonians 4:3-7).

In Proverbs, Solomon gave explicit instructions about how God's people were to deal with appetites. He said, "When thou sittest to eat with a ruler, consider diligently what is before thee: And put a knife to thy throat, if thou be a man given to appetite. Be not desirous of his dainties: for they are deceitful meat" (Proverbs 23:1-3). Desires are to be controlled. Allowing them to wander aimlessly is the cause of much sin, including sexual sin (Ecclesiastes 6:7-9). Solomon's concern was that people not give themselves over to their appetites. Although Proverbs 23:1-3 specifically mentions eating, the principle can be applied to any appetite. When appetites are hooked to unbridled desire, they go out of control.

Notice that the appetite described by Solomon is given a human characteristic: It is deceitful. It misrepresents the truth. It says, "Feed me and I won't make you fat. You won't have any negative consequences attached to satisfying me." Eve fell victim to the negative influence of appetite (Genesis 3:1-7; 1 Timothy 2:14). Satan attempted the same deception with Jesus but did not meet with the success he hoped for (Matthew 4:1-11). Christ tenaciously held himself responsible for obeying the Word of God (Luke 4:1-13). Likewise, biblical counselors should enjoin their counselees to strive for the same level of obedience to God's Word.

Diligence is required if we are to escape such deceitful propositioning. This diligence must be joined to a decision, and the decision and diligence must precede the participation. Solomon doesn't tell us to fast forever in order to deal with the appetite of hunger. Rather, he admonishes us to recognize the power and deceit of appetite, combine careful diligence with decision making, and restructure our environment so that we avoid stimulating the appetite when that stimulation is sin.

A Right Example

The Song of Solomon speaks in poetic form to the issues of sexuality and sex. The poem itself is an exposition of the joy of marital love. A broad expanse of time is covered in the poem, which describes the journey of a young lady from youth to womanhood. In the Song we read, "We have a little sister, and she hath no breasts: what shall we do for our sister in the day when she shall be spoken for? If she be a wall, we will build upon her a palace of silver: and if she be a door, we will enclose her with boards of cedar. I am a wall, and my breasts like towers: then was I in his eyes as one that found favor" (Song of Solomon 8:8-10).

The poem is a celebration of sex and sexuality with virtue. On the young woman's journey to adulthood, two options are open to her in relation to her sexuality: She may be a door, or she may be a wall. If she is a wall, her brothers propose to honor her with a palace of silver. If she is a door, they intend to lock her up in a cage fashioned from boards of cedar. By way of explanation, the figure of the wall is meant to designate a position of honor with reference to her sexual experience, while the door represents a position of dishonor. When she becomes a mature woman, she announces for all to hear, "I am a wall." She is proud of her virginity and the care she took to remain a woman of virtue. How did she do it?

We find the answer in a verse that is repeated three times in the Song of Solomon (2:7; 3:5; 8:4). The verse reads, "I charge you, O ye daughters of Jerusalem, by the roes, and by the hinds of the field, that ye stir not up, nor awake my love, till he please" (KJV). The word "my" is in italics in the text. That means it was supplied by the translators. In this case they shouldn't have supplied the word because they distorted the meaning of the text. She was saying, "I don't want you awakening my love (sexual appetite) before it is the right time." She practiced diligent control over her sexual desires. That is how she maintained her position as "a wall."

This young woman understood the importance of control and commitment. She stated, "Set me as a seal upon thine heart, as a seal upon thine arm: for love is strong as death; jealousy is cruel as the grave: the coals thereof are coals of fire, which hath a most vehement flame. Many waters cannot quench love, neither can the floods drown it: if a man would give all the substance of his house for love, it would utterly be contemned" (Song of Solomon 8:6-7 KJV).

This kind of sexual control is urgently needed today. The young must be taught control by an older generation who model what they teach. Yet promiscuity is not our only dilemma; pornography is cementing a generation of American males to autoeroticism.

Recognizing a Subtle Danger

Some counselors hold the view that masturbation is not harmful. However, masturbation deceives its practitioners with increasingly subtle fantasies, which oftentimes are accompanied by pornographic materials.

Professionals who give young people unqualified permission to masturbate should feel an overwhelming burden to warn them of the dangers inherent in autoerotic sex. Autoeroticism is terrifyingly addictive; it moves its participants away from viewing sex as a gift to be given and shared with another.

Masturbation and other autoerotic forms of sex are a journey into the self. The person closes in on himself or herself and uses the objects of his or her fantasy to heighten his or her sexual satisfaction. When involved with another person, that person merely becomes a masturbatory tool to satisfy the first person's autoerotic urges. Such people treat others as objects, never as people, and rob them of their dignity and specialness.

America is sexually sick because of our tolerance for tools that fuel autoeroticism. Many people have not yet understood that sexual addiction is every bit as imprisoning as addiction to alcohol, drugs, or food. Because we have underestimated the power of sexual addiction to enslave, we have consistently undertreated sexual addicts.

Developing a Right Attitude

In recent decades, Christians have received some valuable resources that help to build biblical attitudes toward the subject of sexuality. The recovery of the Bible as the primary counseling tool for Christian counselors has done wonders for believers' attitudes on sex. Writers such as Jay Adams, Tim LaHaye, and Ed Wheat deserve a major portion of the credit for these important changes in attitudes. They have based their approaches on Scripture, and have accompanied the Scriptures with trustworthy information about sex that has spelled the discovery of sexual joy for many couples.

Sex is a wonderful gift from God to His creatures. God is not against sex, but He has given firm directives governing the proper use of this gift. Believers need to know the directives and how to apply them to their relationships. They also need to know how to deal with the guilt of failure through confession, forgiveness, and the practice of right sexual behaviors.

The Scriptures on Friendship

Oftentimes Christian marriages fail because one or both partners lack an appreciation for the *importance of companioning.* They grow apart because their concept of commitment does not extend to setting aside blocks of time for the purpose of developing their friendship.

Friendship and companioning figure prominently in the Bible's teaching on marriage. Husbands must love their wives as Christ loves the members of His church (Ephesians 5:28). Christ calls us His friends and longs to share His thoughts with us (John 15:15). Christian couples are challenged to share this same level of intimacy with one another. In the Song of Songs we hear the level of desired intimacy described with the words, "This is my beloved, and this is my friend" (Song of Solomon 5:16 KJV). Elsewhere, Jehovah blasts the men of Israel because they have dealt treacherously with their wives. These wives are called "thy companion, and the wife of thy covenant" (Malachi 2:14 KJV). This treachery does great violence to God's mandate to Adam and Eve. In effect, it aborts the godly seed that is close to His heart and intention (Malachi 2:15).

The Foundation of True Friendship

For a friendship to grow, the people involved must be in the same place at the same time (Song of Solomon 8:13; Isaiah 1:18). That seems obvious, but in the closing hours of the fast-paced twentieth century, the need exists to emphasize this requirement for strengthening intimacy. We cannot enhance companioning if we are committed to schedules that place us consistently in different geographical areas. If he is working nights and she is working days, companioning may not be impossible, but it will be difficult. If he is going to church meetings alone every night or she is always off with her friends, companioning will be weakened. In short, companioning demands that the two partners commit themselves to an organization of their time that clearly places the building of their relationship very high on their agenda.

The Reward of True Friendship

When husbands and wives are properly related to God and one another, life is experienced on a higher level. Solomon captured the agony and the ecstacy of marital relationships when he said:

> There is one alone, and there is not a second; yea, he hath neither child nor brother: yet is there no end of all his labor; neither is his eye satisfied with riches; neither saith he, for whom do I labor; and bereave my soul of good? This is also vanity, yea, it is a sore travail. Two are better than one; because they have a good reward for their labor. For if they fall, the one will lift up his fellow: but woe to him that is alone when he falleth; for he hath not another to help him up (Ecclesiastes 4:8-10 KJV).

Reward is the fruit of our laboring together. We derive a special joy from accomplishing tasks together. This joy erupts spontaneously as we recognize the truth that together we represent a force greater than the sum of our individual strengths. Reward is the by-product of our united accomplishments and creates the conviction that whenever possible, we should be working at the accomplishment of tasks together.

The Dedication in True Friendships

Companioning is of great importance to God. It's little wonder that He said, "For this cause a man shall leave his father and his mother, and shall cleave to his wife; and they shall become one flesh" (Genesis 2:24 KJV). Leaving, cleaving, and weaving involves more than commitment. The process also implies the investment of time and energy for the purpose of enriching the relationship.

To ensure the proper investment of time for building the marriage relationship, God gave specific instructions for newlyweds in the Old Testament: "When a man hath taken a new wife, he shall not go out to war, neither shall he be charged with any business: but he shall be free at home one year, and shall cheer up his wife which he hath taken" (Deuteronomy 24:5 KJV). God expected husbands to invest in their wives. The responsibility for this focused investment has never been withdrawn in Scripture.

When the prophet Malachi told Israel that God was intensely angry with His people, the elders in Israel inquired of God to discover the reason for His anger. God said, "Yet ye say, Wherefore? Because the LORD hath been witness between thee and the wife of thy youth, against whom thou hast dealt treacherously: yet is she thy companion, and the wife of thy covenant" (Malachi 2:14). The men in Israel had become hard of heart. They did not see God's unique gifts in their wives. They divorced their wives with calloused indifference, and God hated their attitude.

Paul wrote, "Husbands, love your wives, even as Christ also loved the church, and gave himself for it" (Ephesians 5:25). Seldom do we meet a man who seeks to love his wife with the same selflessness that Christ loves His church. Can you imagine Jesus Christ saving us and then declining to spend any further time with us? Suppose He were to say, "I've secured heaven for you, but now I must be busy with other tasks; don't bother me with the burden of daily dialogue." The Christ of Scripture would never say such a thing. He saved us to have a relationship with us (1 John 1:3-4). Likewise, the marriage relationship was designed for a man and woman to enjoy companionship with one another.

Over the years I have seen many people marry who had no resources with which to build a friendship. These marriages never last; friendship is absolutely essential if marital intimacy is to be developed by a couple. Friends each possess strengths. Each person has things to offer to the other. Each person can be the joyful recipient of the other person's gifts. Neither person needs ever to attain perfection; the celebration of what they bring to each other is enough. That which they can enjoy overshadows any and all inadequacies.

THE PROMISE OF MARITAL FULFILLMENT

Can the Scriptures alone offer couples the insights required for building sound and fulfilling marriages? Based on what we've just observed, the answer is a resounding yes! The Scriptures arm us with sufficient information and principles to guide couples toward true marital fulfillment. This is not surprising when we realize that the founder of the institution of marriage is also the author of the Holy Scriptures.

The Bible provides more than just information. It points us to the One with whom we may have a relationship that results not just in our salvation but also in our transformation. This transformation is accomplished through the enabling power of the living Christ and His Spirit, who dwells in every believer. This progressive process makes possible the suspension of that which hurts relationships, the enactment of behaviors that enrich relationships, and the establishment of great marriages to the glory of God!

TOTALLY SUFFICIENT

9

THE BIBLE AND FAMILY PRACTICE

C. Dwayne Shafer, M.D.

Over the past century, the emphasis placed upon the *art* of medicine has lessened, while the emphasis placed on the *science* of medicine has increased considerably. In the late nineteenth century, the many developments in surgical technology, improved epidemiology, and the emerging understanding of disease mechanisms brought about a startling change in the practice of medicine. Sir William Osler, who was an astute clinician, repeatedly warned his fellow physicians that they must not forget the influence that "caring" can have upon their patients. Unfortunately, Sir Osler's remarks are more often quoted than practiced. During the last two decades, more and more Americans have cried out for the return of the doctor who not only interprets lab data, but who also cares.

SCRIPTURE'S VALUE TO PHYSICIANS

For the physician who is truly concerned about total patient care, the Bible is an unexcelled source for both the *art* and *science* of healing. That's because the Bible is a source not dependent upon the shifting interpretations of obscure facts or the constant revisions of expanding technology. It is, rather, based upon truth, and that truth is not swayed by family history, past medical history, socioeconomic status, or concurrent disease state.

The Bible is useful in the practice of medicine because it has the ability to interpret patient information, to apply both general and specific therapy (counsel), and to serve as a highly specific and sensitive screening tool for a broad group of problems commonly seen in the physician's office. With the high rate of depression-, anxiety-, and patient-induced diseases, as well as those other disease processes that can arise from the *primary diagnosis* of anxiety with depression (ulcerative disease, hypertension, obesity, and so on), the astute, caring physician will not overlook this reliable tool as a primary resource in patient care.

While many people will express derision toward the use of the Bible in patient care, it remains that the *belief systems* held by individuals are of *primary importance in medical care*. This can range from the problem of compliance in a therapy of which the patient is suspicious, to side-effects that are more easily understood. Since belief systems are real, they become very relevant and cannot be ignored in any doctor-patient relationship.

The physician's use of the Bible in counseling must be more than cordial, however. The importance and the validity of the Bible, both historically and practically, makes it an instrument of precision and value.

BIBLICAL COUNSELING AND MEDICINE

The Changing Landscape

The history of biblical counseling is probably as old as the Bible itself. In fact, the book of Proverbs seems to have been written with this specific goal in mind. It was John Baxter, in his book *The Reformed Pastor* (written in the seventeenth century), who first began to systematize biblical counseling and to provide a written resource for ministers to look to for help in solving people's problems. With the exception of Baxter, the written documentation of biblical counseling is rather slim prior to this era. But we know from many historical accounts that the Bible had been widely used by other ministers for counseling purposes as well.

During the early twentieth century, the works of Sigmund Freud and other psychological theorists began to proliferate. Soon, the Bible moved from the physician's pocket to the back of a dusty shelf. What had once been a "discerner of the thoughts and intents" of a man's heart had now been relegated to the pile of archaic mythology.

The long history of the Bible's successful use should have been enough to ensure at least a consideration of validity, but most modern medical schools spend more time training young doctors to understand traditional folk medicine (which is used by very small population groups primarily being found among subcultures) than they spend examining the value of the Scriptures and faith (which a majority of Americans profess to believe).

A Broad-Spectrum Tool

In the diagnosis and treatment of any particular condition, the specificity and sensitivity of the diagnostic measures, as well as their cost, must be considered in the work-up. The treatment is determined based upon the absolute determination of the disease (e.g., a urine culture and sensitivity proving the urine infection, and documenting the efficacy of the prescribed antibiotic) and the weighing of the therapeutic options. The competent physician will seek to choose the safest, most cost-effective alternative (e.g., avoiding penicillin in the allergic patient, and using a generic antibiotic).

In making these determinations and choices, we find that the Bible is both specific ("Thou shalt not steal"—Exodus 20:15 KJV) and sensitive ("All manner of sin and blasphemy shall be forgiven unto men"—Matthew 12:31 KJV). As a therapeutic tool, the Bible can also be considered to be broad-spectrum in its coverage. Psalm 34:4

assures, "I sought the LORD, and he heard me, and delivered me from *all my fears*" (KJV, emphasis added).

The failure to utilize any other tool of comparable experience and efficacy would be considered unethical by any bioethics research committee. Unfortunately, individuals within contemporary theological circles have tended to lessen the authoritative use of the Bible in "professional" situations. The introduction of psychology into seminary curriculums and the popular notion that counseling requires "a professional" has further crippled the attitude of even the most evangelical physician. Often, too, patients may consider their problem to be "much too serious for plain Bible counseling." While most Christians will consider modest urges toward seeking biblical counsel, many have been led to think that the Bible is more of a secondary, salutary resource than a primary tool through which a person can view his or her problems.

THE BIBLE'S USE IN TREATMENT

Application to Believers and Nonbelievers

The uses of the Bible in counseling the believer and the nonbeliever have been described elsewhere in this book, but it is important to understand that the full exploration of the patient's spiritual state may take several visits (if it can be determined at all), and that the postponement of therapy should not wait for this discernment. It is acknowledged, however, that all patients need to have a clear understanding of their own sin nature and the perfect, completed work of Christ in salvation.

The Puritans referred to a concept called *common grace*. While this is not the same as the grace bestowed on us when we are given the gift of eternal salvation, it is significant in many counseling situations. What is common grace? Consider these examples: The vilest of the Israelites was protected by God's law while he endeavored to live according to it. The unbelieving spouse of a believer is spared many horrors because of the believer. God allows rain to pour upon the just and the unjust. Experience has shown that even the individual who does not profess a saving belief in the Lord Jesus Christ can benefit from the practical wisdom offered in the book of Proverbs.

The proverbs of Scripture are applicable to a remarkably wide variety of problems found in the physician's office. As a beginning instrument (for the physician and the patient), they tend to shed "light" on biblical doctrine and are easily applicable because of their plain nature. Their use in "homework" tends to discover previously "undiagnosed" problems. I will never forget the first non-Christian whom I counseled with the Scriptures. The patient was a simple cowboy who had developed panic attacks because of confessedly empty threats made against him by his co-workers. After I prescribed three chapters of Proverbs per day for the treatment and prevention of panic attacks, the man later returned to the office without an appointment, exuberant that he had discovered his problem in Proverbs 12:23: "A prudent man concealeth knowledge: but the heart of fools proclaimeth foolishness." He said, "Doc, I finally figured out that those liars ain't nothin' but fools!"

When we consider the use of Scripture in the physician's office, the scientific observer may initially be dismayed by the seeming lack of reproducibility in clinical situations. But when we consider this usage in the light of the variability of pharmacological effect, a similar pattern of result can be seen. Just as medications must be considered against variables of volume of distribution, route of administration, renal clearance, and strength of concentration, a pattern of result in offering biblical counsel will be seen to emerge based upon the experience of the counselor, the specificity of the scriptures applied, the compounding factors of other sin in the patient's life, the patient's faith or lack of faith in the Bible, and the patient's resistance to change.

Application to a Case Study

The Bible deals with the widest spectrum of material available in any known book, and it reveals for us the spiritual nature of many of the human problems encountered in the physician's office. Whether the problem is a sinful pattern of living, conflict with a spouse or children, illness and death, or one of many other problems people face, the most effective therapy is found in the Word of God. There is also a role for the use of medication and surgery in the treatment of patients with specific problems (e.g., a non-compliant, diabetic patient needing the amputation of a limb). Yet even in such cases, the physician can use the Bible as a primary source to motivate treatment of the diabetes and to overcome the depression commonly associated with the loss of a leg. Spiritual problems must be dealt with spiritually, just as physical problems must be dealt with physically. People are spiritual beings, and all aspects of a person touch upon his or her spirit. To fail to treat this primarily is to fail to treat the person.

The following case study illustrates the importance of discovering the patient's spiritual condition and lifestyle. The case is true, but some specifics have been changed to protect patient confidentiality.

Sandra is a 27-year-old white, female patient who first came to my office in November 1990. At that time her chief complaint was that of a worsening Irritable Bowel Syndrome (IBS), which had previously been diagnosed and treated by a physician in another community. When the patient had called for a refill on her medication, she was told that the prescription could not be refilled without a visit to a physician, so she came to my office on the recommendation of a local acquaintance.

Upon reviewing her medical history, I learned that the young woman had also had a "nervous stomach" that had worsened over the course of her high school years. While an undergraduate, she had experienced occasional bouts of stress-induced diarrhea during exam periods, but she was able to control her symptoms without medical therapy.

After completing her bachelor's degree in business, Sandra was given a well-paid position in a midsized business near her hometown. Over the next four years, her symptoms of IBS became more frequent and severe. When she finally consulted a physician, he prescribed to her some anti-spasmodic drugs. She stated that the medication worked well during the times she had to take it.

Exploring the Possible Causes

A review of Sandra's family history was not helpful. She had broken her ankle in a sports-related injury during high school, and she had an uneventful appendectomy at age 14. She took no regular medications and denied sexual activity. She had been engaged once in high school and once in college, but since then had dated only sporadically, finding most relationships "worrisome."

Sandra was now enrolled in a university graduate program, after having left her job because of stress. She was now halfway through her first semester, and other than being "a little stressed," she felt that she was doing fine.

Sandra denied any use of tobacco and illicit drugs, but she did admit to occasional social usage of alcohol. She reported that she had been intoxicated only once, and that had occurred during "rush" when she was in her first semester in college.

Sandra had attended church only sporadically as a child, but had joined an evangelical congregation during her junior year in high school. After graduating from high school, however, she rarely attended church.

The physical exam was remarkable; Sandra was a healthy-appearing woman who looked well-nourished. She was friendly and seemed quite outgoing and confident. She did have mild left lower-quadrant tenderness, but her gynecological exam revealed no problems and her stool was negative for occult blood. Sandra was then prescribed the same medication she had previously taken and was asked to return in four months for another evaluation.

Two months after the initial visit, Sandra returned to the office complaining of painful, heavy menstrual periods (menometrorrhagia). She added to her previous history that she had occasionally had episodes of painful periods, but only in the previous two months had they become unbearable. She often felt faint during these heavy-flow episodes and would have to stay in bed for one or two days. She added that her IBS symptoms had improved a great deal on the prescribed medication.

Sandra also reported that she was still not dating anyone and specifically denied sexual activity. Her physical exam was found to be normal except for a slightly tender, non-enlarged uterus and seemingly appropriate menstrual flow. She was found to have a hemoglobin of 13.2 gm/dl. After a discussion about the benefits of hormonal therapy, she was started on cyclical contraceptive hormonal therapy. The pap smear test results were diagnosed as "normal."

In June 1991, Sandra returned to the office complaining of epigastric discomfort that her friends had diagnosed as possibly being an ulcer. However, she denied any evidences of gastrointestinal bleeding. She reported that her menstrual periods were normal and that the IBS was still under control with help from her medication. Again, a physical exam showed that everything was essentially normal, with only subjective epigastric tenderness. Pending the performance of an upper GI series, Sandra was started on cimetidine for possible gastritis or ulcers. Her radiographic studies returned as "no evidence of disease," but she was symptomatically improved, so the cimetidine was continued.

Except for an upper respiratory illness in September 1991, the patient was well until she returned to the office again in December 1991 with a complaint about heart palpitations and shortness of breath. She had first noticed the symptoms two nights earlier while preparing a semester project. Initially she had attributed the symptoms to fatigue and excessive caffeine ingestion, but they had reached the point where she could not sit still. Except for school, she denied any other stresses. She had started dating another student, but reported that it was "nothing serious."

Upon examination, Sandra was found to be markedly anxious with rapid, shallow respirations and a rapid pulse. After placing her on oxygen by nasal cannula, she slowed her breathing and expressed significant relief. Her cardiopulmonary exam was normal, and her chest x-ray and electrocardiogram showed nothing amiss. It was felt that Sandra was having an anxiety-induced tachycardia, and since she responded so well to reassurance, it was recommended that she just be observed for the present time.

In January 1992, Sandra returned from the holiday break to follow up on her episode with chest pain. She stated that she had failed a course the previous semester, and that when she found this out the week after Christmas, she had another episode of chest pain and was taken by her family to a metropolitan emergency room. She was diagnosed as having a panic attack and possible mitral valve prolapse. She was prescribed a mild sedative, and told to follow up with her family doctor for a more in-depth cardiac evaluation.

The patient reported taking the sedative four or five times over the previous two weeks with good results. Sandra was a little more fatigued in appearance during this visit, but other than a three-pound weight loss since the December 1991 visit, the physical exam was unremarkable. She had a normal echocardiogram without evidence of mitral valve prolapse. She was warned about the addictive nature of the sedatives that had been prescribed, and was told that if she required frequent use of the medication, she would need to be switched to a nonaddictive medication to control heart rate rather than the benzodiazipine sedative.

During the next seven months, Sandra had episodes of chest pain and panic attacks approximately every one to three weeks, which required her to take a sedative drug. The episodes were generally closely associated with school-related stress. She had started dating a different man and although she found him more supportive, she was concerned that she did not feel as "relaxed" around him.

When Sandra was pressed more deeply about her symptoms of anxiety and depression, she denied any precipitating circumstances other than school stress. She also denied that she had any suicidal thoughts. Psychological profiles obtained in the office revealed her tendencies toward moderately severe anxiety and mild depression. Sandra refused medical therapy for the depression.

Discovering the Real Problem

In September 1992, Sandra returned to school after a summer internship and vacation. She felt more relaxed and stated that over the summer, she had noted a decrease in the frequency and severity of her panic attacks. She had done well until late September, when she began having sudden, severe panic attacks—especially at night. She had been planning a trip with her boyfriend to his home out of state, but canceled it at the last minute because of the attacks. Angry at her loss of control, the boyfriend had gone on the trip without her.

Sandra was unusually anxious and tearful during this visit. She also seemed to be less readily consoled. When asked why she had not gone on the trip, she replied, "Because the car might have broken down." When asked about her concern over this, she related that she was afraid that the car might break down on an isolated stretch of road and that a stranger would stop, kill her boyfriend, rape her, and then bury her alive. When asked what she thought would happen next, she said, "Then I will go to hell for killing my baby."

A re-review of Sandra's history revealed that she had been raped by an acquaintance at age 16. She had been afraid to tell her parents, but friends assured her that because the incident occurred with someone she knew, it was not rape. She had then become sexually active with two partners over the next two years, one of whom she had become engaged to, but he had broken off the engagement after their first intercourse.

During Sandra's first semester at college, she had begun to drink often on weekends and at sorority parties. These episodes often resulted in sexual activity, and eventually she became pregnant at age 19. After an abortion financed by her parents, she decided to get her life "back in line," so she began to drink less and eventually met a boyfriend whom she dated for two years. An engagement resulted from this relationship, but did not last long "by mutual consent." It was at this time that Sandra noted that her IBS symptoms were becoming worse.

After returning to graduate school, Sandra began to date more frequently and had seven sex partners during her first three semesters at school. Each of these new partners was associated with an exacerbation of her physical symptoms of diarrhea, menometrorrhagia, gastritis, or panic attacks.

In retrospect, we see that the patient's symptoms and their progression were a direct result of her actions (which she stated were sinful). Could the course have been altered by an earlier, more biblical approach? The answer is almost certainly yes! In this situation, the application of biblical principles would have made sense. An early recognition that the patient's symptoms were disproportionate to the stressors could have prompted a more aggressive interview and more frequent follow-up with inventories of high-risk behaviors.

The appropriate therapeutic approach in this type of case requires that the counselor not try to change the patient's view of sin, which this individual had already recognized as "ego dystonic." Many secular therapists direct their therapy at altering the patient's view of sin. This presents an even greater set of problems, and to do such would be morally and ethically wrong. There is also the difficulty of deciding just whose moral set that a person would use.

While Sandra had recognized internal conflict over her sexual behavior, she had failed to halt the self-destruction because of the counsel given by her friends, who said, "It's okay; everybody does it."

Applying an Effective Treatment

Upon finding out Sandra's real problem, the first step in her therapy included the recognition that fornication is wrong according to God's standards. As a result, the door was opened for Sandra to repent of her abortion and adultery. She also confessed her anger and bitterness over being raped at age 16, and through Scripture readings and prayer, we focused on God's attributes of love and of mercy.

Over the next two months, Sandra's anxiety attacks decreased in severity and in frequency. There was a definite, recognizable improvement in her condition on a week-to-week basis. She joined a local church and met with the pastor, who had a strong confidence in biblical counseling and was able to provide her ongoing support and guidance.

In May of 1993, Sandra finished her graduate program and secured a good job with expectations of advancement. By this time, she was no longer taking any medications for gastrointestinal symptoms or for her menstrual periods.

The result of bringing Sandra's lifestyle back into synchronization with her spiritual view was more effective and more ethical than it would have been to change her spiritual view. Certainly changing a person's spiritual view would not be easy, especially when it was correct to begin with!

The physician is uniquely situated to provide early detection for physical symptoms that may be the result of spiritual or mental distress. Any suspicion of factors not evident in the first exam should be examined, and an in-depth exploration of the person's spiritual understanding should be considered. In Sandra's case, the failure to locate and understand the impact of spiritual issues upon her health caused a delay in successful treatment.

THE PREPARED PHYSICIAN

Whether in sickness or in health, a person's body will reflect an image of that which dwells within. The Scripture states it so well when it says, "As [a person] thinketh in his heart, so is he" (Proverbs 23:7 KJV). Although sickness is not always caused by sinful thought and actions, sin is more often the cause than most physicians care to admit. A physician is always better prepared, then, when he or she is aware of what Scripture has to say about spiritual matters that can have an effect on a person's spiritual health.

TOTALLY SUFFICIENT

10

THE BIBLE AND THE MISSION OF THE CHURCH

Edward G. Dobson, Ed.D.

I n the book of 2 Timothy, the apostle Paul gave a
final charge to Timothy, his son in the faith. These
are among the last words of the great apostle,
who was preparing Timothy for assuming the responsibility of overseeing many churches. Within this Epistle,
Paul wrote some remarkably simple yet profound words
about the mission and purpose of the church:

> The things which you have heard from me in the
> presence of many witnesses, these entrust to faithful
> men who will be able to teach others also (2 Tim-
> othy 2:2).

Paul wrote this statement to focus Timothy's attention on the central significance of biblical preaching and
teaching, which is central to the mission of the church.

UNDERSTANDING THE MISSION OF THE CHURCH

What is the mission of the church? There are a variety
of ways to define it, but we can be certain that it involves

communicating God's truth from one generation to the next. The church's key role here on earth is to win people to Christ and disciple them. And how do we do that? By proclaiming the Scriptures to others. Thus the teaching and preaching of Scripture is of paramount importance. We're to pass God's truth on to others.

Let's look more closely at 2 Timothy 2:2: "The things which you have heard from me in the presence of many witnesses, these entrust to faithful men, who will be able to teach others also." In that verse, Paul's vision for the mission of the church encompassed *four generations* of believers. Generation *one* was a reference to himself: the things you have heard *me* teach. Generation *two* was *Timothy*: Regarding the things that you have heard from me, now it's your responsibility to entrust it to reliable, *qualified people* (generation *three*) who, in turn, are qualified to teach *others* (generation *four*). At the end of his life's journey, Paul's concern was that God's truth be faithfully transferred not just to one generation, but to the next, and the next, and the next. Central to the mission of the church, then, is the responsibility to pass God's truth on to the next generation of spiritual believers.

Over the course of our lives, we will have the opportunity to do a lot. But nothing that we do will ever count as much as preparing the next generation of believers in the church. Ultimately, when it comes time for a whole new generation to assume the leadership of the church, the question we'll be reflecting on most is this: Did we faithfully pass on the Word of God—*all* of God's Word and *all* of God's truth—to the next generation? That's what matters!

Paul helps us to refine our focus more in 2 Timothy 1:13 when he says, "What you heard from me, keep as the pattern of sound teaching, with faith and love in Christ Jesus" (NIV). He's saying that the passing of God's truth must be Christ-centered. We are not to just pass doctrine and knowledge on to the next generation; rather, we are to teach the truth in such a way that our faith in Christ will be increased and that our love for Christ will be enhanced. We're not passing on truth merely for the sake of truth, but because truth is a means of becoming more like Jesus Christ. Paul went on to say:

> Guard the good deposit [speaking of truth] that was entrusted to you—guard it with the help of the Holy Spirit who lives in us (2 Timothy 1:14 NIV).

Then Paul said:

> Keep reminding them of these things. Warn them before God against quarreling about words; it is of no value, and only ruins those who listen. Do your best to present yourself to God as one approved, a workman who does not need to be ashamed and who correctly handles the word of truth (2 Timothy 2:14 NIV).

By contrast, Scripture reminds us:

> Those who oppose him [that is, those who oppose the truth] he must gently instruct (2 Timothy 2:25 NIV).

When people oppose the truth, we are not to beat them over the head with a giant-print family Bible and beat them into submission. Nor are we to argue with them. Rather, we are to *gently* instruct them "in the hope that God will grant them repentance leading them to a knowledge of the truth" (2 Timothy 2:25 NIV).

In summary, Paul was saying, "I've given you the pattern of sound doctrine, which ought to promote faith and love in Christ. Guard the deposit with the assistance of the Holy Spirit, and do your best to correctly handle God's truth. When people oppose the truth, gently instruct them so that they will come to the knowledge of the truth."

KEEPING OUR FOCUS ON THE TRUTH

The Integrity of the Message

The Bible says this about itself:

> All Scripture is God-breathed and is useful for teaching, rebuking, correcting [bringing a person back to the right path] and training in righteousness [right living], so that the man of God may be thoroughly equipped [or completely equipped] for every good work (2 Timothy 3:16 NIV).

The sufficiency of Scripture is clearly taught in the Scripture. The Bible was inspired by God and is inerrant. When we pay attention to God's Word through teaching, rebuking, correcting, and training in right living, we will find that God's Word is sufficient to equip us completely to do whatever God has called us to do.

Second Timothy 4:1 adds:

> In the presence of God and of Christ Jesus, who will judge the living and the dead, and in view of his appearing and his kingdom, I give you this charge (NIV).

This is serious language. If Timothy's attention had wandered in the course of reading the epistle, these words would have made him sit up and take notice. Paul said to Timothy, in essence, "In the presence of God and Jesus Christ, in view of the future judgment, in light of the coming Christ, and because of Christ's kingdom, let me give you this charge." What was Paul's charge? Simply this:

> Preach the Word; be prepared in season and out of season; correct, rebuke and encourage—with great patience and careful instruction. For the time will come when men will not put up with sound doctrine. Instead, to suit their own desires, they will gather around them a great number of teachers to say what their itching ears want to hear. They will turn their ears away from the truth and turn aside to myths (2 Timothy 4:2-4 NIV).

Timothy was to preach the Word, and entrust it to others who will be qualified, in turn, to teach others. He was to continue spreading the truth from generation to generation. It was as though Paul had said: "Timothy, as I leave this life and I leave you behind, my burning passion is that you always keep the truth of God's Word at the center of your ministry. That's the mission of the church."

Not only was Paul urging us to build up the believers, he was also telling us to proclaim the truth to those who are outside the family of God:

> At my first defense, no one came to my support, but everyone deserted me. May it not be held against them. But the Lord stood at my side and gave me strength, so that through me the message [the gospel] might be fully proclaimed and all the Gentiles might hear it (2 Timothy 4:16-17).

What is our mission? Whatever the program, the classroom, or the function, our ultimate goal is to be passing the truth on to the next generation. In addition, we are to be declaring God's truth to those who need to hear the gospel of Christ.

The Impact of the Message

I am among those joggers who have made a lifetime commitment to running. I very much enjoy running, but there are a couple of irritating distractions I encounter every now and then. First, when someone driving a car recognizes me, sometimes he or she will honk the horn and wave. When that happens, my heart skips several beats because I think that for sure someone is about to run me over! I don't like it when people honk their horn at me. Second, some people want to stop and talk with me. That causes me to lose my rhythm, and then it takes another half mile before I get back into my rhythm. What's worse is that because I'm a pastor, I have to be nice to everyone who stops me!

One Friday at 5:15 p.m. I was running across a bridge over a freeway that was crowded with bumper-to-bumper traffic. I smiled with amusement when I realized that I was going faster than most of the cars on the freeway. As I headed down the hill past the bridge, a car approached. The driver suddenly slammed on the brakes, pulled over to the side of the road, and looked over at me.

"Ed Dobson, right?" he asked.

"Right," I answered.

"Saturday Night Live, right?" he inquired.

"Right," I said again.

He was referring to our church's contemporary Saturday night outreach service. I knew he wanted to talk, so I stopped. Right there, he began to tell me his story.

He said, "I was born and raised in Calvary Church. But years ago I walked away from God. But through 'Saturday Night Live,' I have found the Lord and come back home. I've been wanting to meet you to thank you for that outreach."

He paused, then added, "If I talk to you any more, I'm going to break down and cry. I can't tell you what God has done in my life. It's wonderful!" Then he drove off.

I crossed the road, picked up my running pace, and said, "Thank you, Jesus." I thanked Him not just for the opportunity to communicate His truth to believers, but also to those who are searching and who are in need of the transformation that only the Lord Jesus Christ can offer. That's the mission! Bringing people to Christ, building them up in the faith, and declaring and teaching the truth of God's Word.

STANDING FIRM IN PROCLAIMING THE TRUTH

Facing the Contemporary Challenge

When we fulfill our calling to declare God's truth, we are certain to be challenged. First, we will be challenged by a culture that *denies absolute truth*. Have you discovered that our culture is not truth-friendly? The prevailing idea among people today is that there are no absolutes—that everything is relative. Therefore, there is no such thing as *the* truth. Rather, there are *many* truths, not *one* Truth. When we come along as followers of Christ and declare that this Bible is the inspired, inerrant word of the living God, it's not up for discussion or debate.

When we as Christians tell people that the Bible is the inspired, inerrant Word of the living God, sometimes we'll get the response that the Bible isn't the only source of truth. However, God is not in a negotiating mood with His truth. His truth is forever settled. It transcends culture, language, time, and space. God's Word is the absolute truth of God. And when we proclaim that, we will be taking a stand against the flow of ideas that are popular in our culture. We will be told that Jesus is not the only way to heaven and that we are being narrow-minded and anti-intellectual.

Gandhi believed that all the world's religions are like different branches that extend from the same tree. He believed that Christians were going up one side of the tree, Muslims up another side, and Buddhists up another. Like Gandhi, contemporary culture views all religions as searching for the same thing. In fact, Gandhi said, "I cannot place Christ on a solitary throne for I believe God has been incarnate again and again." And New Agers believe we are all on the same journey.

However, that's not what the Bible says. Jesus Himself said, "I am the way, and the truth and the life. No one comes to the Father except through me" (John 14:6 NIV). Christ alone sits on the heavenly throne, and there is coming a day when every knee will bow and every tongue will confess that Jesus Christ is Lord (*see* Philippians 2:10-11).

One area in which we differ with the world is the increasing tendency to devalue human life through the approval of abortion, genetic engineering, and doctor-assisted suicide. The Bible tells us that all of life is sacred. It is a gift from the Creator from the moment of conception and ought to be valued and protected. Our culture, however, says that people should be free to make their own choices based on their own values. Another area of pressure for Christians is the prevailing sexual practices of people today: premarital sex, extramarital sex, and same-sex relationships. There is increasing pressure on the church to open up the absolutes of Scripture to include those who have chosen to live in disharmony with the biblical model.

The *New York Times* did a major article on our "Saturday Night Live" ministry. A reporter showed up one Saturday night and began taking notes and photographs. Later on, the reporter and I had a phone conversation, and I told him that at our Saturday evening meetings people frequently ask questions related to human sexuality.

The reporter asked, "How do you answer people's questions about being gay or living with somebody?"

I said, "It's pretty simple. We believe that sex is a gift from God—a gift intended for expression solely within the context of a heterosexual marriage. All other expressions of sexuality are outside the boundaries of God's creative intent and the unmistakable teachings of Scripture."

Now such a view is not popular. Many people say that's narrow-minded. But that's what the Word of the living God says. We have a responsibility to love those who choose differently and not berate them, but we're also called to exhort them to repentance and to new life in Christ. We are to declare the love of God, but at the same time we are not to give up proclaiming scriptural truths just because people disagree with them.

Distinguishing Essentials from the Non-essentials

The second way that God's truth is being challenged is by the watering down of doctrine to enhance *Christian unity*. Now, I'm not saying there is anything wrong with unity; anybody who loves Jesus and the Bible is in favor of unity. In fact, Jesus prayed in John 17 that we might all be one. True unity means one Lord, one faith, and one fellowship in the Body of Christ. But we must not strive for unity at the expense of truth. There can be no true Christian unity without the unifying truth of the Scriptures.

Observing the Distinctions

Several years ago, I developed a three-part paradigm to help our church sort out the essentials from the non-essentials of the faith. The first area encompassed *absolute truth*—the fundamentals of the Christian faith. These are the essential doctrines of the New Testament: the deity of Christ, His substitutionary atonement on the cross, His bodily resurrection, and the gospel of salvation by faith based on God's grace. Those are the essentials, the basics, the fundamentals of the Christian faith. Yet there are religious people who deny the deity of Christ or His atonement on the cross. They deny His bodily resurrection and still claim to be Christian. But to deny those essential doctrines is to deny the essence and the absolutes of the Christian faith.

The second area is *convictions*. These are things we believe based on our understanding and interpretation of Scripture. For example, some Christians believe in baptism by immersion after a person commits his life to Jesus Christ. I personally believe that is the biblical interpretation of baptism. A person is to be fully immersed in the water, which identifies him with Christ's death, and then brought up out of the water to identify him with Christ's resurrection. That's my conviction. But there are many genuine Christians who don't believe in total immersion. That doesn't make them more or less Christian. That is not the line that divides whether I'm a Christian or not. But because it is important, it's a matter on which we can develop a conviction based on our understanding of the Bible.

I also believe in eternal security—that when you commit your life to Jesus Christ you are kept by the power of the Holy Spirit until the day of final redemption. There are others who believe you can lose your salvation. Both sides say that their conviction is based on Scripture. Others prefer the term "the preservation of the saints" or "the perseverance of the saints." Each view has its own nuance and emphasis.

Some Christians believe in miraculous gifts of the Spirit. I believe that the sign gifts, such as speaking in

246 • TOTALLY SUFFICIENT

tongues, are gifts that were given for a unique purpose and a unique period of time and are not gifts to be practiced today. But I have many charismatic brothers and sisters who disagree with that. They believe that tongues are for today. Now our convictions don't make me or them a better Christian. Nor is this an issue that determines whether or not a person is a believer. We are brothers and sisters in Christ despite our different convictions.

Third, there are *cultural preferences*. These are things that we do primarily as a result of cultural influence. They often are based not on the Bible, but on tradition. For example, musical style is a cultural preference. There is no biblical basis on which to make a moral decision that one style of music is more spiritual than another. Different styles of music are a matter of preference. You'll find some music that you like, and some that you don't. You can worship God with rock and roll, or Bach, or Beethoven, or anything and everything in between. It's an issue of cultural preference. Some churches sing only psalms. Others prefer gospel songs. Others want only anthems. Some sing only from a hymnal. Others like "praise and worship" music. All of these can be used to the glory of God. But they are all matters of personal preference, not biblical conviction.

The Bible never tells us how loud or soft music should be or even what style it ought to be. Most of us choose our musical preferences based on our own cultural experiences. In the Old Testament, the Hebrews sang, clapped, danced, and waved their arms. Early Christians sang chants. The Puritans sang psalms. The revivalists preferred "gospel songs." In the South, they call it "Southern Gospel" music. Black churches call it "Black Gospel." I'm from Ireland and I like it all!

Our church is not a hand-clapping, hand-waving, pew-jumping sort of crowd. And we probably never will be. But that doesn't make us any more or less spiritual than those who participate in such activities. These are all matters of cultural preference. But, tragically, many Christians get more upset about their preferences than they do their theology. They will tolerate bad theology but they won't tolerate a music style that they don't like.

Keeping a Balance

There are two dangers I see in sorting out our convictions and preferences. The first danger is that we'll take our cultural preferences and convictions and elevate them all to absolutes. This happens when we say things like, "Unless you sing a certain way, you're really not spiritual." That leads to legalism and narrow-mindedness. It leads to exclusivism and to self-righteousness. It allows you to judge everybody else on things that aren't essential truths.

In response to all this, there are some people who say, "Well, you know, doctrine divides, but love unites." This may sound good on the surface, but that's not what Paul is calling for in 2 Timothy. Yes, doctrine divides. It divides the false from the true. It divides the right from the wrong.

The second danger is that we'll set aside our convictions and preferences and declare them as unimportant. We don't want to do that even though we know that real Christian unity recognizes diversity. When we are careful to hold to absolute truths and keep them distinct from our convictions and preferences, then we will have unity in our diversity. That's what will allow me to call a Pentecostal my brother in Jesus Christ even though we differ on our convictions or cultural preferences. That's what allows me to partner with Bethel Pentecostal Church, or First Reformed, or the First AME Church. It allows me to continue doing work for the kingdom with people whose convictions and preferences differ from mine without me becoming like them or them becoming like me.

One of our challenges as believers is to hold on to the absolutes of the faith while loving those believers who do not share our convictions and preferences. We are also challenged to examine our convictions and preferences based on the absolutes of Scripture. We need to do this because our generation needs the truth more than any generation ever. It does not need our cultural "hang ups"—even when we try to repackage them as the truth.

AFFIRMING OUR ULTIMATE PRIORITY

Truth is eternal because it is God's truth. It is essential because it represents His character and nature. It is absolute because He is the ultimate absolute. Its proclamation is our mission, and its fruit is eternal life and righteousness.

TOTALLY SUFFICIENT

11

THE BIBLICAL BASIS OF PASTORAL MINISTRY

W. Wilson Benton, Jr., Ph.D.

Words are things," wrote Lord Byron, "and a drop of ink falling like dew upon a thought is that which causes thousands, perhaps millions to think." Can you think of any better way for God to communicate His truth to us than through the Bible? Sights and sounds fade away. Voices are stilled and forgotten. Acts appear on the stage of human history and then disappear. But the written word endures—it lasts forever! It can be read and reread. It can be copied and contemplated. It can be transmitted from one generation to the next. It can be translated from one language into another.

WHAT MEN HAVE SAID ABOUT THE BIBLE

The Bible is the instrument God has chosen to make visible the invisible, to make tangible the intangible, to make understandable the unfathomable. When we hold a Bible in our hands, we have a private audience with the Ruler of the universe. Just as the virgin birth of Jesus Christ is unique among all other births, so the Bible is unique among all other books.

- Patrick Henry said, "The Bible is worth all other books that have ever been printed."

- Abraham Lincoln said, "I believe the Bible is the best gift God ever gave to man."

- Robert E. Lee said, "In all my perplexes and distresses the Bible has never failed to give me light and strength."

- George Washington said, "It is impossible rightly to govern the world without God and the Bible."

- Napoleon said, "The Bible is no mere book, it is a living creature with a power that conquers all who oppose it."

- Thomas Cranmer, the Archbishop of Canterbury and one of the leaders of the English Reformation, said, "This book which is the word of God is the most precious jewel, the most holy relic that remains on earth."

- Hugh Latimer, an English Reformer martyred for his faith, said, "The excellency of this word is so great and of so high a dignity there is nothing on earth which can be compared to it."

- John Calvin said, "The Word of God must be given a place of unusurped honor within the church."

WHAT THE BIBLE SAYS ABOUT ITSELF

These statements spoken with conviction were made by important men whose lives spanned over a number of centuries; and yet, if we really believe that Scripture is the Word of God, then what the Bible says about itself is far more important than what any man says about the Bible. Consider what the apostle Peter wrote under the inspiration of God's own Spirit in 1 Peter. In verse 23 he said, "You have been born again . . . through the living and enduring word of God" (NIV). The Bible alone has *saving* power. In verse 22 we read, "You have purified yourselves by obeying the truth" (NIV). The Bible alone has *sanctifying* power. And finally, Peter concluded, "The word of the Lord shall stand forever" (verse 25 NIV). The Bible alone has *staying* power.

The Bible's Saving Power

When we open our Bibles and begin to read, we discover not only right human thoughts about God, we also discover God's thoughts about humans. We are told who we really are, where we came from, and where we are going. More importantly, we are told about the One from whom we came. We are told about God our Maker and Creator. The truth that God created us cannot be overemphasized, for it has been called into question and rejected by our society.

Time magazine (Sept. 21, 1993) ran a lead article entitled, "How Man Created God," and this, in part, is what the article stated:

> Who is God; what can we know about God, and if knowing God is possible, how do we comprehend Him: by reason or only through an ecstatic epiphany of faith? These questions have tormented theologians and mystics in the four-thousand-year history of monotheism. Their widely varied answers are explored in an absorbing new book from Britain. Whether or not one accepts the biblical teaching that men and women are made in God's image, argues the author, it is clear that deity is the product of human kind's creative imagination. God may well be our most interesting idea. Down through the ages humans have deposited deity or deities in order to fulfil a pragmatic need primarily to find meaning and value in life.

Do you understand why the Reformers shouted, "*Sola Scriptura*"? That is, "Scripture alone"? Only in Scripture do we find the truth that God created man. When we open our Bibles we soon discover that God is the primary theme of the Bible and man is the secondary theme. God is the loving subject; man is the beloved object. When we open our Bibles we read of God—His sovereignty, power, creation, plan, and purpose for the universe. We read about God's goodness and grace, His mercy and compassion, His light and love. In short, we are told that God is a forgiving, redeeming, saving God. And God's Word reflects God's character, just as your word, whether you know it or not, reflects your character. Hugh Latimer wrote, "The author is so great, that is, God Himself, eternal, almighty, and everlasting so that the Scripture because of Him is also great, eternal, and most mighty."[1]

Because God is a saving God, His Word is a saving Word. That is why Peter said, "You have been born again . . . through the living and enduring word of God" (1 Peter 1:23 NIV). The Bible is not only a living Word, it is a life-giving Word. When Peter made that claim about Scripture, he was reflecting the earlier teaching of Jesus Christ. On one occasion Jesus said, "You believe that I speak to you the truth correctly, so in the words that I speak to you, you have life" (John 5:39). And Peter himself once said, "Lord, to whom shall we go? You have the words of eternal life" (John 6:68).

The Reformers rediscovered the truth that God's Word is a saving Word. They believed that the Bible was the very Word of God to man—the infallible, inerrant, inspired Word of God. The Reformers believed that this Word was given to man primarily to lead man to the Savior, Jesus Christ. They believed that Scripture—the Bible itself—had saving power basically for two reasons: 1) the Bible comes from God, and 2) the Bible leads to Christ.

- Martin Luther wrote, "All Scripture points to Christ alone."[2]

- John Calvin wrote, "The word presents Christ clothed with his gospel that faith may behold God."[3] Elsewhere he said, "Everyone who would enjoy the light of true religion must begin as a disciple of Scripture. If we wish to know of Jesus Christ it is to the written word that we must turn, both for the necessary knowledge of the historical facts and for our understanding of the meaning of those facts. There can be no reliable source either for this knowledge or for this understanding other than the writings of the law, the prophets and the apostles—they are for us the only authoritative witness to Christ. Christ can not be properly known in any other way than from the Scriptures."[4]

- William Tyndale, the man responsible for translating the Bible into English and martyred for doing so, wrote, "The Scripture is that wherewith God draws us to Himself. The Scriptures were given to lead us to Christ. You must, therefore, go along by the Scriptures as by a line until you come to Christ."[5]

- William Whitaker wrote, "The Scriptures are necessary because they contain the necessary doctrine without which we cannot be saved."[6]

- Bishop John Jewel wrote, "If we would believe in God, it is very needful that we hear the word of God. There is no other word that teaches us unto salvation."[7]

- Nicholas Ridley wrote, "The good word of God, that word of truth, is able to save men's souls. By the word of God man is born anew and made the child of God."[8]

I trust that you are blessed by being reminded that the Bible, and the Bible alone, possesses saving power. You understand, of course, why the Reformers were so intent in putting the Bible into the hands of people. They sacrificed their lives to put God's Word in the vernacular because they wanted people to hear the good news of salvation.

On the sixteenth anniversary of William Tyndale's martyrdom for translating the Bible, Hugh Latimer said, "We are much bound to God that He has set out this His will in our natural mother tongue. In English, I say, so that now you and I may not only hear it but also read it ourselves. This I speak to the end to move you to thankfulness toward Him who so lovingly provides His word and in His word all things necessary for our salvation."[9]

Do you understand that it is in the Bible alone that we are introduced to the Savior? Only in the Scriptures alone that we are given the plan of salvation? Only in the Word of God that we receive the call to faith and repentance? If you are saved, if you are a Christian, you can say, "I have been born again by the Word of God." This is the instrument that God used to bring you out of darkness into His marvelous light. D.L. Moody once said, "No conversion ever takes place without the Bible," and yours is no exception.

Victor Nance was an outstanding high school football player. He went to the University of Southern Mississippi on a football scholarship. Because he had a strong body and a bright mind he excelled not only on the gridiron but also in the classroom; but as he would say later himself, he was not smart enough. He was smart enough not to use drugs, but not smart enough not to sell drugs. He was not smart enough to escape the long arm of the law. He was arrested and convicted in his junior year of college and sent to Parchman, the Mississippi State Penitentiary. He had been there a little over a year when I received a letter from him asking that I come by his camp and visit him after the weekly Bible study that I taught there.

When I walked through the gate I met Vic Nance, a very handsome, very engaging young man, and his first words to me were, "Let's walk over to the tree of life." He pointed to a big oak tree in the large compound of the minimum security area. On the way over I asked, "Why do you call it the tree of life?" He told me. Soon after coming to the penitentiary he was given a copy of the New Testament by a fellow inmate. He threw it under his bed and did not even look at it for months. And then out of sheer boredom, because he did have a bright mind and because that mind was not being challenged, he reached under his bed and pulled out that New Testament and began to read it. Every day he would go sit under that tree and read his New Testament, and it was there through the reading of God's Word that he became a Christian.

Victor wanted to talk to me about his experience to be sure he had actually expressed saving faith in Jesus Christ, and I can assure you he had done just that. He was brought to faith through the witness of no one, only through the life-giving Word of God. He was born again by the Word of God. If a person is redeemed, ultimately it is because he or she received the revelation that God has given of Himself in His Word. So I have to ask you a question: Have you been born again by the Word of God? Have you thanked God today for your own Bible? Have you read your Bible today? Day after day, are you seeking to live according to the truth of God's Word?

The Bible's Sanctifying Power

That last question suggests Peter's second point ("You have purified yourselves by obeying the truth"— 1 Peter 1:22 NIV). The Bible has not finished its work when it brings us to faith in Jesus Christ. In fact it has only begun its work then, for the Bible must teach us how to live as those who are true and faithful disciples of Jesus Christ. Peter, therefore, describes the power of God's Word not only as saving power but also as *sanctifying power*. This is his language: "You have purified yourselves by obeying the truth." This is Peter's way of saying that Scripture is the spiritual soap that God uses to wash us and to cleanse us so that we may be the people He wants us to be and enjoy the pleasures He has in store for us. Most likely you know the invigorating and refreshing feeling that comes from taking a shower or bath and scrubbing yourself clean when you are hot, sweaty, and dirty. The Word of God can have a similar effect on our lives. Peter was teaching in a very practical way that the Word of God can help scrub us clean.

In making this claim for Scripture, saying that it possesses sanctifying power, Peter was reflecting the testimony of the psalmist who asked the question centuries ago: "How can a young man keep his way pure?" And the answer given is this: "By living according to your word. . . . I have hidden your word in my heart that I might not sin against you" (Psalm 119:9,11 NIV). Peter was reflecting the teaching of Jesus Christ, who said on one occasion, "You are already clean because of the word I have spoken unto you" (John 15:3 NIV). In His high priestly prayer, the Lord cried on our behalf, "Sanctify them"—wash, cleanse, purify them. How? "By the truth; your word is truth" (John 17:17). Paul picked up the idea in Ephesians 5, where he wrote about Jesus Christ cleansing the church, His bride. He said that Christ sanctifies and cleanses the church by the washing of water through the word (Ephesians 5:26). "*Sola Scriptura*," cried the Reformers—Scripture alone is the instrument that God uses to purify His people that we may then enjoy the pleasures He has for us in life.

It Gives Us a Standard

The question is asked—and it is a logical question —how exactly does God do this? How does the Bible actually purify, cleanse, and sanctify us? Let me suggest two answers. First, the Bible sanctifies us by giving us the *standard* by which we ought to live, that is, the truth of God to which we should conform our lives, those principles we should practice consistently that we may enjoy the blessing of God. In the words of Philip Bliss's great hymn, "Words of life and beauty, Teach me faith and duty."

Many times while I was growing up, I heard my father say, "Son, the Bible is to be your touchstone in everything you do." I knew generally what he was telling me: that I should look to the Bible to give me guidance and direction as I made all the important decisions of life. I was to let the Bible help me as I established important relationships in life and as I endeavored to discern how I should spend my time, energy, and money.

Though I knew generally what my father was saying, I did not know what a touchstone was. So one day I said, "Daddy, what is a touchstone?" He said, "Oh, you know what a touchstone is, don't you?" and I said, "Yes, sir," but I did not have a clue. I had no idea what a touchstone was. But I wanted to know, so I did a little research and discovered that there really is such a thing as a touchstone. It was used extensively at one time in our nation's history. Before we had scientific methods for testing the quality of certain metals, the touchstone was used. It is a hard black rock that was used to test either gold or silver ore. The ore would be rubbed on the black touchstone and the color left by the ore would determine the quality of the metal in that ore. My father was right, then, in telling me that the Bible is to be the touchstone for everything I did in life. It is the standard that God gives us in His word by which we ought to judge the quality of the lives that we are living. Nothing else serves as a valid standard for the judging of life's quality other than the standard we find in Scripture.

The Reformers held to the conviction that Scripture alone contained the standards by which men ought to live.

- John Calvin wrote, "The Bible is not only the sole source of the church's proclamation but also the sole authority that must rule in the life of the church. The Scripture is set over the church by God as the authority that must be allowed full freedom to rule in the life of the church."[10]

- Thomas Cranmer wrote, "May all manner of persons of what estate or condition so ever they be, in this book learn all things that they ought to believe, what they ought to do, and what they ought not to according to Almighty God."[11] There is the standard that purifies us as we conform our lives to its principles and precepts.

- John Bradford wrote, "First we confess and believe all the books of the Old Testament and all the books of the New Testament to be the very true word of God, and to be written by the inspiration of the Holy Ghost and therefore to be heard accordingly as the judge in all controversies in all matters of religion."[12] You and I are not free to decide what is right and what is wrong; even in the practice of our faith we must conform to the standard of God's Word.

- Nicholas Ridley wrote, "This holy and wholesome true word teaches us truly our bounden duty towards our Lord God in every point what is His blessed will and what His pleasure is."[13]

- Bishop Jewel wrote, "Whatever truth is brought to us contrary to the word of God is not truth but falsehood and error. Whatsoever honor done unto God that disagrees from the honor required by His word, it is not honor unto God but blasphemy."[14]

Is it any wonder that the Reformer cried in phrases that sound familiar to us, "The word, the whole word, and nothing but the word"? Is it any wonder that the framers of the Westminster Confession spoke of Scripture as our only infallible rule of faith and practice?

The Scriptures are the only accredited standard by which we are to judge the quality of our lives. That standard is not found in the lifestyles of the rich and famous; it is not found in what they are doing on the latest television sitcom; it is not found in the product being pushed on a 30-second commercial; it is not found in driving the right car, wearing the right clothes, or living in the right house in the right part of town.

It Gives Us Strength

Another way that the Bible sanctifies us is by giving us the *strength* we need to comply with the standard. Isn't God gracious? He gives us the pattern by which we should live, and then having given us the pattern, He also gives us the power to conform to that pattern. And just as the standard is found in the Word, so also is the strength to comply with that standard found in His Word.

John Calvin tells us that our faith in God, Scripture, and the work of the Holy Spirit is increased by the Word of God. He puts it like this: "Faith has a perpetual relationship to the word and can no more be separated from it than the rays from the sun or the fruit from the root. The divine word is the foundation by which faith is sustained and supported."[15] There is no strength to live the Christian life apart from the strength derived from Scripture.

Hugh Latimer, in an interesting and rather prolonged monologue, reminds us of how we receive strength from the Bible so we can confront evil and fight against the devil, who seeks to destroy the pleasure God intends for us. He said,

> Only with the word of God must we fight against the devil; therefore, let us thankfully use the same, for only with God's word shall we avoid and chase the devil and with nothing else. Our Savior, when He was tempted, what were His weapons wherewith He fought? Nothing else but God's word; so likewise we must have God's word to fight with the devil and to withstand his temptations and his assaults.[16]

How is it that God uses His word—the reading of words on a page—to strengthen us? How does He use that to strengthen us so that our faith is increased and we claim the promises He gives us in Scripture, and so that we are able to withstand the fiery darts of the evil one? I do not know. I do not know how it is that God mysteriously uses His Word in this way. I have been a Christian nearly all my life; I am an ordained minister of the gospel. I have a Ph.D. in systematic theology, and I teach in a seminary. Yet I have to tell you I do not know how God does this, but He does it.

Fortunately, we do not have to know how He does it to enjoy the blessing that He communicates to us when we read His Word. We can simply rest in knowing that when we read the Bible, our souls are nourished and strengthened. When we read His Word, we become familiar with the promises and the blessings that He offers and thus are able to claim those promises and enjoy those blessings.

The Bible's Staying Power

Now if you think all of this is outdated, old-fashioned, and that it has no application for today, let me next remind you of what Peter said about the *staying power* of God's Word. The Reformers proclaimed the fact that the Bible was just as true for them in their day as it was in the day that it was written; and you and I ought to believe that it is just as true for us in our day as it was for the Reformers in their day and the apostles in their day.

Peter said this Word of God is the "abiding" Word of God (1 Peter 1:23 NASB), or the "enduring" Word of God (NIV). I do not know which word your version uses to translate the Greek term; both are permissible. The Bible is the abiding, enduring, everlasting Word of God. It is not culturally oriented. To prove his point, Peter quoted a verse that ought to be familiar to all of us: "The grass withers and the flowers fall, but the word of our God stands forever" (Isaiah 40:8 NIV). Peter believed that and the Reformers believed that. "The eternal word of God," wrote Nicholas Ridley, "abides forever."[17] John Jewel wrote:

> The word of God has no end. No force shall be able to decay it. The gates of hell shall not prevail against it. Cities shall fall; kingdoms shall come to nothing; empires shall fade away as the smoke; but the truth of the Lord shall continue forever. Burn it, it will rise again; kill it, it will live again; cut it down by the root and it will spring up again.[18]

What a contrast that presents to the thinking that prevails in our culture! In the words of Henry Lyte's famous hymn, "Change and decay in all around I see." Everything around us is changing. The weather has already changed today. Our circumstances and our situations change; our financial status changes; our relationships change; our age and our health change; presidents change; health care programs change; and on and on we could go. Everything changes, but not God's Word! The Bible, like its Author, is the same yesterday, today, and forever. It never changes its message; it never changes its methods; it never changes its positions on right and wrong, truth and error, good and evil. It never fails to fulfill what it promises; it never fails to accomplish what it predicts; it stands forever. When Peter said that God's Word endures forever, he was echoing the teaching of Jesus Christ, who said on one occasion, "I tell you the truth, until heaven and earth disappear, not the smallest letter, not the least stroke of a pen, will by any means disappear from the Law until everything is accomplished" (Matthew 5:18).

The truth affirmed in those words is our comfort in the midst of the uncertainties around us. The principles of Scripture do not change; the truth of God is a sure foundation upon which we can stake our lives for time and eternity. One of the church's more popular hymns expresses this thought beautifully in the words, "How firm a foundation, ye saints of the Lord, Is laid for your faith in His excellent Word!"

Thomas Cranmer said, "Let us stay, quiet, and certify our consciences with the most infallible certainty, truth, and perpetual assurance of the Scriptures."[19] Do you remember how Jesus Christ concluded His famous Sermon on the Mount?

> Everyone who hears these words of mine and puts them into practice is like a wise man who built his house on the rock. The rains came down, the streams rose, and the winds blew and beat against that house; yet it did not fall, because it had its foundation on the rock (Matthew 7:24-25 NIV).

What is that rock? In the words of Winston Churchill: "We stand with assurance on the impregnable rock of Holy Scripture." Here is certainty for all of our uncertainty; here is the foundation for all of our hope in life and in death: God's Word will stand forever.

Not only is that our comfort, it is also our constraint. Remember, it is this Word that stands forever that will someday judge each and every one of us. Bishop Jewel wrote, "By God's word He makes His will known and by His word He judges us. . . . The word of the Lord is the bush out of which issues a flame of fire."[20] Scripture is a consuming fire.

WHAT DO YOU SAY ABOUT THE BIBLE?

You can ignore God's Word if you want, but you cannot circumvent it. You can break it if you like—transgress it at will—but you cannot circumvent it. You can reject it completely, but you cannot circumvent it. You see, that Word stands, and someday you will stand before that Word and it will either *commend* you or *condemn* you. Every person will be judged, wrote Paul: "This will take place on the day when God will judge man's secrets through Jesus Christ, as my gospel declares" (Romans 2:16).

Will the Word condemn you as one who has rejected God's love and mercy and grace, one who has refused to accept the free gift of forgiveness, one who has declined the offer of salvation through Jesus Christ? Or will that Word commend you as one who took its truth to heart and accepted Jesus Christ as that one who paid the price for your sin, dying in your stead on the cross that you might be forgiven and go to heaven?

Is the Bible something you dread to read, or is it your greatest delight in life? Have you thanked God today for your Bible? Have you read your Bible today? Are you living day by day according to the truth of your Bible? Is it your most prized possession? *Sola Scriptura*—Scripture alone has saving power, sanctifying power, and staying power.

Sing them over again to me,
wonderful words of Life;

Let me more of their beauty see,
wonderful words of Life.

Words of life and beauty,
teach me faith and duty:

Beautiful words, wonderful words,
wonderful words of Life.

Christ, the blessed One,
gives to all wonderful words of Life;

Sinner, list to the loving call,
wonderful words of Life.

All so freely given,
wooing us to Heaven:

Beautiful words, wonderful words,
wonderful words of Life.

Sweetly echo the gospel call,
wonderful words of Life.

Offer pardon and peace to all,
wonderful words of Life.

Jesus, only Savior, sanctify forever:

Beautiful words, wonderful words,
wonderful words of Life.

—*Philip P. Bliss*

TOTALLY SUFFICIENT

12

TOTAL SUFFICIENCY AND BIBLICAL TRUTH

*Howard Eyrich, D.Min. and
Ed Hindson, D.Phil.*

The great themes of the Bible focus on what God does for us, rather than what we do for Him. These themes were the basis of the Reformation, and they form the central beliefs of Protestant Christianity today. Ultimately, they distinguish between a religion of works and one of evangelical faith.

The Bible teaches that we cannot work our way to God. We cannot reach heaven by human self-effort. Rather, God has worked His way to us. He has reached down to meet us at the point of our human inadequacy. That is what the biblical doctrine of grace is all about. It is about God doing for us what we cannot do for ourselves.

Grace has always run counter to unregenerate human nature. Our flesh wants to justify itself—to ourselves, to others, and to God. "I can take care of myself," it wants to shout back at God's grace. "I will find the strength within me to solve my problems," it continues. "Thanks God, but I don't need your help," it insists.

This basic theological issue is at the core of all Christian ministry, including Christian counseling. How we do counseling will be determined by our theology—or lack of theology! A person cannot do distinctively Christian counseling without a distinctively Christian theology. He or she cannot properly evaluate the spiritual legitimacy of secular counseling themes without an adequate grasp of biblical truth.

The doctrine of grace alone eliminates all systems of self-effort, self-love, and self-importance. Grace causes us to see our total inadequacy in light of God's total sufficiency. Grace irresistibly draws us to God, the cross, and the Savior. It is the expression of divine love; it tells us that there is hope. Grace tells us that God loves us in spite of our sins, our failures, our inadequacies, our guilt, and our pain. Grace tells us that God loves us in spite of ourselves.

Dr. Chris Thurman, a licensed psychologist and popular speaker, has recently dealt with this issue in his book *Self-Help or Self-Destruction?*[1] In the book, Thurman candidly shares about the struggles he faced in his attempts to balance biblical truth with popular psychology. As his own understanding of theology matured, he became less confident in many of the concepts he had learned in school. He said, "It wasn't until I had been out of school for a number of years that it began to dawn on me . . . that some—maybe a lot—of what I had been taught was simply not valid."[2]

In his book, Thurman attacks what he calls "ten pop psychology myths that could destroy your life," arguing that each one is unbiblical and, therefore, untrue. Here is his list of dangerous pop psychology myths:

1. People are basically good.
2. You need more self-esteem and self-worth.
3. You can't love others until you love yourself.
4. You shouldn't judge anyone.
5. All guilt is bad.
6. You need to think more positively.
7. Staying in love is the key to a great relationship.

8. You have unlimited power and potential.
9. Your happiness is the most important thing.
10. God can be anything you want Him to be.

Years ago, I (Ed) heard a wise old preacher say: "Knowing the Bible will unfit you for a lot of preaching!" The same could be said for a lot of counseling. Just because something sounds good doesn't mean it is true. And if it isn't true, then it doesn't really work.

TRUTH IS THE BOTTOM LINE

Businessmen are known for asking each other to cut through the sales pitch and "get to the bottom line." In Christianity, truth is the "bottom line." Truth and truth alone decides what is valid and what is invalid. The Christian faith sits on the pillars of basic truth claims. Without these basic truths there is no basis for claiming that what we believe really matters.

The essential truths of the Christian faith include:

1. The Divine Inspiration of the Bible

If the Bible is not the divinely inspired, inerrant Word of God, then it does not really matter what it says. It is nothing more than a collection of ancient myths, traditions, and human wisdom. Any counselor who claims to be a Christian yet doesn't believe in the divine inspiration of Scripture will not take it seriously when it comes to telling a client what the Lord desires for our lives.

2. The Existence of an Infinite, Personal God

If the God of the Bible is not the true and only God, then it does not matter what He thinks or what He has said. If each person can fashion his own "god" to meet his own needs, then counselees do not need a personal relationship with the God of the Bible. If they can subjectively find "god" within themselves, then they do not need objective faith in a God who is outside themselves. Counselors who do not hold a biblical view of God will have no incentive to introduce counselees to that God.

3. The Uniqueness of Jesus Christ

If Jesus is not really the divine Son of God, the promised Messiah, or the Savior of mankind, then He was nothing more than a fallible human being. In fact, He was a liar and a deceiver. Yet He claimed to be God (John 8:58), He received worship (John 9:38), He claimed to be able to forgive sins (Matthew 9:2-6), and He promised people eternal life (John 5:24). Either He was who He said He was or He was in desperate need of psychological help! As. C.S. Lewis remarked, "Jesus was a liar, a lunatic, or Lord of lords!"[3]

4. Salvation by Grace

If our personal salvation is not by grace alone, then we must teach people to work their way to heaven. There can be no legitimate Christian counseling that does not understand the biblical nature of God's grace. Both legalism and liberalism miss the mark on the issue of grace. God must initiate the process of salvation by extending His unmerited favor to us. Any attempt at Christian counseling that falls short of understanding and emphasizing the grace of God is doomed to humanistic self-effort and failure.

5. Substitutionary Atonement

If Jesus Christ did not die in our place, taking the wrath of God for our sins, then we have no hope of eternal salvation. It does not matter if your religion satisfies you; what matters is that which satisfies God! And God is satisfied only with the substitutionary blood atonement of His Son. There is no other payment for sin that satisfies the righteousness of God. There is no other way to heaven. Jesus alone is the "Lamb of God who takes away the sin of the world" (John 1:29). Until our counselees come face to face with the Savior, there is no hope of helping them to permanently resolve their problems in this life or the life to come.

6. Personal Spiritual Regeneration

The Bible teaches that we must be "born again" (John 3:3,7) by the regeneration of the Holy Spirit. The Bible views all people as spiritually dead (unregenerate). They can come to life only by the quickening process of the new birth. The Holy Spirit must regenerate us, infuse faith in our hearts, enable us to believe the gospel, convict us of sin, call us to the Savior, and seal us to God forever. Without personal regeneration there is no hope of permanent change for anyone. Every Christian counselor who believes this must seriously present the gospel message to unsaved counselees and call them to faith in Christ as a part of any true Christian counseling effort. To fail to do this is to leave people hopelessly in their sins.

7. Personal Spiritual Sanctification

Sanctification follows regeneration, and is the process by which the Holy Spirit progressively conforms us into the image of Christ (Romans 8:29; 12:1-2). It is that spiritual process by which the Spirit produces personal holiness within our hearts and lives. As with our salvation, our sanctification is His work, not ours. We are not saved by good works, nor are we sanctified by good works. We cannot work our way to a better life any more than we can work our way to heaven. Jesus said to the Father, "Sanctify them by the truth; your word is truth" (John 17:17 NIV).

TOTALLY SUFFICIENT FOR SANCTIFICATION?

It is this doctrine that is at stake more than any other in the "sufficiency debate" within Christian counseling. Most people would agree that the Bible is sufficient for salvation. But many are not sure that it is sufficient for sanctification. Instead of relying on biblical truth to help people with their problems, they are quick to offer the "insights" of psychoanalysis, long-term therapy, transactional analysis, behavior modification, selective abstraction, unconditional acceptance, dream analysis, hypnosis, and so on.

If biblical sanctification through spiritual growth is God's goal for our lives, then why don't counselors spend more time exploring this vital process? How can Christian psychological counselors skip over the issue of sanctification in the hope that some secular psychological exercise will bring the counselee the growth and maturity he or she needs?

It is our sincere desire to appeal to all Christian counselors (biblical or psychological) to re-examine the importance of Christian sanctification. We need to ask ourselves if we are really serious about the work of the Holy Spirit in the believer's life.

In his classic book *The Work of the Holy Spirit*, Octavius Winslow made this comment:

> Sanctification has its commencement and its daily growth in a principle of life implanted in the soul by the eternal Spirit. . . . The necessity for sanctification also springs from the work of Christ. The Lord Jesus became incarnate, and died as much for the sanctification as for the pardon and justification of His church; as much for her deliverance from the indwelling power of sin as from the condemnatory power of sin.[4]

The Bible assures us in 2 Thessalonians 2:13, "God has chosen you from the beginning for salvation through sanctification by the Spirit and faith in the truth." Again, we notice the importance of biblical truth as an essential agent in the process of sanctification, which involves a progressive conformity of the whole person to the divine nature. We are to become like Christ in personal holiness as we "let the word of Christ richly dwell within [us]" (Colossians 3:16).

Without regeneration and sanctification, there can be no permanent spiritual change in people. Christian counselors know this is true, but often forget it in practice. As soon as we begin exhorting an unbeliever to forgive his or her spouse, accept his or her responsibilities, or live by some spiritual principle, we are asking him or her to do something that is impossible for unregenerate people to do.

Ask yourself: When was the last time I seriously challenged a counselee to examine his or her faith? When was the last time I shared the life-changing gospel of Jesus Christ with a counselee? When was the last time I turned to the Bible to help my client evaluate his or her behavior, attitudes, or decisions? Then, ask yourself: Am I *really* doing *Christian* counseling, or just counseling?

AN APPEAL TO CHRISTIAN COUNSELORS

We have come to a time in the Christian counseling enterprise where we must begin asking ourselves the really tough questions about what we are doing. Is our counseling truly Christian? Is it firmly rooted in God's truth? Does our counseling really work? Can it be used of God to change lives?

We suggest that it is time for Christian counselors to take the following steps:

1. Self-Evaluation of Biblical Counseling

The time has come for those within the field of biblical counseling to provide a better self-analysis of the strengths and weaknesses of our counseling methodology. We cannot merely assume that because our approach is "biblical" that it is beyond critical evaluation. More research is necessary to develop guidelines that help validate the success and effectiveness of biblical counseling. There are several areas of counseling for which more resources are needed; for example, little has been written on counseling children or adolescents. Clearer guidelines need to be established to distinguish between psychically caused and spiritually caused problems. More emphasis needs to be placed on dealing with addictive patterns in counselees.

2. Projection of the Future of Biblical Counseling

Those of us working within the field of biblical counseling need to better develop a "self-portrait" of biblical counseling. John MacArthur and Wayne Mack have helped clarify many issues in their book *Introduction to Biblical Counseling* (1994). Ed Bulkley's works have also helped clarify several issues of concern for biblical counselors. His case studies especially illuminate the differences between biblical and non-biblical approaches. We would encourage more people to write from the biblical perspective. David Powlison and Edward Welch have much more to contribute to the future of biblical counseling in the days ahead.

3. Further Discussion Between Biblical and Psychological Counselors

We sincerely need more honest discussion and interaction between Christian biblical and psychological counselors—especially those who are actually doing counseling. Presently, there have been precious too few attempts for both "camps" to speak effectively to one another. We need more examination of each other's concerns with intellectual integrity and a renewed commitment to the sufficiency of Scripture in our professional and personal lives. We believe that many Christian psychological counselors have moved further away from their biblical roots than they ever intended initially. Many, like Chris Thurman, are now reevaluating whether they have gone too far and need to return to a more biblical approach. We need to encourage fellow counselors to feel free to discuss such matters without fear of criticism, rejection, intimidation, or closed-mindedness. Opening lines of communication and discussion will be helpful to the Christian community in general. What is at stake is greater than our individual differences. We who are committed to helping others must be committed to helping one another to deal more effectively with the implications of Scripture.

4. Elimination of Incorrect Caricatures of Others' Views of Counseling

It is time to eliminate closed-mindedness and pejorative labeling of representatives on both sides of the debate. Labels like "anti-intellectualism" or "psychoheresy" only further alienate us and prevent honest interaction. Godly counselors may differ in their views, but they are not the "enemy." Men like James Dobson, Larry Crabb, Jay Adams, and Wayne Mack have all made substantial contributions to the evangelical cause in America. Biblical and psychological Christian counselors are brothers and sisters in the faith whether or not they agree with one another. At the same time, being Christians does not exempt us from the need to question, evaluate, and hold one another accountable to the standards of biblical truth.

5. Renewed Commitment to Helping Hurting People

Most Christian counselors, whether biblical or psychological, genuinely want to help the people they counsel. Most sincerely believe their particular theory or methodology is helping people or they would discard it. Sometimes, however, in the theoretical debate over counseling theory and practice, it is easy to lose sight of the counselees themselves. They are the ones who need to benefit from the counsel we provide. We all need to commit ourselves afresh to helping those who are hurting. We need to ask ourselves if God is truly pleased with our counseling methods. Is our advice consistent with biblical truth? Are we really seeing progress in our counselees? Are they resolving their basic life issues? Are they maturing in their walk with God and their relationships with others?

6. Strengthen the Theological Basis of All Christian Counseling

One of the essential commitments of those who are biblical counselors is that they maintain theological integrity. If we do not have a solid grasp of theology, then we really cannot do counseling that is distinctively Christian in nature. Therefore, we appeal to Christian psychological counselors to strengthen their understanding of biblical theology. Theological study and research will help your counseling, not hurt it. Those lacking a formal theological background need to pursue alternate theological study—personal reading, external degree programs, or video, audio, and correspondence study. Some counselors may live in communities where they can attend an evangelical seminary to further their education or expand their personal knowledge of a consistent biblical theology. Without such a basis, there can be no real interaction of theology and psychology that is meaningful and purposeful.

7. Improve Biblical Exegesis in Order to Determine Counseling Theory and Methodology

Most evangelical Christians affirm a belief in the divine inspiration of Scripture. Yet, few are willing to do the hard work of biblical exegesis. If we are going to be consistent with biblical truth in our counseling, we must carefully examine the biblical passages on marriage, divorce, remarriage, family life, child-rearing, care for the elderly, personal responsibility, and spiritual growth. These are subjects on which the Bible speaks very clearly. We cannot neglect the biblical truths on these matters and expect to do truly Christian counseling. Tragically, many "Christian" counselors are woefully lacking in this regard. They are quick to adopt every new fad in counseling whether it is biblical or not, and they use psychological definitions rather than biblical. For example, the Bible speaks of worry as a sin (that is, lack of faith), whereas psychology defines sin as anxiety. In reality, they are one and the same. Philippians 4:6-7 deals with both worry and anxiety cognitively (thoughts), emotionally (feelings), and behaviorally (actions).

Biblical counselors believe that one of the great weaknesses of non-biblical Christian counselors is that their lack of theological or biblical expertise causes them to use the Bible devotionally, analogically, and often incorrectly. True exegesis involves much more than simply trying to read into a passage of Scripture a possible psychological parallel. Calling Peter a sanguine or suggesting that Moses suffered from rejection is eisegesis and not true exegesis of the text.

NO PREMIUM ON IGNORANCE

Several years ago while I (Howard) was a student at Dallas Theological Seminary, we had an exchange day with some students from Southern Methodist University. When we tried to discuss theological issues, we often found ourselves in totally different worlds. We didn't even "do theology" in the same way. But as our discussions progressed, it became obvious they were completely unaware of our beliefs and positions. At least some of us had read some of the more liberal theological works and knew where the students from the other university stood in terms of biblical truth.

Finally, I suggested, "I don't find any of our books in your library. Your institution functions as if we don't exist!"

Too many times, that same problem has been prevalent in Christian counseling circles. We can choose to ignore those with whom we differ, but to do so is to function in ignorance. In 1982, I (Ed) had the opportunity to lecture on biblical fundamentalism at the Harvard Divinity School as the guest of Dr. Harvey Cox. After a one-hour lecture and an hour of questions from the floor, I received a standing ovation from the divinity school student body. One student remarked afterwards, "I have never seen a real fundamentalist before!" To which Dr. Cox added, "Or read one either!"

Later that evening, Harvey, myself, Cal Thomas, and Richard Lovelace went to dinner together at the Harvard Faculty Club to discuss the evening's events.

"Ignorance is the great enemy of fundamentalism," Dr. Cox announced.

"What do you mean?" Cal Thomas asked.

"Ignorance of what fundamentalists really believe," Dr. Cox responded. "Most of our students know fundamentalism only through the lens of the secular media and liberal academia. Many of them have never spoken to a real one face to face before today!"

What was true on that occasion is all too often true in the debate between Christian biblical and psychological counselors. Many who are quick to criticize biblical counseling have never even talked to a real biblical counselor, nor have they seen biblical counseling in process. Their criticism is often based on speculation or assumption, not hard facts or personal observation.

WHERE DO WE GO FROM HERE?

It is our hope that in the future, non-biblical counselors will have a better and more informed understanding of who biblical counselors are and what they do. Our purpose in this volume has not been to rehash old arguments but to clarify the issues that distinguish our position. Biblical counseling is done by a wide range of professionals who work in various capacities. All of us, however, are equally committed to the sufficiency of Scripture as the absolute source of truth which defines *who* we are and *what* we do. Our ultimate confidence in helping people is not based upon any current psychological fad but upon the infallible truths of an inerrant Scripture.

As Dr. Leonard Poom of the University of Georgia has so aptly said, "'Therefore, we may conclude' does not apply in the social sciences. We can only say, 'It seems to be true that. . . .'"[5]

Scientific social research certainly has its legitimate place, but we all must recognize that we can never fully conclude that we have discovered ultimate truth from it. Its veracity is limited by its very nature. Therefore, it is too simplistic to suggest that "all truth is God's truth." In the arena of the social sciences, from a purely psychological perspective, we have no way of knowing when we have discovered God's truth—except as it is revealed in His Word.

Biblical truth is the ultimate truth. It is the propositional revelation of God's will for our lives. Without hesitation, the Bible proclaims its total sufficiency to provide "everything pertaining to life and godliness" (2 Peter 1:3). Scripture speaks to every area of personal and practical living; it is God's blueprint for our lives. Yes, it tells us how to get to heaven, but it also tells us how to make the journey until we get there.

TOTALLY
SUFFICIENT

CONTRIBUTORS

Gary L. Almy, M.D. is Associate Chief of Staff at Edward Hines, Jr. Hospital, Department of Veteran Affairs. He is also Associate Clinical Professor in the Department of Psychiatry at the Stritch School of Medicine at Loyola University in Chicago. Dr. Almy coauthored *Addicted to Recovery* (Harvest House). He received his M.D. from the University of Nebraska and his psychiatric training at the University of California in San Francisco and the U.S. Naval Hospital in Oakland, California.

Wilson Benton, Jr. is the senior pastor of the Kirk of the Hills Presbyterian Church in St. Louis, Missouri. He is also an adjunct professor at Covenant Theological Seminary and is a past moderator of the Presbyterian Church of America. He holds an M.Div. degree from Columbia Theological Seminary and a Ph.D. in New Testament from the University of Edinburgh (Scotland). Dr. Benton is a national leader among evangelical pastors.

Edward G. Dobson is the senior pastor of Calvary Church in Grand Rapids, Michigan. He is also a consulting editor with *Leadership Journal* and Senior Editor for *Christianity Today*. Ed holds B.S. and M.A. degrees in religion and an Ed.D. in higher education from the University of Virginia. Moody Bible Institute recently honored Dr. Dobson, naming him "Pastor of the Year" in 1993. Ed has authored several books, including *Simplicity: Finding Order, Freedom and Fulfillment* (Zondervan).

Howard A. Eyrich is the senior pastor of Knollwood Presbyterian Church in Sylacauga, Alabama. Dr. Eyrich also serves as Dean of Biblical Counseling for Trinity Theological Seminary and Professor of Biblical Counseling at Birmingham Theological

Seminary in Alabama. He was formerly Professor of Practical Theology at Covenant Theological Seminary in St. Louis, Missouri. He holds an M.A. from Liberty University; Th.M., Dallas Theological Seminary; D.Min., Western Conservative Baptist Seminary. Howard is the author of the highly successful premarital counseling text *Three to Get Ready* (Baker) and *The Christian Handbook on Aging* (Growth Advantage).

Ronald E. Hawkins is the president of Western Seminary, Portland, Oregon. He previously served as Dean of the Seminary at Liberty University in Virginia. Dr. Hawkins holds a B.A. degree from Barrington College; M.Div., Gordon-Conwell Seminary; D.Min., Westminster Theological Seminary; Ed.D. from Virginia Polytechnic Institute and State University. Ron is a licensed professional counselor, educator, administrator, and ordained minister.

Edward E. Hindson is the associate pastor of the 9,000-member Rehoboth Baptist Church in Atlanta, Georgia. Dr. Hindson is also adjunct professor of religion at Liberty University in Virginia. He holds an M.A. degree from Evangelical Divinity School; Th.M., Grace Theological Seminary; D.Min., Westminster Seminary in Philadelphia; D.Phil, University of South Africa. He has authored numerous books, edited a Bible commentary and a study Bible, and served on the translation committee for the New King James Version. Ed is also one of the co-hosts for the nationally syndicated *Care Givers* radio broadcast.

Arnold G. Hyndman earned an A.B. in Biology from Princeton University and a Ph.D. in Biology from the University of California, Los Angeles (UCLA). His expertise is the development of the nervous system. He has authored numerous articles in technical journals. He is currently a professor of Biological Sciences and the dean of Livingston College, Rutgers University in New Jersey.

Wayne A. Mack is the chairman and professor of Biblical Counseling at The Master's College in Santa Clarita, California. Wayne holds an A.B. from Wheaton College; M.Div., Philadelphia Theological Seminary; D.Min., Westminster Theological Seminary. He has authored numerous books, including *Strengthening Your Marriage, Your Family God's Way, How to Pray Effectively,* and he coauthored *Introduction to Biblical Counseling* (Word) with John MacArthur, Jr. Wayne has over 25 years of counseling experience.

Paul Madtes, Jr. earned an M.S. in biophysics and a Ph.D. in biochemistry from Texas A & M University and a Ph.D. in biblical counseling from Trinity Theological Seminary. He has studied the development of the nervous system and has published extensively in this field. He is presently serving as the chairman of the Biology Department for Mount Vernon Nazarene College in Mount Vernon, Ohio, and is adjunct professor at the Ohio State University College of Medicine in Columbus, Ohio.

David Powlison is the editor of the *Journal of Pastoral Counseling*, counsels at the Christian Counseling & Educational Foundation, and teaches pastoral counseling at Westminster Theological Seminary in Philadelphia. He holds an A.B., Harvard College; M.Div., Westminster Seminary; Ph.D. University of Pennsylvania. Dr. Powlison has written numerous articles on the philosophy of biblical counseling and is recognized for his contributions to the development of a philosophy of biblical counseling.

C. Dwayne Shafer, M.D. is a medical doctor in the practice of family medicine in Stephenville, Texas (near Fort Worth) and he also serves as the pastor of the Stephenville Baptist Church. He holds a B.S. from Texas Tech University, an M.D. from the University of Texas at Houston, and a Ph.D. from Trinity Theological Seminary. Dr. Shafer did his family practice residency at the Baylor College of Medicine in Waco, Texas.

Chris Thurman is a licensed psychologist in private practice in Austin, Texas. He holds a Ph.D. in counseling psychology from the University of Texas at Austin. Dr. Thurman is the author of the bestsellers *The Lies We Believe, If Christ Were Your Counselor,* and *Self-Help or Self-Destruction?* (Thomas Nelson). Chris is currently one of the co-hosts on the nationally syndicated *Care Givers* radio broadcast. He is a powerful communicator and popular seminar speaker.

Edward T. Welch is a counselor and lecturer at the Christian Counseling & Educational Foundation in Philadelphia, Pennsylvania and serves as adjunct professor at Westminster Theological Seminary. He holds an M.Div. from Biblical Theological Seminary and a Ph.D. in neuropsychology from the University of Utah. He is the coauthor of *Addictive Behavior* (Baker).

BIBLIOGRAPHY

Adams, Jay E.

— *Competent to Counsel.* Grand Rapids, MI: Baker Book House, 1970.

— *The Christian Counselor's Manual.* Phillipsburg, NJ: Presbyterian & Reformed, 1973.

— *The Use of the Scriptures in Counseling.* Grand Rapids, MI: Baker Book House, 1975.

— *More Than Redemption.* Phillipsburg, NJ: Presbyterian & Reformed, 1979.

— *Ready to Restore: A Layman's Guide to Christian Counseling.* Grand Rapids, MI: Baker Book House, 1981.

— *How to Help People Change.* Grand Rapids, MI: Zondervan Publishing House, 1986.

Almy, Gary

— *Addicted to Recovery.* Eugene, OR: Harvest House Publishers, 1994.

Benner, David G., ed.

— *Christian Counseling and Psychotherapy.* Grand Rapids, MI: Baker Book House, 1987.

— *Baker Encyclopedia of Psychology.* Grand Rapids, MI: Baker Book House, 1985.

Bobgan, Martin and Deidre

— *The Psychological Way/The Spiritual Way.* Minneapolis: Bethany Fellowship, 1979.

— *How to Counsel from Scripture.* Chicago: Moody Press, 1985.

Bulkley, Ed

— *Why Christians Can't Trust Psychology*. Eugene, OR: Harvest House Publishers, 1993.

Collins, Gary

— *Christian Counseling: A Comprehensive Guide*. Dallas: Word Books, 1980.
— *Helping People Grow: Practical Approaches to Christian Counseling*. Santa Ana, CA: Vision House, 1980.
— *Psychology & Theology*. Nashville: Abingdon Press, 1981.

Crabb, Lawrence J.

— *Basic Principles of Biblical Counseling*. Grand Rapids, MI: Zondervan Publishing House, 1975.
— *Effective Biblical Counseling*. Grand Rapids, MI: Zondervan Publishing House, 1977.
— *Understanding People*. Grand Rapids, MI: Zondervan Publishing House, 1987.
— *Inside Out*. Colorado Springs: NavPress, 1988.

Dobson, James

— *Dr. Dobson Answers Your Questions*. Wheaton, IL: Tyndale House Publishers, 1982.
— *Emotions: Can You Trust Them?* Ventura, CA: Regal Books, 1980.

Farnsworth, Kirk

— *Wholehearted Integration: Harmonizing Psychology and Christianity Through Word and Deed*. Grand Rapids, MI: Baker Book House, 1985.

Jeeves, Malcom A.

— *Psychology & Christianity: The View Both Ways*. Downers Grove, IL: InterVarsity Press, 1976.

Jones, Stanton & R. Butman

— *Modern Psycho-Therapies: A Comprehensive Christian Appraisal*. Downers Grove, IL: InterVarsity Press, 1991.

Kilpatrick, William K.

— *Psychological Seduction*. Nashville: Thomas Nelson, 1983.

Koteskey, Ronald L.

— *General Psychology for Christian Counselors*. Nashville: Abingdon Press, 1983.

Kruis, John

— *Quick Scripture Reference for Counseling*. Grand Rapids, MI: Baker, 1988.

LaHaye, Tim

— *Spirit-Controlled Temperament*. Wheaton, IL: Tyndale House Publishers, 1970.
— *Transformed Temperaments*. Wheaton, IL: Tyndale House Publishers, 1971.

MacArthur, John, Jr.

— *Our Sufficiency in Christ*. Dallas: Word Publishing, 1991.

MacArthur, John, Jr. & Wayne A. Mack

— *Introduction to Biblical Counseling*. Dallas: Word Publishing, 1994.

Mack, Wayne A.

— *A Homework Manual for Biblical Counseling*, 2 vols. Phillipsburg, NJ: Presbyterian & Reformed, 1980.

McGee, Robert

— *The Search for Significance*. Dallas: Word, 1985.

McMinn, Mark R.

— *Psychology, Theology and Spirituality* (AACC Counseling Library). Wheaton, IL: Tyndale House Publishers, 1996.

Minirth, Frank B.

— *Christian Psychiatry*. Old Tappan, NJ: Fleming H. Revell, 1977.

Minirth, Frank & Paul Meier

— *Happiness Is a Choice*. Grand Rapids, MI: Baker Book House, 1978.

Owen, James

— *Christian Psychology's War on God's Word*. Santa Barbara, CA: East Gate Publishers, 1993.

Powlison, David

— "Integration or Inundation?" in *Power Religion*, ed. Michael Horton. Chicago: Moody Press, 1992, pp. 191-218.
— "How Shall We Cure Troubled Souls?" in *The Coming Evangelical Crisis*, ed. John H. Armstrong. Chicago: Moody Press, 1996, pp. 207-226.
— "Which Presuppositions? Secular Psychology and Categories of Biblical Thought," *Journal of Theology & Psychology*, 12, no. 4 (1984), pp. 270-78.

Thurman, Chris

— *The Lies We Believe*. Nashville: Thomas Nelson, 1989.
— *Self-Help or Self-Destruction?* Nashville: Thomas Nelson, 1996.

Vitz, Paul C.

— *Psychology as Religion: The Cult of Self-Worship*. Grand Rapids, MI: Wm. B. Eerdmans Publishing Company, 1977.

Welch, Edward & Gary Shogren

— *Addictive Behavior*. Grand Rapids, MI: Baker Book House, 1994.
— *Counselor's Guide to the Brain and its Disorders*. Grand Rapids, MI: Zondervan, 1991.

Wright, Norman.

— *Training Christians to Counsel*, Eugene, OR: Harvest House, 1977.

NOTES

Chapter 1—Is the Bible Really Enough?

1. Mark R. McMinn, *Psychology, Theology, and Spirituality in Christian Counseling* (Wheaton, IL: Tyndale House, 1996). McMinn is to be commended for the spirit and tone of this volume as well as its practical application to specific counseling cases.

2. See Jay E. Adams, *Competent to Counsel* (Grand Rapids: Baker Book House, 1970); *The Christian Counselor's Manual* (Phillipsburg, NJ: Presbyterian & Reformed, 1973); *More Than Redemption* (Phillipsburg, NJ: Presbyterian and Reformed, 1979); *The Use of Scripture in Counseling* (Grand Rapids: Baker Book House, 1975).

3. See, for example, Larry Crabb, *Understanding People* (Grand Rapids: Zondervan Publishing House, 1987), pp. 54-58, 129. Crabb refers to biblical counseling as "a nonthinking and simplistic understanding of life and its problems . . . (filled with) superficial adjustments while psychotherapists, with or without biblical foundation . . . do a better job than the church of restoring troubled people to more effective functioning."

4. "Roots and Shoots of Christian Psychology," *Christianity Today*, 40:10 (Sept. 16, 1996), p. 77. The chart appears within the longer article "Hurting Helpers" by Steve Rabey (pp. 76-80, 108-10).

5. John MacArthur, Jr., and Wayne A. Mack, *Introduction to Biblical Counseling* (Dallas: Word Publishing, 1994), pp. 10-12.

6. See Heinrich Meng and Ernst Freud, eds., *Psychoanalysis and Faith* (New York: Basic Books, 1963), pp. 63, 110.

7. John MacArthur, Jr., *Our Sufficiency in Christ* (Dallas: Word Publishing, 1991), p. 20.

8. Steve Rabey, "Hurting Helpers," *Christianity Today*, 40:10 (Sept. 16, 1996), p. 78.

9. Gary Collins as quoted in *Christianity Today*, 40:10 (Sept. 16, 1996), p. 80.

10. John Murray, *Collected Writings of John Murray* (Edinburgh: Banner of Truth, 1976), p. 22.

11. Chris Thurman, *Self-Help or Self-Destruction?* (Nashville: Thomas Nelson, 1996), p. 167.

12. Larry Crabb, *Effective Biblical Counseling* (Grand Rapids: Zondervan, 1977), pp. 47-52. Crabb suggests a model for Christian counseling that combines nouthetic confrontation with paraklitic comfort and exhortation (pp. 147-48).

13. Cornelius Van Til, *Christian Theistic Evidences* (Phillipsburg, NJ: Presbyterian & Reformed, 1976), p. 67.

14. See Mark McMinn, *Psychology, Theology, and Spirituality*, p. 25. Writing as a representative of the American Association of Christian Counselors, McMinn reflects on the struggle of Christian counselors on the issue of sufficiency, though he does not use this term. McMinn acknowledges that "a Christianized form of therapy can be built on flawed, misleading and damaging worldview assumptions." Nevertheless, he later admits on page 34, "Most of us do not want to replace our theoretical commitments to behavioral, cognitive, psychodynamic, family systems, and other forms of therapy."

15. Noel Weeks, *The Sufficiency of Scripture* (Edinburgh: Banner of Truth, 1988), p. 167.

16. Ibid., p. 182.

Chapter 2—What Is Biblical Counseling?

1. John MacArthur, Jr., *Our Sufficiency in Christ* (Dallas: Word Publishing, 1991), pp. 27, 72. In the last paragraph quoted, MacArthur is referring to attempts to help people based on secular humanistic theories, techniques, and therapies. He is not referring to the kind of counseling being described in this chapter, as is evidenced from many of his other writings and his coauthored book entitled *Introduction to Biblical Counseling*, as well as the facts that the church he pastors has a very active counselor training program and counseling ministry, and that the Master's College, of which he is president, has an undergraduate major in biblical counseling and a graduate program leading to an M.A. in biblical counseling.

2. More about the role of the church in the lives of believers may be found in the book *Life in the Father's House: A Member's Guide to the Local Church*, Wayne Mack and David Swavely (Phillipsburg, NJ: Presbyterian and Reformed, 1996).

3. *Introduction to Biblical Counseling*, eds. John MacArthur and Wayne Mack (Dallas: Word Publishing, 1994), pp. 3-20.

4. Ibid., p. 69.

5. J. Harold Ellens, *Biblical Themes*, as cited in *Introduction to Biblical Counseling*, p. 71.

6. J. Harold Ellens, *Journal of Psychology and Theology*, 9:4, 1981, p. 320.

7. Doug Bookman, in *Introduction to Biblical Counseling*, p. 79.

8. Ibid., p. 90.

9. English, *Integrationist's Critique*, as cited in *Introduction to Biblical Counseling*, p. 229.

10. Important critiques related to integrationist attempts are found in *Introduction to Biblical Counseling*, pp. 63-97; *Power Religion*, ed. Michael S. Horton, see David Powlison, author of chapter 8, and Edward Welch,

author of chapter 9 (Chicago: Moody Press, 1992), pp. 191-218, 219-43; David Powlison, *Journal of Psychology and Theology* 12, no. 4, (1984): 270-78; Jay Adams, *Competent to Counsel* (Grand Rapids, MI: Zondervan, 1970); Jay Adams, *A Theology of Christian Counseling* (Grand Rapids, MI: Zondervan, 1979); Jay Adams, *Teaching to Observe* (Woodruff, SC: Timeless Texts, 1995); Ed Bulkley, *Why Christians Can't Trust Psychology* (Eugene, OR: Harvest House, 1993); David F. Wells, *No Place for Truth* (Grand Rapids, MI: Eerdmans, 1993); John MacArthur, Jr., *Our Sufficiency in Christ* (Dallas: Word Publishing, 1991); John MacArthur, Jr. *The Vanishing Conscience* (Dallas: Word Publishing, 1994); John MacArthur, *Reckless Faith* (Wheaton, IL: Crossway Books, 1994); Noel Weeks, *The Sufficiency of Scripture* (Edinburgh: Banner of Truth, 1988), pp. 3-46, 167-82; James Owen, *Christian Psychology's War on the Word* (Santa Barbara, CA: East Gate Publishers, 1993).

11. Russell Baker, "Education's Duplicity, Uselessness," *The New York Times*, March 16, 1996.

12. Ibid.

13. The word *noetic* is related to the Greek word *nous*, which is translated by the English word mind. This word denotes "the seat of reflection, consciousness, comprising the faculties of perception and understanding, and those of feeling, judging, and determining," as defined in W.E. Vine, *An Expository Dictionary of New Testament Words* (Westwood: Revell, 1957), p. 69.

14. *See* Romans 1:18-2:23; 1 Kings 8:46; Psalm 51:5; 58:3; Isaiah 53:6; 64:6; Psalm 14:1-13; Ephesians 2:1-3; Romans 8:8.

15. Edward Reynolds, *The Sinfulness of Sin* (Ligonier, PA: Sola Deo Gloria, 1992 reprint of 1826 ed.), p. 123.

16. David Powlison, in *Introduction to Biblical Counseling*, pp. 365-66.

17. Wayne Mack, in *Introduction to Biblical Counseling*, p. 254.

18. Richard Pratt, *Every Thought Captive* (Phillipsburg, NJ: Presbyterian & Reformed, 1979), p. 17.

19. Ibid.

20. Ibid.

21. Jay Adams, *How to Help People Change* (Grand Rapids, MI: Zondervan, 1986), pp. 23-24.

22. *See* Adams' book *How to Help People Change* for a fuller explanation and application of 2 Timothy 3:14-17.

23. Michael Green, *Second Epistle of Peter and the Epistle of Jude* (Grand Rapids, MI: Eerdmans, 1968), p. 64.

24 David Powlison, in *Introduction to Biblical Counseling*, p. 365.

25. In *Introduction to Biblical Counseling*, eds. MacArthur and Mack, chapters 10-16, 20. Wayne Mack has developed many books and audio and videotapes of counseling courses, including tapes dealing with a biblical approach to counseling on a variety of specific issues (a catalog listing these materials is available by writing to him at 21726 W. Placerita Canyon Rd., Santa Clarita, CA 91322); Christian Counseling and Educational Foundation West has videotapes of several counseling courses, and they offer

many training courses (3495 College Avenue, San Diego, CA 92115); Christian Counseling and Educational Foundation East offers courses on biblical counseling and produces an excellent journal—*The Biblical Counseling Journal*—for biblical counselors (1803 East Willow Grove Ave., Laverock, PA 19118); the National Association of Nouthetic Counselors (NANC) sponsors conferences, produces a biblical counseling publication, and has audio and videotapes on numerous "how to" issues (NANC, 5526 State Road 26 East, Lafayette, IN 47905); Jay Adams has written numerous books and produced many audio and videotapes on various biblical counseling issues (Woodruff, SC: Timeless Texts); Gary Almy, *Addicted to Recovery* (Eugene, OR: Harvest House); Ed Bulkley, *Only God Can Heal the Wounded Heart* (Eugene, OR: Harvest House); David Powlison, *Power Encounters* (Grand Rapids, MI: Baker Book House); Edward Welch, *Counselor's Guide to the Brain and Its Disorder: Knowing the Difference Between Sin and Disease* (Grand Rapids, MI: Zondervan); William Playfair, *The Useful Lie* (Wheaton, IL: Crossway Books); D. Martyn Lloyd-Jones, *Spiritual Depression: Its Causes and Its Cure* (Grand Rapids, MI: Eerdmans); Michael Bobick, *From Slavery to Sonship: A Biblical Psychology for Pastoral Counseling* (available from Grace Book Shack, 13248 Roscoe Blvd., Sun Valley, CA 91352); Sound Word Cassettes carries many audio and videotapes on counseling various problems biblically (430 Boyd Circle, P.O. Box 2035, Mail Station, Michigan City, IN 46360); Westminster Theological Seminary (Chestnut Hill, P.O. Box 27009, Philadelphia, PA 19118, and 1725 Bear Valley Parkway, Escondido, CA 92027) offers many counseling courses that provide a biblical approach on various counseling issues; degree programs are available in biblical counseling at Trinity College and Theological Seminary, 4233 Medwel Dr., Box 717, Newburgh, IN 47629-0171.

Chapter 3—Does Biblical Counseling Really Work?

1. C.S. Lewis, as commonly quoted in numerous works.

2. In the first part of the twentieth century, American Bible-believers concentrated their apologetic energies in two directions. First, they argued for classic theological orthodoxy (e.g., A.C. Dixon, ed., *The Fundamentals*, and J.G. Machen, *Christianity and Liberalism*). Second, they took on geology and evolutionary biology. I have wondered what would have happened if Bible-believers in the 1920s had concentrated their apologetic energies on psychology, psychotherapy, and the mental health system rather than on biology and geology.

3. "Lois" is a composite of various real people with similar problems and histories. All the details have been altered, but the thematic unity of her life has been maintained.

4. I've written at much greater length on the Bible's view of these "First Great Commandment" issues in "Idols of the Heart and 'Vanity Fair'" (*The Journal of Biblical Counseling*, 13:2, Winter 1995, pp. 35-50) and "How Shall We Cure Troubled Souls?" in John Armstrong, ed., *The Coming Evangelical Crisis* (Chicago: Moody, 1996), pp. 207-25.

5. J. Budziszewski, "The Illusion of Moral Neutrality," *First Things* (August/September 1993), p. 36.

6. Jay Adams' *Christian Counselor's Manual* (Philadelphia: Presbyterian & Reformed, 1973) abounds with specific analyses and descriptions of behavioral and attitudinal lifestyles, and the biblical way of "putting off and putting on."

7. An earlier version of this section was published as "Critiquing Modern Integrationists," *Journal of Biblical Counseling*, XI:3 (Spring 1993), pp. 24-34. My shift to "we" and "our" reflects my participation in a widespread biblical counseling movement.

8. See, for example, Jay Adams' *What About Nouthetic Counseling?* (Grand Rapids: Baker, 1976), p. 12. Question: "Don't you think that we can learn something from psychologists?" Answer: "Yes, we can learn a lot; I certainly have. That answer surprised you, didn't it? If it did, you have been led to believe, no doubt, that nouthetic counselors are obscurantists who see no good in psychology." Adams goes on to clarify what he opposes, what he embraces, and why.

9. This brief history summarizes my article "Integration or Inundation?" in Michael Horton, ed., *Power Religion* (Chicago: Moody Press, 1992), pp. 191-18. For further reading on the relationship of biblical counseling to the integrationistic Christian psychologists, see Jay Adams, "Reflections on the History of Biblical Counseling," in Harvie Conn, ed., *Practical Theology and the Ministry of the Church, 1952–1984: Essays in Honor of Edmund P. Clowney* (Phillipsburg, N.J.: Presbyterian and Reformed, 1990). For background reading, see E. Brook Holifield, *A History of Pastoral Care in America: From Salvation to Self-Realization* (Nashville: Abingdon, 1983). Holifield's subtitle tells it all. He ends his narrative with the mainline churches, circa 1960. The integration movement in conservative churches since then is a further illustration of Holifield's thesis. Biblical counseling is a movement to counter the tide.

10. Frank Minirth, Paul Meier and Robert Hemfelt, *Love Is a Choice: Recovery for Codependent Relationships* (Nashville: Thomas Nelson, 1989); David Seamands, *Healing for Damaged Emotions* (Wheaton: Victor Books, 1981); Robert Schuller, *Self-Esteem: The New Reformation* (Waco, TX: Word Books, 1982); William Backus and Marie Chapian, *Telling Yourself the Truth* (Minneapolis: Bethany House, 1980).

11. Stanton Jones and Richard Butman, *Modern Psychotherapies: A Comprehensive Christian Appraisal* (Downers Grove, IL: InterVarsity Press, 1991), p. 411 and pp. 29ff.

12. Stanton Jones and Richard Butman (see Note 11); Siang-Yang Tan, *Lay Counseling: Equipping Christians for a Helping Ministry* (Grand Rapids: Zondervan, 1991). Jones and Butman teach at Wheaton College, and Tan teaches at Fuller Seminary.

13. Larry Crabb, *Understanding People: Deep Longings for Relationship* (Grand Rapids: Zondervan, 1987).

14. These comments apply consistently to Crabb's books up through *Inside Out*. His recent book, *Men and Women: Enjoying the Difference*, seems to replace the needs model with a sin model: self-justifying self-centeredness and demandingness are the biggest problems, therefore forgiveness is the greatest need. If this shift proves enduring, then Crabb's stated desire to

be biblical, not integrationist, is bearing tangible fruit, and his counseling theory is shifting in a more biblical direction.

15. James Davison Hunter, *American Evangelicalism: Conservative Religion and the Quandary of Modernity* (New Brunswick, NJ: Rutgers University Press, 1983). Note the chapter, "Accommodation: The Domestication of Belief," in particular, pages 91-99.

16. Ibid., p. 95.

17. Ibid., p. 99.

18. Ibid., p. 94.

19. It is curious that opponents of psychologizing the church are often characterized as basically mean-spirited, while the psychologists who eviscerate biblical Christianity with self-conscious intent are portrayed as full of truth, wisdom, and love for people. This is no excuse for mean-spirited biblical counselors, but let's recognize that secularism demonstrates the more significant and characterological hostility.

20. Jay E. Adams, *Competent to Counsel* (Presbyterian & Reformed, 1970), p. xxi. Compare *Christian Counselor's Manual* (Presbyterian & Reformed, 1973), pp. 76-93; "Counseling and the Sovereignty of God" in *Lectures on Counseling* (Grand Rapids: Zondervan, 1975, 1976, 1977), pp. 59-72. "Integration," *Journal of Pastoral Practice*, VI:1 (1983), pp. 3-7 (reprinted in *How to Help People Change* [Grand Rapids: Zondervan, 1986, pp. 33-40]).

21. Adams and other biblical counselors have sometimes used psychology in a third way, as a co-belligerent. The intramural critiques one psychologist makes of another—e.g. Szasz's and Mowrer's indictments of the psychiatric establishment—have buttressed the normative presuppositional critique made from Scripture. This is a subset of both the provocative and illustrational uses. For example, O.H. Mowrer's belligerency to the psychodynamic establishment played a provocative role in the founding of nouthetic counseling as a distinctively biblical "anti-psychiatry." For example, when Carol Tavris criticizes hydraulic energy models of anger and the therapeutic practice of catharsis for anger, she buttresses a biblical critique of the same things. Among the critics of psychology, Martin and Deidre Bobgan are the ones who most frequently use psychology as their co-belligerent. They frequently muster counter-evidential research from secular psychologists to debunk the speculative pop psychology Christians drink in.

22. See Jay Adams, *More Than Redemption: A Theology of Christian Counseling*, p. 101 and *Communicating with 20th Century Man* (Phillipsburg, NJ: Presbyterian & Reformed, 1979) for discussions of the descriptive utility of sociology if under the reign of biblical presuppositions.

23. See Jay E. Adams, *The Christian Counselor's Manual* (Philadelphia: Presbyterian & Reformed, 1974), pp. 76-93, for a fuller portrayal of how biblical presuppositions demand seeing the antithesis and enable a reinterpretive labor. For specific examples of reinterpretation of secular observation, see David Powlison, "Human Defensiveness: The Third Way," *The Journal of Pastoral Practice*, VIII:1 (1985), pp. 40-55; "Idols of the Heart and 'Vanity Fair'" (*The Journal of Biblical Counseling*, Winter 1995, pp. 35-50); and "How Shall We Cure Troubled Souls?" in John Armstrong, ed., *The Coming Evangelical Crisis* (Chicago: Moody, 1996), pp. 207-25. "Integration

or Inundation?", in Michael Horton, ed., *Power Religion* (Chicago: Moody Press, 1992), pp. 191-218; and "What Do You Feel?" *The Journal of Pastoral Practice*, X:4 (1992), pp. 50-61.

24. Jay E. Adams, *The Christian Counselor's Manual*, pp. 124ff.

25. Of course we do not always need to utilize that intervening *re*interpretive step, if we begin with biblical categories. Ideally, we—and any psychologists worthy of the name—will gather data about people with biblical categories operative from the start.

26. Jay E. Adams' *Studies in Preaching, Volume II: Audience Adaptation in the Sermons and Speeches of Paul* (Philadelphia: Presbyterian & Reformed, 1976) presents a challenge to ministers of the Word to labor at adapting truth without accommodating it.

Chapter 5—Is There a Psychiatrist in the House?

1. *Diagnostic and Statistical Manual of Mental Disorders*, 3d ed. rev. (Washington, D.C.: American Psychiatric Association, 1987).

2. Kaplan & Sadock, *Comprehensive Textbook of Psychiatry*, 5th ed. (Baltimore: Williams & Wilkins, 1989).

3. Leff, "International variations in the diagnosis of psychiatric illness," *British Journal of Psychiatry* (131:329-38, 1977).

4. N. Kreitman, "The reliability of psychiatric diagnosis," *Journal of Mental Science* (107:876-86, 1961).

5. Taylor, Sierles, and Abrams, *General Hospital Psychiatry* (New York: The Free Press, 1985). This textbook is an excellent example of the kind of thinking that's behind the phenemenological approach to psychiatry. A reading list on that approach would include these titles:

    M.A. Taylor and J.P. Heiser, "Phenomenology: An alternative approach to the diagnosis of mental illness," *Comprehensive Psychiatry* (12:480-486, 1971).

    Karl Jaspers, *General Psychopathology* (Manchester, England: Manchester Univ. Press, 1963).

    Kurt Schneider, *Clinical Psychopathology* (New York: Grune & Stratton, 1959).

6. Frank Fish, *An Outline of Psychiatry*, 2d ed. (Bristol, England: John Wright & Sons, 1968).

7. Taylor, Sierles, and Abrams, *General Hospital Psychiatry*, p. 218.

8. Ibid., p. 287.

9. J.B. Kurionsky, et al., "Trends in the frequency of schizophrenia by different diagnostic criteria," *American Journal of Psychiatry* (134:631-36, 1977).

10. J.P. Feighner, E. Robins, S.B. Guze, et al., "Diagnostic criteria for use in psychiatric research," *Journal of General Psychiatry* (26:57-63, 1972).

11. Wilson, et al., *Harrison's Principles of Internal Medicine*, 12th ed. (New York: McGraw-Hill, 1991).

12. Ibid.

13. Ibid.

14. Ibid.

15. *See* 2 Corinthians 12:7: "To keep me from becoming conceited . . . there was given me a thorn in my flesh . . . to torment me" (NIV).

16. *See* Hebrews 12:7,10-11: "Endure hardship as discipline; God is treating you as sons. . . . for our good that we may share in his holiness. . . . produc[ing] a harvest of righteousness and peace for those who have been trained by it" (NIV).

17. Moses, Miriam, Uzzah, Jeroboam, Gehazi, Ananias and Sapphira, and Herod were all subject to punitive suffering delivered by God for their sins. Paul said to Elymas (child of devil, full of deceit, enemy of the right and perverter of truth), "Now the hand of the Lord is against you. You are going to be blind, and for a time you will be unable to see the light of the sun" (Acts 13:11 NIV).

18. *See* John 9:1-4, especially verse 3: "This happened so that the work of the God might be displayed in his life" (NIV).

19. *See* Genesis 1:27: "God created man in his own image, in the image of God he created him" (NIV).

20. *See* 2 Corinthians 4:16: "Do not lose heart. Though outwardly we are wasting away, yet inwardly we are being renewed day by day" (NIV).

21. *See* 2 Corinthians 4:18: "We fix our eyes not on what is seen, but on what is unseen. For what is seen is temporary, but what is unseen is eternal" (NIV).

22. *See* Matthew 10:28: "Do not be afraid of those who kill the body but cannot kill the soul" (NIV).

23. *See* Jeremiah 17:9: "The heart is deceitful above all things and beyond cure. Who can understand it?"

24. *See* Genesis 3:5: "God knows that when you eat of it your eyes will be opened, and you will be like God, knowing good and evil."

25. Sigmund Freud, *An Outline of Psychoanalysis* (New York: W.W. Norton, 1949).

26. *See* Jeremiah 17:10: "I the LORD search the heart and examine the mind, to reward a man according to his conduct, according to what his deeds deserve."

27. *See* John 15:22: "If I had not come and spoken to them, they would not be guilty of sin. Now, however, they have no excuse for their sin"; and Romans 1:20: "Since the creation of the world God's invisible qualities— his eternal power and divine nature—have been clearly seen, being understood from what has been made, so that men are without excuse" (NIV).

28. *See* Romans 3:19: "Now we know that whatever the law says, it says to those who are under the law, so that every mouth may be silenced and the whole world held accountable to God" (NIV).

29. *See* Proverbs 30:11-12 (NIV): "There are those who curse their fathers and do not bless their mothers; those who are pure in their own eyes and yet are not cleansed of their filth." Also, Ezekiel 18:20: "The soul who sins is the one who will die. The son will not share the guilt of the father, nor will

the father share the guilt of the son. The righteousness of the righteous man will be credited to him, and the wickedness of the wicked will be charged against him" (NIV); and Exodus 20:12: "Honor your father and your mother, so that you may live long in the land the LORD your God is giving you" (NIV).

30. *See* John 3:21: "Whoever lives by the truth comes into the light, so that it may be seen plainly that what he has done has been done through God" (NIV).

31. *See* Genesis 1:27-28: "So God created man in his own image . . . [to] rule over . . . every living creature"; and Genesis 2:7 (NIV): "The LORD God formed the man from the dust of the ground and breathed into his nostrils the breath of life [spirit], and the man became a living being" (NIV). *See also* Psalm 8:5-8: ". . . a little lower than the heavenly beings . . . ruler over the works of your hands; you put everything under his feet" (NIV); and Romans 8:14,16: "Those who are led by the Spirit of God are sons of God. . . . The Spirit himself testifies with our spirit that we are God's children" (NIV).

32. *See* 1 Corinthians 5:5: ". . . sinful nature [flesh] may be destroyed and his spirit saved on the day of the Lord" (NIV).

33. *See* James 2:26: "As the body without the spirit is dead, so faith without deeds is dead" (NIV).

34. Throughout Scripture "heart" (Hebrew *leb*, or *lebab*; Greek *kardia*) generally refers to the mind of man: his character, emotions, thinking, will, understanding, reflection, and memory ability. Throughout the New Testament the various Greek words translated "mind" refer to the same mental faculties. Similarly, spirit (Greek *pneuma*) and soul (Greek *psuche*) refer repeatedly to those very same mental faculties. Note that Hebrews 4:12 says, "The word of God is . . . sharper than any double-edged sword, it penetrates even to dividing soul and spirit, joints and marrow; it judges the thoughts and attitudes of the heart" (NIV). Only God can distinguish between heart, soul, spirit, and mind, but we do understand all these to be the "mind" of man, the seat of his spirit and clearly differentiated from but inseparable in this life from the body.

35. *See* Ezekiel 16:30: "How weak-willed you are" (NIV); *see also* Romans 6:19: "You are weak in your natural selves" (NIV).

36. *See* Genesis 3:16-19f (NIV): "pains in childbearing; with pain you will give birth . . . painful toil . . . thorns and thistles for you . . . sweat of your brow . . . to dust you will return" (NIV).

37. *See* Jeremiah 17:9-10.

38. *See* Colossians 2:8: "See to it that no one takes you captive through hollow and deceptive philosophy, which depends on human tradition and the basic principles of this world rather than on Christ" (NIV).

39. G. Zilboorg & G.W. Selesnick, *A History of Medical Psychology* (New York: Norton, 1941).

40. Franz Alexander & S.T. Selesnick, *The History of Psychiatry* (New York: Harper Row, 1961).

41. Wilhelm Greisinger, *Mental Pathology and Therapeutics* (1817–1868).

42. Edward Welch, "12-Steps and Co-Dependency," workshop at National Association of Nouthetic Counselors annual meeting, October 4-6, 1993; Greenville, South Carolina.

43. M.F. Folstein, et al., "Minimental State," *Journal Psychiatric Research* (12:189-198, 1975).

44. An up-to-date listing of biblical counselors certified by the National Association of Nouthetic Counselors is available; you can write to their office at 5526 S.R. 26, East Lafayette, IN 47905.

45. *See* Joshua 1:7.

46. *See* Proverbs 9:20.

47. *See* Proverbs 3:6.

Chapter 6—What's the Brain Got to Do with It?

1. "Neuronal" refers to the cells or neurons of the brain.

2. Jerome Kagan, "Three Pleasing Ideas," *American Psychologist*, 1966, 51:905.

3. Peter Kramer, *Listening to Prozac* (New York: Viking, 1993).

4. Simon LeVay, "A difference in hypothalamic structure between heterosexual and homosexual men," *Science*, 1991, 253:1034-37.

5. M. Bailey and R. Pillard, "A genetic study of male sexual orientation," *Archives of General Psychiatry*, 1991, 48:1089-97.

6. D. Hamer, S. Hu, V. Magnuson, N. Hu, and A. Pattatucci, "A linkage between DNA markers on the X chromosome and male sexual orientation," *Science*, 1993, 261:321-27.

7. These comments on homosexuality are in no way intended to single out this sin as being worse than others. But this area of research is in dire need of biblical oversight. Otherwise, Christians who are struggling with homosexuality have little hope for change.

Chapter 7—What About Biomedical Research?

1. Victor H. Fiddes, *Science and the Gospel* (Edinburgh; Scottish Academic Press, 1987), p. 4.

2. Ibid.

3. Robert Chasnov, "Natural Sciences," in W. David Beck, Ed., *Opening the American Mind: The Integration of Biblical Truth in the Curriculum of the University* (Grand Rapids, MI: Baker Book House, 1991), pp. 153-54.

4. Alexander Solzhenitsyn, *From Under the Rubble* (Boston: Little, Brown & Company, 1975), pp. 145-47).

5. Jacques Ellul, *What I Believe* (Grand Rapids, MI: William B. Eerdmans Publishing , 1989), p. 43.

6. J.P. Moreland, *Christianity and the Nature of Science* (Grand Rapids, MI: Baker Book House, 1984).

7. William Keeton, *Biological Science*, 3d ed. (New York: W.W. Norton, 1980), p. 3.

8. John J. O'Dwyer, *College Physics*, 2d ed. (Belmont, CA: Wadsworth, 1984), p. 2.

9. Robert Chasnov, "Natural Sciences" in *Opening the American Mind,* pp. 159-60.

10. Henry Margenau and Roy Abraham Varghese, eds., *Csomos, Bios, Theos: Scientists Reflect on Science, God, and the Origins of the Universe, Life, and Homo Sapiens* (La Salle, IL: Open Court, 1992).

11. Ibid., p. 171.

12. Ibid., pp. 29-30.

13. Ibid., p. 62.

14. Ibid., p. 65.

15. Ibid., p. 72.

16. Robert Chasnov, "Natural Sciences" In *Opening the American Mind,* p. 157.

17. Ibid.

18. J.P. Moreland, *Christianity and the Nature of Science,* p. 70.

19. Victor H. Fiddes, *Science and the Gospel,* p. 93.

20. S.I. McMillen, *None of These Diseases* (Old Fleming, NJ: Revell, 1984), pp. 19-22.

21. Jack J. Kanski, *Clinical Ophthalmology: A Systematic Approach* (Boston: Butterworth-Heinemann, 1989), p. 302).

22. Ibid., pp. 302-04, 328-31.

23. Hans-Walther Larsen, M.D., *The Ocular Fundus* (Philadelphia: W.B. Saunders, 1976), pp. 54-59, 64-65, 68-77, 94-109, 146-47.

24. Joseph Lechner, personal communication.

25. S.I. McMIllen, *None of These Diseases,* pp. 19-22.

26. James L. Fletcher, Jr., "The case for routine neonatal circumcision," *Journal of Biblical Ethics in Medicine* (6:11-18), 1992.

27. S.I. McMillen, *None of These Diseases,* pp. 87-96.

28. Victor H. Fiddes, *Science and the Gospel,* p. 108.

Other recommended reading:

Dr. Paul Brand and Philip Yancey, *In His Image* (Grand Rapids, MI: Zondervan Publishing House, 1987), p. 66.

M. Conrad Hyers, *The Meaning of Creation* (Atlanta: John Knox Press, 1984), pp. 1-8.

Henry M. Morris, *The Biblical Basis for Modern Science* (Grand Rapids, MI: Baker Book House, 1984), pp. 236, 370-71.

Chapter 8—Marriage and Family Counseling

1. Robert N. Bellah et al., *Habits of the Heart* (Berkeley: University of California Press, 1985).

2. Paul C. Vitz, *Psychology As Religion: The Cult of Self Worship* (Grand Rapids: Eerdmans Publishing Co., 1977) and William Kirk Kilpatrick, *Psychological Seduction: The Failure of Modern Psychology* (Nashville: Thomas Nelson Publishers). These writers clearly identify the roots of client-centered and existential psychology in liberal Protestant theology.

This helps to explain some of the tension between psychology and theology. We are both clearly on the same turf, yet often with vastly different mindsets.

3. D. Yankelovich, *New Rules* (New York: Random House, 1981), and *see also* Yankelovich and B. Lefkowitz, "Work and American Expectations," *National Forum*, 62 (2), 3-5. Yankelovich does a good job of evaluating the impact of Abraham Maslow's human potential psychology upon American culture.

4. Aaron T. Beck, *Love Is Never Enough* (New York: Harper and Row Publishers, 1988). Aaron Beck advanced a cognitive explanation for the etiology of most depressions. It is wonderful to hear from a man who offers the fruit born from years of experience.

5. Ronald H. Nash, *Faith and Reason: Search for a Rational Faith* (Grand Rapids, MI: Zondervan, 1988); *see also* Gary Collins in *The Biblical Basis of Christian Counseling for People Helpers* (Colorado Springs: NavPress, 1993), which does a good job of discussing the importance of counselors understanding the worldviews of people with whom they counsel. He develops the elements that should be examined when seeking to assess the content of a person's worldview as well as what elements are of critical importance as we seek to develop a worldview that is truly Christian (see pages 11-24).

6. I have been engaged in the practice of pastoral and professional counseling for over three decades. It is a source of puzzlement to me that many pastors and professors who give lip service to the authority of Scripture never use a Bible or biblical passages as a component of their actual counseling practice. Integration has sometimes been at the expense of the primacy of Scripture and has frequently undermined the relevance of God's Word for the actual practice of counseling.

7. The search for the "edenic place" is often at the root of the restlessness we see in those who come for marital counseling. Solomon counsels us to remind ourselves and others, "Better is the sight of the eyes than the wandering of the desires" (Ecclesiastes 6:9 KJV). Paul surely embodies the realities advanced in this text when he states, "I have learned, in whatsoever state I am, therewith to be content" (Philippians 4:11).

8. Larry Christenson, "The Christian Family" (audiotape series). In this excellent series, Larry Christenson describes a technique he labels "empathetic repentance." Larry teaches the partners to stop when they find themselves criticizing their mate and consider whether he or she has any of the same faults in themselves. It is far easier to get someone to repent of a hurtful behavior when we acknowledge sensitively our own need of participation in such repentance.

9. Ed Wheat, *Intended for Pleasure* (Old Tappan, NJ: Fleming H. Revell, 1981), p. 21.

Chapter 11—The Biblical Basis of Pastoral Ministry

1. Hugh Latimer, *Words*, vol. 1, p. 85.

2. Martin Luther, "Preface to the New Testament," 1546.

3. John Calvin, *Institutes*, III, ii, 6.

4. John Calvin, *Institutes*, I, vi, 3.

5. William Tyndale, *Works*, vol.1, p. 43.

6. William Whitaker, *Dissertation on Holy Scripture*, p. 235.

7. Bishop John Jewel, *Works*, vol. IV, p. 1179.

8. Nicholas Ridley, *Works*, p. 56.

9. Hugh Latimer, *Works*, vol. 1, p. 369.

10. John Calvin, *Institutes*, III, xxiii, 2).

11. Thomas Cranmer, *Memorials of Archbishop Cranmer*, vol. III, p. 85.

12. John Bradford, *Writings*, vol. 1, p. 370.

13. Nicholas Ridley, *Works*, p. 56.

14. Bishop John Jewel, *Works*, vol. IV, p. 1163.

15. John Calvin, *Institutes*, III, ii, 6.

16. Hugh Latimer, *Works*, vol. 1, p. 369).

17. Nicholas Ridley, *Works*, p. 56.

18. Bishop John Jewel, *Works*, vol. IV. p. 1163.

19. Thomas Cranmer, *Homilies*, p. 9.

20. Bishop John Jewel, *Works*, vol. IV, p. 1164.

Chapter 12—Total Sufficiency and Biblical Truth

1. Chris Thurman, *Self-Help or Self-Destruction?* (Nashville: Thomas Nelson, 1996). Thurman quotes Dutch theologian Abraham Kuyper in the frontispiece of the book: "When principles that run against your deepest convictions begin to win the day . . . you must at the price of dearest peace, lay your convictions bare before friend and enemy, with all the fire of your faith."

2. Ibid., p. xxi.

3. C.S. Lewis, *Mere Christianity* (New York: MacMillan, 1960), p. 56. Quoted in Richard Lee and Ed Hindson, *No Greater Savior* (Eugene, OR: Harvest House, 1995), p. 77.

4. Octavius Winslow, *The Work of the Holy Spirit* (London: Banner of Truth, 1972 reprint of 1840 edition), pp. 105, 108.

5. Comment by Dr. Leonard Poom, Director of Center for Gerontology, University of Georgia (Athens, GA) course lecture, 1985.

Other Good Harvest House Reading

MEN OF THE PROMISE
by *Ed Hindson*

Discover the refreshingly simple and fulfilling calling God designed especially for men. Hindson's inspirational study of Old Testament figures encourages men to discover the many ways God wants to use them today. Excellent for groups.

ONLY GOD CAN HEAL THE WOUNDED HEART
by *Ed Bulkley*

Many Christians genuinely desire to overcome hurts that stem from past experiences. Pastoral counselor Ed Bulkley offers biblical solutions that promise true freedom and genuine inner peace for those who hurt.

WHY CHRISTIANS CAN'T TRUST PSYCHOLOGY
by *Ed Bulkley*

Where should Christians go to heal the deep hurts in their hearts? Some say we need the Bible plus psychology; others say the Bible alone is sufficient. Here's both sides of the issue with biblical answers.

THERE'S HOPE FOR THE HURTING
by *Richard Lee*

Using illustrations from everyday life as well as examples from the lives of Bible personalities, Dr. Lee reminds us that God will restore and redeem those who cry to Him "out of the depths."

Dear Reader,

We would appreciate hearing from you regarding this Harvest House nonfiction book. It will enable us to continue to give you the best in Christian publishing.

1. What most influenced you to purchase *Totally Sufficient?*
   - ❏ Author
   - ❏ Subject matter
   - ❏ Backcover copy
   - ❏ Recommendations
   - ❏ Cover/Title
   - ❏ Other_____

2. Where did you purchase this book?
   - ❏ Christian bookstore
   - ❏ General bookstore
   - ❏ Department store
   - ❏ Grocery store
   - ❏ Other_____

3. Your overall rating of this book?
   ❏ Excellent ❏ Very good ❏ Good ❏ Fair ❏ Poor

4. How likely would you be to purchase other books by this author?
   ❏ Very likely ❏ Not very likely ❏ Somewhat likely ❏ Not at all

5. What types of books most interest you? (Check all that apply.)
   - ❏ Women's Books
   - ❏ Marriage Books
   - ❏ Current Issues
   - ❏ Christian Living
   - ❏ Bible Studies
   - ❏ Fiction
   - ❏ Biographies
   - ❏ Children's Books
   - ❏ Youth Books
   - ❏ Other_____

6. Please check the box next to your age group.
   ❏ Under 18 ❏ 18-24 ❏ 25-34 ❏ 35-44 ❏ 45-54 ❏ 55 and over

Mail to: Editorial Director
Harvest House Publishers
1075 Arrowsmith
Eugene, OR 97402

Name _____

Address _____

State _____ Zip _____

Thank you for helping us to help you in future publications!